After a career in advertising, **Christopher Turner** took a sabbatical to visit many European cities. Discovering that few guidebooks were 'user friendly', he decided to write one himself. His first book, *London Step by Step*, won the London Tourist Board's Guidebook of the Year Award for 1985 and is now in its third edition. Five more London books followed in the series. In 1991, his first books on continental cities, *Paris Step by Step* and *Barcelona Step by Step*, were published, to be followed, in 1992, by *The Penguin Guide to Seville*. He is now completing a guide to India.

## Acknowledgement

The author wishes to acknowledge the great assistance provided by Els Wamsteeker, of the VVV Amsterdam Tourist Office.

*Lascelles City Guides*

# AMSTERDAM
## STEP BY STEP

Christopher Turner

**Roger Lascelles,** Cartographic and Travel Publisher
47 York Road, Brentford, (Middx) TW8 0QP. Tel: 081 847 0935  Fax: 081 568 3886

# Publication Data

| | |
|---|---|
| **Title** | Amsterdam Step by Step |
| **Printing** | Typeset and Printed by Kelso Graphics, Kelso, Scotland. |
| **Photographs** | By the Author or courtesy of VVV Amsterdam Tourist Office as indicated |
| **Maps** | Page 220 by John Gill. Inside back cover licensed from Falkplan – Suurland BV (Eindhoven). |
| **ISBN** | 1 872815 22 7 |
| **Edition** | First edition August 1992 |
| **Publisher** | Roger Lascelles |
| | 47 York Road, Brentford, Middlesex, TW8 0QP. |
| **Copyright** | Christopher Turner |

# Distribution

| Africa: | South Africa | Faradawn, Box 17161, Hillbrow 2038 |
|---|---|---|
| Americas: | Canada | International Travel Maps & Books, P.O. Box 2290, Vancouver BC V6B 3W5. |
| | U.S.A. | Available through major booksellers with good foreign travel sections |
| Asia: | India | English Book Store, 17-L Connaught Circus, P.O. Box 328, New Delhi 110 001 |
| Australasia: | Australia | Rex Publications, 15 Huntingdon Street, Crows Nest, N.S.W. |
| Europe: | Belgium | Brussels – Peuples et Continents |
| | Germany | Available through major booksellers with good foreign travel sections |
| | GB/Ireland | Available through all booksellers with good foreign travel sections. |
| | Italy | Libreria dell'Automobile, Milano |
| | Netherlands | Nilsson & Lamm BV, Weesp |
| | Denmark | Copenhagen – Arnold Busck, G.E.C. |
| | Finland | Helsinki – Akateeminen Kirjakauppa |
| | Norway | Oslo – Arne Gimnes/J.G. Tanum |
| | Sweden | Stockholm/Esselte, Akademi Bokhandel, Fritzes, Hedengrens.Gothenburg/Gumperts, Esselte. Lund/Gleerupska |
| | Switzerland | Basel/Bider: Berne/Atlas; Geneve/Artou; Lausanne/Artou: Zurich/Travel Bookshop |

# Contents

# Introduction

As in most important cities, strangers to Amsterdam soon despair of ever finding their way around without the aid of a large, unwieldy map, which always seems to open at the wrong section. An important feature of this guide, therefore, is the inclusion of precise directions, which will help visitors to see all the city's attractions without getting lost or retracing their steps.

He, or she, is led around the exterior and, wherever possible, the interior, of each location, and points of detail are described exactly as they are reached. Directions are then given for proceeding further on foot. Admittedly, the multiplicity of directions does not make for thrilling reading, but this guidebook is primarily intended for use in the city; it is not simply a travel book to be read in the comfort of your own home – there are plenty of those already.

Much of Amsterdam's architectural interest is centred on the brick gables of its ancient houses, and the examples of greatest interest are described as they are passed. Readers will soon become expert 'gable-gogglers'! Most routes have been planned to run from north to south, partly because Central Station, sited at the northernmost limit of the old city, is an easily located starting point, but also because a wind from the North Sea can blow icily down the main canals for much of the year, and it is significantly more comfortable to have your back to it, facing, hopefully, the sun.

In general, following long stretches of any one canal at a time are avoided, otherwise, a certain degree of tedium would be risked. Instead, short streets of interest, which link with other canals, are taken as they are reached, both to add variety and to encompass the outstanding shops and small museums that are located within them.

An important aim of this guide is to help the tourist discover the less obvious features, which contribute to much of the charm of this uniquely charming, human-scale city.

Christopher Turner

# Amsterdam and the Amsterdammer

## The City

Although it is known that for most English-speaking tourists, Amsterdam, after Paris, is the most popular European city to visit, few of them have more than a hazy notion of its content. The main reason for this is that Amsterdam displays a wealth of great architecture, but there are few great buildings. With the single exception of the former Town Hall, now the Royal Palace, those commissioning private and civic structures up to the 19th century considered reticence to be a virtue, and the Calvinist ecclesiastical authorities insisted on austere, undemonstrative purity for the city's churches. Delights of a more intimate nature are primarily what Holland's capital city has to offer.

Described by publicists as the 'Venice of the North', Amsterdam is nothing of the kind. Accepted, it is, like Venice, a city built on canals, but here the similarity ends. Amsterdam's canals are treelined, whereas trees in Venice are few and far between, and the buildings that overlook the canals are completely different, with their variety of decorative brick gables. Moreover, again unlike Venice, members of the public with sensitive olfacts can be assured that fresh water flushes Amsterdam's canals every three nights and even in the hottest summer no objectionable smells waft up from them.

Apart from the charming canals and venerable brick houses, what else is generally known about the city? The Rijksmuseum, with its great Rembrandt paintings, which include *The Nightwatch*, are a magnet for art lovers, as is the Vincent Van Gogh Museum, currently the city's biggest single draw. Consistently long queues indicate the location of The Anne Frank House, an unsettling reminder of the Nazi Holocaust, and in spring, of course, there are the tulip fields nearby. Other, more worldly visitors make straight for the red light district, more often to observe than to participate in its seamy attractions, and those who greatly enjoy a 'smoke' find Amsterdam's soft-drug liberalism much to their taste. The city is also particularly welcoming to homosexuals.

What is not generally known is that Amsterdam boasts more than 50 museums, with subjects ranging from money boxes to trams; brightly painted barrel organs that entertain at ever-changing venues; and an extraordinary variety of shops. No other city has so many singleminded shopkeepers – only buttons, only beads, only kites, only toothbrushes, only condoms... the range seems endless. The multiplicity of taverns, particularly the 'brown bars', are also a revelation; dating back to the 17th century, many possess great vats, timber beams, sand on the floor and a generally venerable ambience, which will make connoisseurs of the English country pub feel very much at home.

Above all, Amsterdam, like most continental cities, is lived in, with no wholesale desertion of the city centre for the suburbs when the offices close, as is the case in most large English and American towns. Another surprise is that although Amsterdam is rightly considered to be the intimate city par excellence, it has a larger historic core than any other European capital. Try walking the length of Singelgracht, which marks its boundary, and you will find that 'tourist Amsterdam' is certainly not small.

## The People

Dutch cheeses are a byword for blandness; one's palate will not normally be disturbed or excited. And then, discover Limburger; at its peak of maturity one of the world's most pungent and idiosyncratic cheeses. So it is with the Dutch people: kindly, phlegmatic and eminently sensible in the main, until, without warning, an eccentric materializes.

Stubborn rebelliousness is perhaps the most common expression of the non-conforming Dutchman's individuality, a trait most commonly displayed in Amsterdam, a city with a long tradition of opposing authority. Only in Amsterdam, for example, did the citizens of an occupied European city unite in open opposition to the German deportation of the Jews. Since the end of the Second World War, Amsterdammers have organised a series of massive protests against, notably: redeveloping the former Jewish quarter; the Town Hall/ Opera project; and expenditure on the coronation of Queen Beatrix.

Inadequate low-cost housing in the city led to organised squatter activities and it was estimated that almost 10,000 citizens were illegally occupying accommodation in 1982.

One amusing recent example of the Amsterdammers' 'bolshy' nature is that when the city sent an official delegation to make a bid for the 1992 Olympic Games it was uniquely accompanied by an unofficial delegation, whose sole object was to oppose it!

Personal freedom has always been a major aspiration of the Amsterdammer, who never permitted the country's rulers to have effective power over the civilian population except in time of war. Whilst neighbouring Roman Catholics in what is now Belgium enforced their strict views on the whole nation (with a little help from the Spanish Inquisition), the Dutch Calvinists expressly permitted freedom of religious thought. True, they would not officially tolerate public worship by non-Protestants, but very soon a blind eye was turned to the many 'secret' churches and synagogues gradually set up by minority religions.

However, it is for their belief that sex and soft drugs are strictly personal matters that the Dutch are, at present, particularly renowned. This consensus has been achieved through the post-war efforts of pressure groups, and most visitors to Holland are surprised to learn that prostitution and marijuana are still technically illegal; another example of Dutch officialdom turning a blind eye to the letter of the law. Amsterdam is now regarded as the gay capital of Europe, but this is a comparatively recent development, as homosexuals of both sexes were rigorously persecuted until the 1960s. Even though many members of the Dutch Reformed Church support these laissez-faire views, it is undoubtedly the modern lack of Dutch enthusiasm for religion, and thereby orthodox religious standards of morality, that have led to these changes in attitude. British visitors, in particular, must be prepared to be quizzed by their hosts in a friendly, but non-comprehending, way about their country's attitude to private morality, which the Dutch believe to be hypocritical and out-dated.

Sometimes in Amsterdam, particularly after the odd tipple of *oude genever*, I have had the strong impression that my flight across the North Sea never actually took place and that I am, in reality, just a stone's throw from my home. Virtually everyone speaks English, albeit with a softly guttural, slightly American accent. Sometimes they even speak it amongst themselves, and many of the television programmes and signs are also in English. Partly due to this lack of a language problem, in no other European country will the English-speaking visitor feel quite so much at home. An added bonus is that there is still a residue of Dutch gratitude for their liberation by the Allies in the Second World War. Add to this that the Dutch vie with the British in producing Europe's blandest food, and the deep affection for the country expressed by most Anglo-Saxons can well be understood.

It is to be hoped that a contest, which has recently evolved between the English and the Dutch to establish which country can produce the world's worst football hooligans, is, like the 17th-century naval battles between them, just a passing phase.

## Suggested Reading

The following books are currently available in the UK:

*The Diary of Anne Frank*, Pan Books, 1954.
*Dutch Painting*, R. H. Fuchs, Thames and Hudson, 1978.
*The Dutch Revolt 1559-1648*, Peter Limon, Longman, 1989.
*The Dutch Seaborne Empire 1600-1800*, C. R. Boxer, Penguin, 1990.
*Patriots and Liberators*, Simon Schama, Fontana, 1992.
*An Excess of Riches*, Simon Schama, Fontana, 1991.

Only generally available in Holland and Belgium:
*Amsterdam Architecture A Guide*, Guus Kemme, Uitgeverij.
Thoth, 1989 (over 550 buildings are illustrated).

# A Brief History

## Early developments

Not until the level of the North Sea fell significantly in the eleventh century did the western seabord of the Netherlands become habitable. Prior to this, most of the land had been under water. Fens were drained and forests cleared, permitting farmsteads to be built along the river banks. Amsterdam developed at this time, with two streets running parallel to each other, one on either side of the Amstel.

The country's earliest recorded inhabitants, the Batavi, had lived around the mouth of the Rhine, to the south-west of Amsterdam, and were subjugated by the Romans in AD12. A spirited revolt under their leader Claudius Julius Civilis, from AD69 to 70, is an event that is still regarded with much pride by the Dutch, who named what is now Jakarta, Batavia, when they colonised Java in the 17th century. From 1798 to 1806, throughout much of the French occupation, the Netherlands (then Holland and Belgium) was itself called the Bataafsche Republiek.

A major flood in 1170 created the Zuider Zee, and there followed a long period of reclaiming low-lying banks of sand, known as polders, from the sea, and protecting them with mounds created by excavating ditches. Rather confusingly, the Dutch refer to both the mound and its ditch as a dike.

The province of Holland became established under the hegemony of the Holy Roman Empire, administered by Counts of Holland. In the 17th century, the province, with Amsterdam its capital, became so dominant that other countries referred to the entire country formed by the Seven United Provinces as Holland, and continue to do so, even though the Dutch call their country the Netherlands (Lowlands). At roughly the same time, incidentally, the English began to refer to the inhabitants as Dutch. The source of the word, which means those who speak Low German, was the same as that of the German Deutsch; i.e. German people.

It is believed that the Amstel river was dammed c.1270, and the earliest known reference to the settlement there is to be found in a toll privilege granted to the citizens of Amstelledamme by Count Floris of Holland in 1275. Twenty-five years later, the city received its first charter.

The peaty soil of western Holland is soft and often waterlogged. Foundations for any form of construction, therefore, have to overcome these problems by adopting special methods. Until modern techniques were developed in the late 19th century, the emphasis had to be on lightweight structures. Amsterdam's early buildings, all entirely of timber, were single-storey, aisled houses, resting on floats. For higher buildings, piling was necessary, wooden piles being forced manually into the layers of sand beneath the peat. A series of catastrophic fires, particularly those of 1421 and 1423, inspired an edict that all side walls of houses had to be built of masonry, in order to limit the spread of conflagrations. Although timber façades and thatched roofs were never outlawed, only two houses with timber fronts have survived in the city.

The cost and time involved in providing effective foundations for more permanent, masonry-built structures was generally prohibitive and there are few Gothic buildings in the city. However, Old Church (1339) and The New Church (1400) are exceptions. Both are built of masonry, but even here, in order to keep the weight down, the main vaults are of timber, and window glass forms much of the wall area.

## Medieval growth

In the Middle Ages, drinking water was frequently polluted and led to outbreaks of disease. Beer was considered a much safer alternative: its processing and alcoholic content killing many of the dangerous germs. From the mid-13th century, beer was made from hops in Haarlem, Gouda and Delft and exported from Amsterdam, giving an early boost to the city's maritime trade. By 1400 grain, cloth, wood, furs, fish and spices were being exported and Amsterdam's importance had become established. As was common in Europe during the Middle Ages, craftsmen, shopkeepers and purveyors of food formed powerful trade guilds, later to be joined by printers and the Civic Guards Companies, which formed three militia guilds. Members of the Civic Guards were well-heeled burghers, who were permitted to carry arms in order to protect the city against attacks from without or within, also acting as a private police force. They became extremely powerful politically, few would-be opponents wishing to argue with a cluster of firearms.

Like most medieval cities, Amsterdam was protected by a rampart. However, less usually, the outer ditch, which was dug to provide material for the wall, gave additional protection, as it was flooded to form a moat. On both occasions when the city was expanded significantly, the wall and its moat were moved outward. Not until 1425 was the rampart first built of brick. Nothing remains of any of the city's walls today, the last vestiges being demolished in 1848, but a few of their gateways – in the form of towers subsequently adapted to other uses – have survived.

## Religious turmoil and independence

Through inheritance, the country fell under the rule of the Hapsburgs in 1482. In 1555, the Holy Roman Emperor Carlos V presented the Netherlands (then including what is now Belgium) to his son Philip II of Spain, a Roman Catholic bigot, who was responsible for the Spanish Inquisition's persecution of Protestants. Protestantism had already gained ground in Northern Europe, where Lutherans and Calvinists attacked the superstition and ceremony of the Roman Catholic church. A riot by an early group of Amsterdam Protestants, known as Anabaptists, led to their occupancy of the old town hall in 1535. This proved too much for the authorities, who repulsed the rebels and executed those that had survived on scaffolds hastily erected in De Dam. Calvinism, although strong in most of Holland, made little impact in Amsterdam until after 1560. A harvest failure in 1565 resulted in a winter famine amongst the labouring class, most of whom were Calvinist and, later that year, iconoclastic attacks on the churches led to the destruction of much ornamentation, particularly altarpieces.

Rebellion against the Roman Catholic church and Philip II gathered slowly throughout the northern Netherlands, where Protestantism had gained its strongest hold and, in 1572, Willem the Silent, Prince of Orange, led a revolt. His forces, however, were greatly outnumbered, and the dubious Amsterdammers remained loyal to Philip until 1578, when it became apparent that Willem was about to prevail. The following year saw the creation of the Republic of the Seven United Provinces and a truce with Spain was ratified in 1609. It was not until the Treaty of Munster, in 1648, however, that Spain formally relinquished its authority over the northern Netherlands. The ten provinces of the southern Netherlands, now known as Belgium, remained under Spanish influence, which only permitted the Catholic religion. Almost immediately on siding with Willem, Amsterdam switched from Catholicism to Protestantism, an act that is referred to in Amsterdam not as the Reformation but the Alteration.

The Dutch Reformed Church, following Calvinist principles, permitted freedom of religious belief, but initially would not tolerate any other form of worship in public. In spite of this, the authorities soon began to turn a blind eye to sects that had set up their own 'hidden' places of worship and, by the 1670s, Lutheran churches and Jewish synagogues had been constructed in Amsterdam, although they had to be built without towers. At the Alteration, Catholic administrators and priests were dismissed and monasteries put to secular use. Roman Catholic churches were not officially permitted until the French occupation at the end of the 18th century established complete freedom of worship.

## Administration

The foundation of the Seven United Provinces made little difference to the city's administration, which, from 1400 to 1795, varied little in form, important families ensuring a virtual 'closed shop' of patrician rulers. From 1477, the situation hardened: council members were not only appointed to advise the burgomasters for life, but also permitted to appoint successors. Burgomasters served for one year and were chosen by a college comprising former burgomasters and aldermen. The country's stadholder officially appointed Amsterdam's sheriff and aldermen, but he was required to seek the advice of the city council.

Willem I, Prince of Orange, whose martial skills had gained independence for the North Netherlands from Philip II, became the country's first stadholder. This position, although hereditary, was not as powerful as that of a monarch. The stadholder only had general authority over the civilian population in time of war; his task was primarily military. The Orange dynasty, which still rules Holland, heralded from the town of Orange in the South of France, and became a vassal of the Holy Roman Empire as early as the 12th century. By marriage, its princes were united with the German House of Nassau in the 16th century and thus began their relationship with the Netherlands. Supporters of the princes, known as the Orange Party, comprised the aristocracy, orthodox Calvinists and rural communities. The party rarely gained the full support of the patricians, who ran the larger cities; for them, trade was all important, certainly too important to be disturbed by religious strife and heavy military expenditure. Amsterdam, in particular, had a series of disputes with the stadholder, Willem II even threatening the city with attack in 1649 unless its plan to disband the military garrison was cancelled. Probably due to the Amsterdammers' strong independent quality, no powerful lobby has ever attempted to transfer either the seat of national government or the sovereign's main residence from the Hague to the capital: a situation analogous with that in England, where both establishments have been located in the City of Westminster rather than the City of London since the 11th century. During the periods 1650-72 and 1702-47 Holland was without a stadholder.

## Immigration and rapid expansion

Amsterdam's religious tolerance led to the city becoming a magnet for persecuted minorities, as well as those seeking greater business opportunities; most of the latter coming from elsewhere in Holland. Jews were welcomed from many sources, particularly Portugal, where the Inquisition had recently been introduced. Nevertheless, as has been mentioned, they were not initially allowed to worship in public, and, unlike other groups, each generation had to purchase rather than inherit citizenship. By the end of the 18th century, Jews made up ten per cent of Amsterdam's population. Protestants migrated en masse from Antwerp, which remained under Philip II's sovereignty. That city's trade, in any case, was critically damaged by the Dutch blockade of the river Scheldt, on which it stands. Lutherans mostly came from Germany and Scandinavia, their descendants eventually comprising 16 per cent of all Amsterdammers.

Between 1570 and 1640, the city's population rose from 30,000 to 139,000 and Amsterdam was bursting at the seams. In 1613, the capital's greatest expansion scheme began, one of the most sensitive that any European city has ever put into effect. It comprised the concentric Canal Girdle of Herengracht, Keizersgracht and Prinsengracht and an adjacent area for workers to the west, now known as the Jordaan. The canals were laid out in three stages, which were not concluded until the 18th century, when Nieuwe Herengracht was finally linked with the IJ. From the very beginning, the scheme was a great success; wealthy merchants abandoned their cramped Warmoestraat mansions for the new residences, each of which was provided with a long garden and space for a coachhouse.

## The evolution of the Amsterdam house

Relatively few of the surviving canal houses have completely retained their 17th century appearance externally, although many original structures survive beneath later remodelling. Plots of land continued to be narrow, mainly because house owners were taxed according to the size of their frontages. Furthermore, the maximum length of timber that could be transported on the canals was 18 feet, thereby limiting the width of undivided areas to that dimension. Rooms, therefore, tended to be high and long, with deep windows forming most of the frontage. Due to their general narrowness, and Dutch conservatism, few possibilities existed for architectural splendour, and most embellishment was confined to the gable. The earliest masonry gable, triangular in shape, continued the simple outline of Amsterdam's timber houses in brickwork and is known as a spout gable. Step gables were created in the mid-16th century to disguise the steeply pitched roofs of the narrow houses, which were then being built. Many of the early gables of this type were decorated with scrolls; the step gable continued to make its appearance until the end of the 17th century.

Hendrick de Keyser (1563-1613), Amsterdam's greatest architect, introduced trapezium-shaped gables early in the 17th century. These were built of soft red brick, profusely decorated with yellow Bentheimer stone. It was also de Keyser who developed the Dutch Renaissance style, which resulted in Amsterdam's most appealing houses and churches.

Around 1625, Classical elements began to dominate, with Italian pattern books being followed closely. The Vingboons brothers were important early exponents, favouring a central feature emphasised by a neck gable, which was usually surmounted by a small pediment forming the 'head'. A further development, similarly favoured by the brothers, was the raised neck gable, the 'neck' often encompassing three storeys. Supporting volutes (scrolls) and other stone carvings frequently linked this form of gable to the remainder of the façade.

The most devoted Classicist was Jacob van Campen, who began to replace gables with pedimented cornices as early as 1633. His Town Hall, now the Royal Palace, built in the mid-17th-century, remains the city's most imposing Classical building. Its internal sculptures by Quellien are amongst the finest to embellish a public edifice in Europe. A more austere form of Classicism became popular after 1665, promoted by Adriaan Dortsman (1625-82).

During the 18th century, the population of the city increased little and most building activities were restricted to the remodelling of existing properties. Initially, the heavy Baroque style of Louis XIV was favoured, but, as the century progressed, Baroque's development – Rococo – with its asymmetrical qualities, proved unsuitable for embellishing neck gables, and the much wider bell gable was introduced. Neck gables, however, continued to be built, generally following pattern book designs. These did not always adapt happily to wider-fronted properties, and additional side decoration, frequently in the form of Classical vases, was employed. For houses more than three bays wide, however, a straight cornice was generally preferred to a gable and, towards the end of the century, the Louis XVI style, dependant on symmetry and strength, became popular. Simultaneously, many brick façades were rendered with stucco.

Throughout the different styles of gable treatment, it was always necessary to incorporate a centrally-positioned hoist, with its beam at the apex, because the narrowness of most Amsterdam staircases made it impossible, internally, to raise large items such as furniture to the upper storeys. As goods had to be passed from outside the building into the room, this was another reason, in addition to that of weight, why the windows were so large. Many houses with three or more bays were provided with double entrance steps, giving direct entrance to the raised hall floor. The semi-basement floor below provided the servants' quarters.

## The 'Golden Age'

It was the 17th century that witnessed Holland's 'Golden Age', the country benefiting from internal strife in England, France and Germany. Its fleet was vastly superior in size to those of all its neighbours put together and wealth was soon engendered in the new colonies, particularly those administered by the Dutch East Indies Company, which was set up in 1602.

As so often happens, great wealth was accompanied by great art. Dutch painters who are still household names, led by Rembrandt, Vermeer and Hals, all worked during the first half of the 17th century. The Dutch School betrayed the influence of Italian Baroque and, at an early stage, many of its members were known as 'Carravagists' after Caravaggio, the Italian master. Soon, however, realism became an even more important element. Evelyn, the English diarist, visited Holland in 1641 and postulated that the Dutch owned so many paintings because it was difficult for all but the richest to demonstrate their wealth in the form of property. In any case, the average citizen's interest in architecture was very limited. Tremendous expenditure on paintings inspired a huge output; it has been estimated that the average Amsterdam household owned more than five paintings. In addition, a Europe-wide market developed for works by the leading masters. A feature of Dutch paintings of this period was the illusion of depth achieved by dramatic chiaroscuro, and the popularity of genre themes that recorded everyday life at the time. Not only did the Dutch have little interest in architecture, they also displayed a disregard for sculpture and, with the exception of Hendrick de Keyser (better known as an architect), their sculptors never approached the quality of contemporary Flemish masters.

As the century progressed, England and France became more belligerent in safeguarding their trade, and Holland was involved in a series of battles, mostly naval. New Amsterdam, in North America, was lost to England in 1664 and renamed New York, but Surinam, in South America, was gained from the English three years later - at the time a good swap! Louis XIV eventually invaded the Netherlands and, in 1672, his army had advanced to within 14 miles of Amsterdam before being repulsed; a peace treaty was signed at Rijswijck in 1697. In spite of their eventual victory, wars had drained Dutch energy, and Holland was never again to regain its position of dominance. Towards the end of the century, Holland and England were allied against France, and stadholder Willem III became William III of England, reigning jointly with his consort Mary II.

## French occupation – an independent kingdom

Throughout the 18th century, in spite of their diminished importance, the Dutch maintained a higher standard of living than their neighbours, even though they completely ignored the Industrial Revolution that had arrived in England. In 1795, a huge French army brought its revolutionary liberty, equality and fraternity to the country, and Willem V, a weak stadholder, destined to be Holland's last, fled to England. The country passed from revolutionary to Napoléonic domination, with the Emperor's brother Louis-Napoléon briefly serving as king. In 1813, Holland and Belgium were once again united and Willem V's son Willem I ruled, not as stadholder but as king, from 1815-40. The reunion, however, was short-lived, Belgium proclaiming its independence once more in 1830.

## The 19th century

By the 1820s, as ships were being built that were too large to navigate the shallow Zuider Zee, Amsterdam's port faced ruin in the face of competition from Rotterdam. To overcome this, the North Sea Canal was opened in 1876 and the Merwede Canal, to the Rhine, in 1896. Amsterdam then regained its position as a major port, serving the Dutch merchant fleet but leaving international shipping to Rotterdam. Between 1850 and 1900, improvements in public health led to the city's population almost doubling. After a century of delay, industrialisation at last began, Holland's earlier refusal to countenance this having meant that the Dutch standard of living, formerly the highest in the world, now lagged well behind that of its more go-ahead neighbours.

French occupation had established freedom of worship in Holland, and Roman Catholic churches were built, the addition of towers to them being permitted from 1853. The most impressive new building in Amsterdam, however, was the Paleis voor Volksvlijt, completed in 1854, but which, like London's Crystal Palace, on which it was modelled, eventually burnt down. Fortunately, two other important buildings, both built in the 1880s, have survived: the Rijksmuseum and Central Station, both the work of P.J.H. Cuypers. As in many other European countries, most architecture was Revivalist in style, with Gothic and, later, Dutch Renaissance providing most inspiration in Amsterdam. The ancient core of the city fortunately escaped wholesale 19th century 'improvements', although, partly for health and partly for communication reasons, many canals were filled and transformed into streets. At the turn of the century, the Art Nouveau style, which had a brief international vogue, was never favoured by the undemonstrative Dutch. A less exuberant version, Nieuwe Kunst, occasionally made use of Art Nouveau motifs, but had a greater

affinity with the contemporary English Arts and Crafts movement
than genuine Art Nouveau.

## The 20th century

The 20th century saw the first major break away from Revivalist
architecture, when Hendrik Berlage completed his enormous Trade
Exchange in 1903. Berlage believed in purity of structure
unconcealed by style or decoration. His work is recognised as the
chief inspiration for the Amsterdam School of Architects, created in
the office of Ed Cuypers, mainly due to the massive areas of crisp
brickwork and fondness for towers that it employed. However, the
Amsterdam School gave far more emphasis to form, and depended
almost entirely on brickwork for decoration. Maritime House, by van
der Mey, Michel de Klerk and Pieter Kramer was built in 1916 and is
recognised as the first of the School's buildings. Most examples of
their work are to be found in South Amsterdam, where the 1917
municipal housing scheme of Berlage was put into effect during the
1920s.

Holland remained neutral throughout the First World War, but
Amsterdammers suffered grievously during the German occupation
of 1940-45 although, unlike Rotterdam, little structural damage was
done. Many died in Amsterdam from malnutrition during the last
year of the war (partly due to a long transport strike called by Queen
Wilhelmina, when, in 1944, it seemed that Holland would soon be
liberated). The city was not freed, in fact, until 4 May 1945, the day
before Germany's unconditional surrender.

As in London, Rationalism, developed by Le Corbusier, The
Bauhaus and Frank Lloyd Wright in the 1920s, made no impact in
Amsterdam until the Second World War had ended. Most examples
of this style, generally in the form of high blocks built of concrete or
stainless steel together with glass, are to be found outside the central
area, thus preserving the traditional low-rise appearance of the city
centre. However, virtually all of the former Jewish quarter has been
redeveloped. Its focal point is Waterlooplein, for centuries an open
space, but now filled with the controversial Opera House/Town Hall.
Largely due to the loss of most of its 80,000 pre-war Jewish citizens,
the population of Amsterdam has declined, although the pressure on
centrally-located accommodation remains high. Much effort is now
concentrated on rehabilitating existing buildings; the conversion of

canal-side warehouses for domestic use being particularly successful. As in virtually all European capitals, conservation is of prime importance, strict controls being placed on alterations to listed buildings. Hopefully, no more historic gables will be lost, or the uniquely intimate quality of Holland's capital city threatened within the foreseeable future.

# Timing Your Trip

Like Paris, Amsterdam is at its most enchanting in the spring, when fresh leaves create a green filigree over the ancient houses, yet without completely obscuring them. It is during April that the tulips are permitted to bloom in the nearby fields for around three weeks before being executed. In general, summers are slightly cooler and winters very much colder than in London. However, in contrast to London, rainfall is much lower between November and February than it is in the summer months. A mid-winter trip, therefore, can be most enjoyable as long as warm clothing is taken.

## Public holidays

Banks and most shops are closed on public holidays. Museums and art galleries close on New Year's Day, Christmas Day and Boxing Day, but on other holidays most will follow Sunday opening hours.

Holidays are: 1 January, Good Friday, Easter Monday, Ascension Day, 30 April (Queens Day), Whit Monday, 25 and 26 December.

## Special events

**February 25, J. D. Meierplein**:  Commemoration of the 1941 protest strike against deportation of Jews by the Nazis.

**March**:  Sunday nearest the 15th; 'Silent' Procession from the Begijnhof to commemorate the 14th century 'Amsterdam Miracle'.

**April 30, Queens Day**:  Held throughout Amsterdam to celebrate the official birthday of Queen Beatrix. The sovereign was actually born in January, hardly a suitable time for rejoicing in the streets, and the birthday of her mother and predecessor, Queen Juliana, has therefore continued to be used. Events take place in Vondelpark and De Dam, but it is in the bars and streets that most of the atmosphere develops. It is really just one big booze-up; the event is more enjoyable for foreigners if accompanied by Dutch friends.

**June 1st to 30th**:  Holland Festival at various venues. Music, dance and drama performed by international artists.

**July 1st to 21st**: Summer Festival. This is also mainly an arts festival but concentrates on the avant-garde and is less formal.

**August**: Amsterdam 700 takes place throughout one weekend, consisting of a football tournament between leading Dutch professional teams.

**September**: Aalsmeer to Amsterdam Flower Pageant. Held in the city centre, particularly around De Dam.
During the penultimate week the Jordaan street festival takes place.

**November**: Mid-November, St. Nicholas Parade.

## How to get to Amsterdam

The cost of getting to Amsterdam is almost precisely related to the time taken. Standard airfares are disgracefully high for the distance covered, but shopping around at cut-price specialists usually leads to significant reductions.

Amsterdam's Schiphol airport is just a 45-minute flight from London. Situated approximately eight miles south-west of the city, three trains per hour run from the airport's station, and the journey to Amsterdam's Central Station is made in less than 20 minutes. A KLM bus also runs to the city centre and, although the journey takes at least twice as long and the route is dreary, stops are made at the more important hotels thus saving a taxi fare for some. There is, of course, a taxi rank outside the airport, chiefly of advantage to those with excessively heavy luggage, as naturally, fares to Amsterdam centre are comparatively high. Car hire may also be arranged from the airport's concourse.

A train from London Victoria to Dover, and thence across the Channel to Ostend by Jetfoil, continuing by train to Amsterdam, is the quickest alternative to flying.

Hoverspeed City Sprint, from Victoria Coach Station to Calais, uses modern coaches, making the sea crossing by the new SeaCat catamaran, the fastest passenger vessel ever to cross the Atlantic.

P&O ferries (formerly Townsend Thoressen) cross from Dover to Ostend, or from Felixstowe to Zeebrugge. Olau ferries depart from Sheerness to Flushing (Vlissingen). All these ferries connect with trains to and from London or Amsterdam.

From the north of England, travellers may prefer to take ferries from Hull, but the sea journey is very long.

## City Transport

A full-colour plan of Amsterdam's public transport system is available, free of charge, from the GVB ticket office in front of Central Station. Advice will also be given on the type of ticket that will best suit your needs. Transport continues until 24.00 hours, after which time there are night buses (covered by a separate GVB brochure).

### Tickets

Tickets are interchangeable on all routes of trams, buses and trains. Few tourists will need to travel outside the Central Zone (Zone Centrum).

Single or strip tickets may be purchased on the tram or bus, valid for one hour after they have been cancelled. Strips of two, three or 10 tickets are sold at a cheaper rate, but the cheapest rate strip of 15 tickets, available at GVB offices and the VVV office, are an even better buy. On buses, the driver will cancel your ticket, but on trams and at Metro stations passengers are expected to cancel their own.

Within the central zone, fold the strip and cancel the second ticket. When another zone is entered an additional ticket must be cancelled. Spot-checks by inspectors are made and those without a ticket or who have not cancelled their ticket may be fined up to 100 guilders, which must be paid immediately.

Tickets in daily units covering up to nine days are valid for unlimited journeys throughout all zones and systems. However, long stay visitors will probably find that a seven-day pass for the central zone is the most economical buy; a passport-sized photograph must be supplied. The shop in the American Hotel in Leidseplein and the VVV office at 106 Leidestraat also stocks most types of ticket.

### Trams

Trams are the most frequently used transport system in Amsterdam and the service is excellent. Those generally used by tourists start at Central Station and then head due south following Damrak or N.Z. Voorburgwal before their routes diverge once Singel has been crossed. Exceptions are 13, 14 and 17, which follow a westward route through the Jordaan. The ticket cancelling machine is sited near the entrance.

## Buses

Although most buses also begin their journeys at Central Station they immediately proceed away from the city centre. Eastbound routes, however, are useful for reaching the Maritime Museum.

## Metro

The Metro system is of limited use to tourists, as it covers only four stations in the centre, and these are located towards its eastern extremity: Stationsplein, Nieuwmarkt, Waterlooplein and Weesperplein. Ticket cancelling machines are to be found near the stairways to the platforms. Standard and one-day tickets are available from dispensers; other types are sold at the ticket office.

## Taxis

Taxi fares are slightly lower than in London, but it can be difficult to hail a cab in the street. Telephone 6777777 or pick up from ranks at Central Station, Leidseplein, Rembrandtplein or Westermarkt.

## Water Transport

Unlike Venice, Amsterdam has never fully utilised its canals for transporting people, only goods. A 'Canal Bus' operates, stopping at Central Station, City Hall, Rijksmuseum, Leidseplein, Leidsestraat and Westerkerk. However, the one or two-day ticket price is high and the service cannot be regarded as public transport. The Museum Boot operates a similar service at a similar price, stopping at Prinsengracht, Museumplein, Herengracht, City Hall and the Maritime Museum. A one day ticket only is issued; with both services the ticket is available for as many journeys during the day as required, but the standard Museum Boot ticket also entitles the holder to a 50 per cent reduction on all museums' admission fees and, by paying a supplement, the Combi-ticket gives free admission to any three museums.

Canal bikes (pedaloes) may be hired for two or four people for one hour; rain shields are provided in wet weather. Moorings are at Leidseplein, Rijksmuseum, Westerkerk and Keizersgracht/ Leidsestraat. Canal bikes may be hired from and returned to whichever mooring is most convenient. A deposit will be required. Canal-boat excursions, with commentaries, begin at Damrak and Rokin. Most of the boats are glass-covered but some can now be completely opened in fine weather.

## Bicycles

'Very flat Holland' to paraphrase Noel Coward, and very suitable for cyclists. One of the great complaints of the Dutch on the arrival of the German occupying forces in 1940 was that they took away their bicycles. There are now half a million in Amsterdam and visitors can hire one for either a day or a week from Central Station. A hefty deposit is required, due to the high rate of bicycle thefts in the city; always lock the bicycle up. Other fairly central hiring points are Rent-a-Bike, Pieter Jacobsdwarsstraat 17 and Koenders, Utrechtsedwarsstraat 105. Take your passport when hiring. Cyclists-only lanes are indicated by a sign displaying a white circle on a blue background, or a rectangular black shape; when approaching pedestrians who appear to be tourists, slow down as they are probably not used to cyclist lanes.

## Car parking in Amsterdam

The Amsterdam Tourist Office gives one word of advice to those proposing to tour Amsterdam by car – don't! However, it is appreciated that some will visit the city as part of a motoring tour of the country and, for them, it is recommended that their vehicle is parked, in safety, in a garage. Parking, at meters only, is usually permitted, but will cost around 3 guilders per hour: risks of clamping are great for those who transgress the regulations and fines are high. If a fine is not paid within 24 hours vehicles may be towed away. A proposal to ban all private vehicles from central Amsterdam was approved by the local authority in 1992, but narrowly defeated by a referendum; the scheme, however, may be revived.

## Parking Garages

Bijenkorf, Beursplein
Byzantium, Stadhouderskade (facing Leidseplein)
Europarking, 250 Marnixstraat
Grand Hotel Krasnapolsky, St. Jansstraat
Muziektheater, 22 Waterlooplein
RAI, Europaboulevard
Victoria, Prins Hendrikkade.

## Shopping

Most shops in Amsterdam are closed on Monday mornings and Sundays, with late opening on Thursdays. Smaller shops may close on Wednesday afternoons. Travellers cheques are rarely accepted.

A recent survey named Amsterdam as Europe's best buy for clothes. Amsterdam's fashion shops refreshingly concentrate on Dutch rather than internationally-renowned designers. P.C. Hooftstraat, Van Baerlestraat and Beethovenstraat, adjacent thoroughfares, have the best, although the priciest selection. Also not far from the Rijksmuseum, but to its north, is the 'Spiegelkwartier', with Spiegelstraat and Kerkstraat providing the world's greatest concentration of antique shops.

Purchases are, of course, a matter of taste, but many will wish to return home with a pack of smoked eels, best bought from a wet fish shop, not a street stall, where they are much more expensive. A mature Oud Gouda cheese will be a tasty revelation to those who only know the standard bland version. For the very brave, Limburger cheese, one of the world's most pungent, will prove of interest. Dutch chocolates are delicious, with Droste, for example, offering a much wider range than they do in England. Some may acquire a taste for Dutch gin (genever), but a bottle will cost much less at duty-free shops in Schiphol Airport, or on the boat, at least until 1999, when EC regulations may put a stop to this bonus. Decorated clogs make gifts that appeal to young children. Dutch toy shops are in general a delight, displaying far less plastic junk than their British equivalents.

## Summary of Selected Shops

Most of the following shops specialise in a limited range of products, often just one. Department stores, fashion boutiques and international chains are not included. Page numbers indicate fuller information.

Allert de Lange (page 66) books.
André Coppenhagen, 1001 Krabe (page 175) beads.
Berkhoff Tea Rooms (page 159) chocolates, biscuits.
Condomerie Het Gulden Vlies (page 116) condoms.
Dikker and Thijs (page 182) delicatessen (highest quality).
Eicholt (page 159) delicatessen.
Flying Objects (page 173) kites.
Gallerie d'Arte (page 176) delftware.
Hajenius (page 88) cigars, cigarettes etc.
Jacob Hooey (page 117) herbs.
Kerkhof (page 155) braid.
't Klompenhuisje (page 123) clogs.
Knopen Winkel (page 155) buttons.

Laura Dols (page 155) 'vintage' ladies clothing.
Old Prints (page 213) prints.
Patisserie Pompadour (page 156) chocolates, glacé fruits, gateaux.
Posthumus (page 87) rubber stamps.
Pyramid (page 124) bespoke leather goods.
Roxanne (page 121) shoes.
De Slegte (page 104) second-hand books.
Smit Volendammer Vishandel (page 160) smoked eels.
Toko (page 175) spices for oriental cooking.
H.P. de Vreng (page 64) Dutch spirits, particularly very old genevers.
Witte Tandenwinkel (page 156) toothbrushes.
Ziekenfondsbrillen (page 171) spectacle frames.

## Services

### Theatres/concert reservations
Advance bookings may be made, in person, at the VVV office in
Stationsplein. From abroad, the National Reservations Centre (tel: 70
3202500) will accept bookings by telephone.

### Telephones
Public kiosks accept 25 cent, 1 guilder and 2.5 guilder coins, and
most bars will have a telephone, which takes the same units. Two 25
cent coins will generally be sufficient for an Amsterdam call. Hotels
will make international calls for you but it is more economical to
telephone from Telehouse, 48 Raadhuisstraat; open daily, 24 hours.
The dialling code to the UK is 09 44. A cheap rate operates for
international calls daily, 20.00-08.00 hours. Since 1991, all
Amsterdam numbers have had seven digits, most being given a 6
prefix.

### Postage
Queues at Amsterdam post offices always seem to be long and slow-
moving. Ensure, therefore, that postcards are purchased with the
necessary stamp. Not all postcard shops have stamps, so ask first.

At post boxes make sure to use the 'Overige' slot.

### Money Exchange
Banks are open Monday to Friday, from 09.00-16.00; some also now
open on Saturday mornings. They give the best exchange rates, all
accepting Travellers Cheques and, most of them, Eurocheques.

Avoid hotel exchange services, which usually give very poor rates. At weekends, there will be a Bureau de Change open somewhere for most of both days; Change Express at Central Station and various offices in Damrak, Leidsestraat and Leidseplein are conveniently sited. American Express Travellers Cheques, changed at their Amsterdam office, 66 Damrak, will not entail a commission charge and are, therefore, a good buy, particularly as their replacement service is uniquely speedy and quibble-free. Eurocheques may be a good buy for long stays, but the conversion rate to sterling is not advantageous.

## Toilet facilities

Sentimentalists will be happy to learn that the circular, gentlemen's urinals, discreetly shielded by decorative ironwork and once so common in Paris (where they were known as *pissotières*), are alive and well but living in Amsterdam. Plastic units, which have replaced all but a handful of the Paris versions, do exist in Amsterdam but are few and far between. However, all bars and hotels permit those in dire need to use their facilities without insisting that a purchase is made.

## Tourist Information

VVV, the Dutch tourist organisation, has two offices in the city: Stationsplein, immediately facing Central Station (telephone 6266444). Open daily in the high season 09.00-23.00. Open daily at other periods 10.00-17.00.

The second, at 106 Leidsestraat, is open daily in the high season 09.00-22.30. At other periods Monday – Saturday 09.00-17.00.

The Netherlands Board of Tourism Office (United Kingdom) is at 25-28 Buckingham Gate, London, SW1E 6LD, (tel: 071 630 0451). Telephone lines are woefully inadequate during the season and a letter or personal visit may well be necessary.

# Accommodation

Unless lower grade accommodation or a long stay are being sought it is generally more economical for two people sharing a room to take the travel/accommodation deals offered by package specialists. Whilst most UK travel agents are able to book hotels, their reservation service is generally limited to the more expensive establishments and an additional booking fee may be charged. Complete lists of hotels are provided by the Netherlands Tourist Board, but it will usually be simpler to make arrangements on arrival at the VVV office, facing Central Station. However, most Amsterdam hotels are fully booked for some time in advance during the spring, particularly on Queens Day (30 April) and at Easter, and difficulties might then be expected if no booking has been made. A wide selection of accommodation available in 1992 follows below.

Amsterdam's accommodation, now totalling 29,000 beds, is slightly cheaper than London's or New York's, but the more economically-priced rooms are significantly dearer than in Paris. Many hotels are located to the south of Leidseplein, but some tourists may prefer to stay within the old city's boundary. Proximity to a tram route to Central Station is advantageous. Canal-side rooms understandably carry a premium, but no matter what grade of accommodation is selected, the rooms will always be clean and reasonably furnished. As may be expected, not all lower-grade rooms have private facilities, but some form of heating will be provided.

## Hotels

The following information is based on the 1992 criteria established by the Benelux Hotel Classification Industrial Catering Board. Prices shown, in Dutch guilders, are for a double room per night in the high season, and represent an average for each grade; some establishments will charge significantly more, some significantly less. Breakfast, service and taxes are included. Single occupancy reductions, if available, will not generally be great. The star(*) indicates a central Amsterdam situation, ie. bounded by the IJ and Singelgracht. A free advance booking service for accommodation in Amsterdam is operated by National Reserverings Centrum Postbus 404, 2260AK Leidschendam, Holland (tel: (3170) 3202500).

## De luxe hotels (five star) 400-500 guilders

| Name of Hotel | Address | Postcode | Telephone |
|---|---|---|---|
| Amsterdam Inter Continental* | Prof. Tulpplein 1 | 1018GX | 6226060 |
| Amsterdam Hilton | Appollolaan 138-40 | 1077BG | 6780780 |
| Amsterdam Marriott* | Stadhouderskade 12 | 1054ES | 6075555 |
| Forte Crest Amsterdam | Apollolaan 2 | 1077BA | 6735922 |
| The Grand* | OZ Voorburgwal 197 | 1012EX | 5553111 |
| Golden Tulip Barbizon Centre | Stadhouderskade 7 | 1054E | 6851351 |
| Golden Tulip Barbizon Palace* | Prins Hendrikkade 59-72 | 1012AD | 5564564 |
| Holiday Inn Amsterdam | De Boelelaan 2 | 1083HJ | 6462300 |
| Holiday Inn Crowne Plaza* | NZ Voorburgwal 5 | 1012RC | 6200500 |
| De l'Europe* | Nieuwe Doelenstraat 2-8 | 1012CP | 6234836 |
| Garden Hotel | Dijsselhofplantsoen 7 | 1077BJ | 6642121 |
| Okura Amsterdam | Ferdinand Bolstraat 333 | 1072LH | 6787111 |
| Pulitzer* | Prinsengracht 315-331 | 1016GZ | 5235235 |
| Ramada Renaissance Amsterdam* | Kattengat 1 | 1012SZ | 6212223 |
| SAS Royal Hotel* | Rusland 17 | 1012CK | 6231231 |

## First-class hotels (four star) 250-400 guilders

| Acca International | Van der Veldestraat 3a | 1071CW | 6625262 |
|---|---|---|---|
| American* | Leidsekade 97 | 1017PN | 6245322 |
| Apollofirst | Apollolaan 123 | 1077AP | 6730333 |
| Swissôtel Amsterdam Ascôt* | Damrak 95-98 | 1012LP | 6260066 |
| Atlas | Van Eeghenstraat 64 | 1071GK | 6766336 |
| AMS Hotel Beethoven | Beethovenstraat 43 | 1077HN | 6644816 |
| Pullman Hotel Capitool* | NZ Voorburgwal 67 | 1012RA | 6275900 |
| Caransa Karena* | Rembrandtplein 19 | 1017CT | 6229455 |
| Jolly Hotel Carlton* | Vijzelstraat 2-18 | 1017H | 6222266 |
| Cok First Class | Koninginneweg 28-32 | 1075CZ | 6646111 |
| Damrak* | Damrak 49 | 1012LL | 6262498 |
| Delphi | Apollolaan 101-105 | 1077AN | 6795152 |
| Dikker & Thijs* | Prinsengracht 444 | 1017KE | 6267721 |

| Name of Hotel | Address | Postcode | Telephone |
|---|---|---|---|
| Doelen Karena* | Nieuwe Doelenstraat 24 | 1012CP | 6220722 |
| Estheréa* | Singel 303-309 | 1012WJ | 6245146 |
| Galaxy | Distelkade 21 | 1031XP | 6344366 |
| Grand Hotel Krasnapolsky* | Dam 9 | 1012JS | 5549111 |
| AMS Hotel Lairesse | De Lairessestraat 7 | 1071NR | 6719596 |
| De Roode Leeuw* | Damrak 93-94 | 1012LP | 6240396 |
| Jan Luyken Hotel & Residence | Jan Luykenstraat 58 | 1071CS | 5730730 |
| Memphis | De Lairessestraat 87 | 1071NX | 6733141 |
| Novotel Amsterdam | Europaboulevard 10 | 1083AD | 5411123 |
| Parkhotel | Stadhouderskade 25 | 1071ZD | 6717474 |
| Die Port van Cleve* | NZ Voorburgwal 178-180 | 1012SJ | 6244860 |
| Rembrandt Karena* | Herengracht 255 | 1016BJ | 6221727 |
| Sander | Jacob Obrechtstraat 69 | 1071KJ | 6627574 |
| Schiller Karena* | Rembrandtplein 26-36 | 1017CV | 6231660 |
| Scandic Crown Victoria* | Damrak 1-6 | 1012LG | 6234255 |
| Nicolaas Witsen | Nicolaas Witsenstraat 4 | 1017ZH | 6266546 |

## Three star hotels (150-250 guilders)

| Name of Hotel | Address | Postcode | Telephone |
|---|---|---|---|
| Aalborg | Sarphatipark 106-108 | 1073EC | 6760310 |
| Aalders | Jan Luykenstraat 13-15 | 1071CJ | 6620116 |
| Altea Amsterdam | Joan Muyskenweg 10 | 1096CJ | 6658181 |
| Ambassade* | Herengracht 341 | 1016AZ | 6262333 |
| Mercure Arthur Frommer* | Noorderstraat 46 | 1017TV | 6220328 |
| Avenue Hotel* | NZ Voorburgwal 27 | 1012RD | 6238307 |
| Barbacan* | Plantage Muidergracht 89 | 1018TN | 6264073 |
| Bastion Amsterdam Centrum Noord | Rode Kruisstraat 28 | 1025KN | 6323131 |
| Bastion Amsterdam Centrum Zuid-West | Nachtwachtlaan 11 | 1058EV | 6691621 |
| Belfort | Surinameplein 53 | 1058GN | 6174333 |
| Borgmann | Koningslaan 48 | 1075AE | 6735252 |
| The Bridge Hotel* | Amstel 107-111 | 1018EM | 6237068 |
| Canal House* | Keizersgracht 148 | 1015CX | 6225182 |
| Casa 400 | James Wattstraat 75 | 1097DL | 6651171 |
| Amsterdam Classic Hotel* | Gravenstraat 14-16 | 1012NM | 6233716 |
| Cok Tourist Class | Koninginneweg 34-36 | 1075CZ | 6646111 |
| Concert-Inn | De Lairessestraat 11 | 1071NR | 6750051 |
| Cordial* | Rokin 62-64 | 1012KW | 6264411 |
| Delta* | Damrak 42 | 1012LK | 6202626 |

| Name of Hotel | Address | Postcode | Telephone |
|---|---|---|---|
| Eden* | Amstel 144 | 1017AE | 6266243 |
| Eureka* | 's Gravelandseveer 3-4 | 1011KM | 6246607 |
| Falcon Plaza* | Valkenburgerstraat 72-74 | 1011LZ | 6382991 |
| Flipper | Borssenburgstraat 1-5 | 1078VA | 6761932 |
| Heemskerk | J. W. Brouwersstraat 25 | 1071LH | 6794980 |
| Prins Hendrik* | Prins Hendrikkade 53 | 1012AC | 6277931 |
| Hestia | Roemer Visscherstraat 7 | 1054EV | 6180801 |
| AMS Hotel Holland | P. C. Hooftstraat 162 | 1071CH | 6764253 |
| Lancaster | Plantage Middenlaan 48 | 1018DH | 6266544 |
| De Looier* | Derde Looiersdwarsstraat 75 | 1016VD | 6251039 |
| Maas* | Leidsekade 91 | 1017PN | 6233868 |
| Marianne | Nicolaas Maesstraat 107 | 1071PV | 6797972 |
| De Molen* | Prinsengracht 1015 | 1017KN | 6231666 |
| AMS Museum Hotel* | PC Hooftstraat 2 | 1071BX | 6621402 |
| Nes* | Kloveniersburgwal 137 | 1011KE | 6244773 |
| Nova* | NZ Voorburgwal 276 | 1012RS | 6230066 |
| Owl | Roemer Visscherstraat 1 | 1054EV | 6189484 |
| De Paris* | Marnixstraat 372 | 1016XX | 6225587 |
| Prinsen | Vondelstraat 36-38 | 1054GE | 6162323 |
| Rho Hotel* | Nes 11-23 | 1012KC | 6207371 |
| Roemer Visscher | Roemer Visscherstraat 10 | 1054EX | 6125511 |
| San Francisco* | Nieuwendijk 100 | 1012MR | 6259076 |
| Singel* | Singel 13-17 | 1012VC | 6263108 |
| Slotania | Slotermeerlaan 133 | 1063JN | 6134568 |
| Smit* | PC Hooftstraat 24-28 | 1071BX | 6714785 |
| AMS Terdam Hotel | Tesselschadestraat 23 | 1054ET | 6126876 |
| Terminus* | Beursstraat 11-19 | 1012JT | 6220535 |
| Toren* | Keizersgracht 164 | 1015CZ | 6226352 |
| Toro | Koningslaan 64 | 1075AG | 6737233 |
| AMS Trianon Hotel | J. W. Brouwersstraat 3 | 1071LH | 6732073 |
| Vondel | Vondelstraat 28 | 1054GE | 6120120 |
| Vondelhof | Vondelstraat 24 | 1054GD | 6122221 |
| Westropa I | 1e Const. Huygensstraat 103-105 | 1054BV | 6188808 |
| Westropa II* | Nassaukade 387-390 | 1054AE | 6834935 |
| Zandbergen | Willemsparkweg 205 | 1071HB | 6769321 |

## Two star hotels (75-150 guilders)

| | | | |
|---|---|---|---|
| Van Acker | J. W. Brouwersstraat 14 | 1071LJ | 6790745 |
| Acro | Jan Luykenstraat 44 | 1071CR | 6620526 |
| Agora* | Singel 462 | 1017AW | 6272200 |
| Amstel Botel Hotel* | de Ruyterkade pier 5 | 1011AA | 6264247 |
| Amstelzicht* | Amstel 104 | 1017AD | 6236693 |

| Name of Hotel | Address | Postcode | Telephone |
| --- | --- | --- | --- |
| Amsterdam Wiechmann* | Prinsengracht 328-332 | 1016HX | 6263321 |
| D'Amsterdam | Tweede Helmersstraat 4 | 1054CH | 6160125 |
| Apple Inn | Koninginneweg 93 | 1075CJ | 6627894 |
| Armada | Keizersgracht 713-715 | 1017DX | 6232980 |
| Arsenal | Frans van | | |
| | Mierisstraat 97 | 1071RN | 6792209 |
| Asterisk* | Den Texstraat 16 | 1017ZA | 6262396 |
| Bodeman* | Rokin 154-156 | 1012LE | 6201558 |
| Van Bonga | Holbeinstraat 1hs | 1077VB | 6625218 |
| Casa-Cara | Emmastraat 24 | 1075HV | 6623135 |
| Central Park West Hotel | Roemer Visscherstraat 27 | 1054EW | 6852285 |
| Cynthia | Vondelstraat 44-48 | 1054GE | 6188553 |
| City Hotel* | Prins Hendrikkade 130 | 1011AP | 6230836 |
| Destiné | Sarphatikade 17 | 1017WV | 6236822 |
| Engeland | Roemer Visscherstraat 30a | 1054EZ | 6129691 |
| De Filosoof | Anna Vondelstraat 4-6 | 1054GZ | 6833013 |
| Fita | Jan Luykenstraat 37 | 1071CL | 6790976 |
| Freeland* | Marnixstraat 386 | 1017PL | 6227511 |
| Friendship* | van Eeghenstraat 22 | 1071GG | 6644011 |
| Groenhof | Vondelstraat 74 | 1054GN | 6168221 |
| Imperial* | Thorbeckeplein 9 | 1017CS | 6220051 |
| ITC (gay)* | Prinsengracht 1051 | 1017JE | 6230230 |
| Jupiter | Tweede Helmersstraat 14 | 1054CJ | 6124964 |
| De Gouden Kettingh* | Keizersgracht 268-272 | 1016EV | 6248287 |
| De Korenaer* | Damrak 50 | 1012LL | 6220855 |
| Middelberg | Koninginneweg 149 | 1075CM | 6765392 |
| De Munck* | Achtergracht 3 | 1017WL | 6236283 |
| New York (gay)* | Herengracht 13 | 1015BA | 6243066 |
| Sint Nicolaas* | Spuistraat 1a | 1012SP | 6261384 |
| Omega | Jacob Obrechtstraat 31 | 1071KG | 6645182 |
| Parklane | Plantage Parklaan 16 | 1018ST | 6224804 |
| Parkzicht | Roemer Visscherstraat 33 | 1054EW | 6181954 |
| Piet Hein | Vossiusstraat 53 | 1071AK | 6628375 |
| Int. Police Hotel | Voorburgstraat 250 | 1059VD | 6157026 |
| De La Poste* | Reguliersgracht 3-5 | 1017LJ | 6237105 |
| The Golden Regal | Korte van Eeghenstraat 8 | 1071ER | 6762131 |
| Rembrandt | Plantage Middenlaan 17 | 1018DA | 6272714 |
| La Richelle | Holbeinstraat 41 | 1077VC | 6717971 |
| Rokin* | Rokin 73 | 1012KL | 6267456 |
| Savoy | Michelangelostraat 39 | 1077BR | 6790367 |
| Sipermann | Roemer Visscherstraat 35 | 1054EW | 6161866 |
| Stadhouder | Stadhouderskade 76 | 1078AE | 6718428 |
| Thorbecke* | Thorbeckeplein 3 | 1017CS | 6232601 |
| Verdi | Wanningstraat 9 | 1071LA | 6760073 |
| Vijaya* | OZ Voorburgwal 44 | 1012GE | 6269406 |

| Name of Hotel | Address | Postcode | Telephone |
|---|---|---|---|
| The Village* | Kerkstraat 25 | 1017GA | 6269746 |
| Vullings | P. C. Hooftstraat 78 | 1071CB | 6712109 |
| The Waterfront* | Singel 458 | 1017AW | 6239775 |
| Wilhelmina | Koninginneweg 167-169 | 1075CN | 6640594 |

## One star hotels (70-125 guilders)

| | | | |
|---|---|---|---|
| Abba | Overtoom 122 | 1054HM | 6183058 |
| Acacia* | Lindengracht 251 | 1015KH | 6221460 |
| De Admiraal* | Herengracht 563 | 1017CD | 6262150 |
| Adolesce | Nieuwe Keizersgracht 26 | 1018DS | 6263959 |
| Albert | Sarphatipark 58 | 1073CZ | 6734083 |
| Aspen* | Raadhuisstraat 31 | 1016DC | 6266714 |
| Atlanta* | Rembrandtplein 8-10 | 1017CV | 6253585 |
| Belga* | Hartenstraat 8 | 1016CB | 6249080 |
| Bema | Concertbegouwplein 19b | 1071LM | 6791396 |
| Biervliet | Nassaukade 368 | 1054AB | 6188404 |
| Boshoek* | Groenburgwal 27 | 1011HR | 6248429 |
| Clemens* | Raadhuisstraat 39 | 1016DC | 6246089 |
| Corner House* | NZ Voorburgwal 121 | 1012RH | 6241326 |
| L'Espérance | Stadhouderskade 49 | 1072AA | 6714049 |
| Fantasia* | Nieuwe Keizersgracht 16 | 1018DR | 6238259 |
| Fox* | Weteringschans 67 | 1017RX | 6228338 |
| Galerij* | Raadhuisstraat 43 | 1016DD | 6248851 |
| De Gerstekorrel* | Damstraat 22-24 | 1012JM | 6249771 |
| Vincent van Gogh | van der Veldestraat 5 | 1071CW | 6796002 |
| Granada* | Leidsekruisstraat 13 | 1017RE | 6236711 |
| Van Haalen* | Prinsengracht 520 | 1017KJ | 6264334 |
| De Harmonie* | Prinsengracht 816 | 1017JL | 6228021 |
| De La Haye* | Leidsegracht 114 | 1016CT | 6244044 |
| Hegra* | Herengracht 269 | 1016BJ | 6237877 |
| Hemony | Hemonystraat 7 | 1077BK | 6714241 |
| Hoksbergen* | Singel 301 | 1012WH | 6266043 |
| PC Hooft* | P C Hooftstraat 63 | 1071BN | 6594979 |
| Het Witte Huis* | Marnixstraat 382 | 1016XX | 6646500 |
| Impala* | Leidsekade 77 | 1017PM | 6234706 |
| Interland | Vossiusstraat 46 | 1071AJ | 6622344 |
| Internationaal* | Warmoesstraat 1-3 | 1012HT | 6245520 |
| Janson | Frans van Mierisstraat 69a | 1071RL | 6797203 |
| Kap* | Den Texstraat 5b | 1017XW | 6245908 |
| Van de Kasteelen | Frans van Mierisstraat 34 | 1071RT | 6798995 |
| King* | Leidsekade 85-86 | 1017PN | 6249603 |
| Kitty | Plantage Middenlaan 40 | 1018DG | 6226819 |

| Name of Hotel | Address | Postcode | Telephone |
|---|---|---|---|
| Kooyk* | Leidsekade 82 | 1017PM | 6230295 |
| De Lantaerne* | Leidsegracht 111 | 1017ND | 6232221 |
| Het Leidseplein* | Korte Leidsedwarsstraat 79 | 1017PW | 6272505 |
| De Leydsche Hof* | Leidsegracht 14 | 1016CK | 6232148 |
| Linda | Stadhouderskade 131 | 1074AW | 6625668 |
| Museumzicht | Jan Luykenstraat 22 | 1071CN | 6715224 |
| Old Nickel* | Nieuwe Brugsteeg 11 | 1012AG | 6241912 |
| Van Onna* | Bloemgracht 102 | 1015TN | 6265801 |
| Oosterpark | Oosterpark 72 | 1092AS | 6930049 |
| Van Ostade Bicycle Hotel | Van Ostadestraat 123 | 1072SV | 6715213 |
| Pax* | Raadhuisstraat 37 | 1016DC | 6249735 |
| Perséverance | Overtoom 78-80 | 1054HL | 6182653 |
| Peters* | Nicolaas Maesstraat 72 | 1071RC | 6733454 |
| Prinsenhof* | Prinsengracht 810 | 1017SL | 6231772 |
| Ronnie* | Raadhuisstraat 41 | 1016DD | 6242821 |
| Van Rooyen | Tweede Helmersstraat 6 | 1054CH | 6184577 |
| Schirmann* | Prins Hendrikkade 23 | 1012TM | 6241942 |
| Schröder* | Haarlemmerdijk 48b | 1013JE | 6266272 |
| Seven Bridges* | Reguliersgracht 31 | 1017LK | 6231329 |
| Sphinx* | Weteringschans 82 | 1017XR | 6273680 |
| De Stern* | Utrechtsestraat 18 | 1017VN | 6265619 |
| Titus* | Leidsekade 74 | 1017PM | 6265758 |
| Victorie | Victorieplein 40-42 | 1078PH | 6623233 |
| Het Wapen van Amsterdam* | Damrak 58 | 1012LL | 6249263 |
| Washington | Frans van Mierisstraat 10 | 1071RS | 6797453 |
| Weber* | Marnixstraat 397 | 1017PJ | 6270574 |
| De Westertoren* | Raadhuisstraat 35 | 1016DC | 6244639 |
| Wijnnobel* | Vossiusstraat 9 | 1071AB | 6622298 |

## Economical hotels (no star rating) 80-110 guilders

| | | | |
|---|---|---|---|
| Beursstraat* | Beursstraat 7 | 1012JT | 6263701 |
| La Bohème* | Marnixstraat 415 | 1017PK | 6242828 |
| Brian* | Singel 69 | 1012VE | 6244661 |
| Damhotel* | Damrak 31 | 1012LJ | 6240945 |
| Florence | Van Eeghensstraat 44 | 1071GJ | 6793798 |
| Hotel 83* | OZ Achterburgwal 83 | 1012DC | 6262089 |
| Van Hulssen* | Bloemgracht 108 | 1015TN | 6265801 |
| De Bloeiende Ramenas* | Haarlemmerdijk 61 | 1013KB | 6246030 |
| The Regal* | Binnen Wieringerstraat 9 | 1013EA | 6274390 |
| San Luchesio | Waldeck Pyrmontlaan 9 | 1075BT | 6716861 |
| Senova Dinar* | Frederiksplein 15 | 1017XK | 6206425 |
| The Veteran* | Herengracht 561 | 1017BW | 6202673 |

## Youth hotels/hostels

| Name of Hotel | Address | Postcode | Telephone |
|---|---|---|---|
| Adam & Eva | Sarphatistraat 105 | 1018GA | 6246206 |
| Aroza* | Nieuwendijk 23 | 1012LZ | 6209123 |
| Bob's Youth Hostel* | NZ Voorburgwal 92 | 1012SG | 6230063 |
| Hans Brinker* | Kerkstraat 136 | 1017GR | 6220687 |
| Eben Haëzer | Bloemstraat 179 | 1016LA | 6244717 |
| Kabul* | Warmoesstraat 38-42 | 1012JE | 6237158 |
| Keizersgracht* | Keizersgracht 15 | 1015CC | 6251364 |
| Jeugdhotel Meeting Point* | Warmosstraat 14 | 1012JD | 6277499 |
| The Shelter* | Barndesteeg 21 | 1012BV | 6253230 |
| Stadsdoelen (IYHF)* | Kloveniersburgwal 97 | 1011KB | 6246832 |
| Vondelpark (IYHF)* | Zandpad 5 | 1054GA | 6831744 |
| Sleep-in Mauritskade* | 's Gravesandestraat 51 | 1092AA | 6947444 |
| Zeezicht | Piet Heinkade 15 | 1019BR | 6178706 |

## Camping

| | | | |
|---|---|---|---|
| Het Amsterdamse Bos | Kleine Noorddijk 1/ Aalsmeer | 1432CC | 020-6416868 |
| De Badhoeve | Uitdammerdijk 10/ Amsterdam | 1026CP | 02904-294 |
| Gaasper Camping | Loosdrechtdreef 7/ Amsterdam | 1108AZ | 020-6967326 |
| Vliegenbos | Meeuwenlaan 138/ Amsterdam | 1022AM | 020-6368855 |
| Zeeburg | Zuider IJdijk 44/ Amsterdam | 1095KN | 020-6944430 |

## Apartments

| | | | |
|---|---|---|---|
| Amsterdam Apartments* | Kromme Waal 32 | 1011BV | 6265930 |
| Amsterdam House Apartments* | Staalkade 4 | 1011JN | 6262577 |
| Canal Apartments* | Nieuwe Achtergracht 67 | 1018WL | 6257238 |
| Briefcase Home Tip* | Sarphatistraat 116-118 | 1018GW | 6254443 |
| Gasthuismolen Apartments* | Gasthuismolensteeg 10 | 1016AN | 6240736 |
| GIS Apartments* | Keizersgracht 33 | 1015CD | 6250071 |
| Holbein Studio's | Holbeinstraat 5 | 1077VB | 6628832 |
| IDA Housing Services* | Den Texstraat 30hs | 1017ZB | 6248301 |
| Intercity Room Service | Van Ostadestraat 348 | 1073TZ | 6750064 |
| Riverside Apartments* | Amstel 138 | 1017AD | 6279797 |
| Toff's Apartments | Ruysdaelkade 167 | 1072AS | 6738529 |

# Food & Drink in Amsterdam

## Food

Specifically Dutch dishes are very limited in number, and few Amsterdammers wish to eat them when dining out. Therefore, as in Britain, where a similar situation exists, most Amsterdam restaurants are 'international' or ethnic, but with particular emphasis on the former Dutch colony of Indonesia. A few restaurants, however, do offer some local dishes, which are little-known elsewhere, and a summary of Dutch cuisine is therefore given. Also discussed briefly is Indonesian food, which is still hard to find in many other European countries. Hotels generally include Dutch breakfasts, varying little in their content, and for lunch and 'space-fillers' most tourists will rely, like the locals, on fast foods.

### Breakfast

Mid-way between the traditional English and the sparse 'continental' breakfast, the spread is likely to contain: Dutch cheese (of a very bland variety), ham, salami, an egg boiled or fried, preserves and peanut butter. Bread, toast and unsalted butter complete the meal. Coffee is almost always expresso and strong. Tea, made from tea bags, is almost always weak. Few Dutch contemplate drinking either of these beverages without sugar, and they tend to serve sweet, evaporated milk 'koffiemelk' with coffee – check before pouring. No milk is usually offered with tea; ask for it if required.

### Lunch/Fast Food

It is uncommon for the Amsterdammer to eat a formal lunch, even as part of business entertaining, and few restaurants open before 17.00 hours. Health and diet considerations have convinced most of the Dutch that a snack is all that is required to keep the system going. Consequently, the fast food range offered is wide, much wider than in England. Herring stalls, found throughout the city, offer small portions of fish, including raw herring, which will be fresh from late spring to early summer or, salted throughout the rest of the year. In Amsterdam, the herring is cut into bite-sized pieces and served with chopped onion and cucumber pickled in dill – not as frightening as it sounds! Lovers of smoked fish will find that the slim fillets of smoked eel are one of the great delights of eating in Holland; they are subtle in flavour and less salty than most smoked salmon. In the home, the eels are eaten with buttered toast – neither lemon nor pepper is added, but rolls are always offered.

Chips (French fries), very popular in Amsterdam, are sold at various outlets. They are smothered in a sauce, usually mayonnaise, an unusual combination for many, but quite tasty and satisfying, even though the snack is very high in calories.

Butchers and fishmongers also get in on the hot fast food act, many offering, respectively, meatballs fried in batter and fried fish fillets.

*Broodjes* indicates that soft roll sandwiches are sold and there are, of course, the usual hamburgers and pizzas, varying in quality. The Dutch are very fond of hot desserts; delicious small pancakes, waffles, etc., are widely available. Look for the signs 'poffertjes' and 'wafels'.

# Dinner

## Dutch dishes

As in England, Dutch food depends on the simple preparation of first-rate raw materials. However, the emphasis on vegetables and boiling, rather than meats and roasting tends to result in even blander flavours. All the dishes are only really suitable for consumption in the cooler months, but some restaurants will offer them all the year round. Probably due to the damp, northern climate, specialities are usually heavy, the meal often beginning with a thick pea, brown bean or potato soup. Mashed potatoes form the basis of *stampots* and are blended with another mashed vegetable, such as endive, cabbage, sauerkraut, etc. Smoked sausage or bacon is usually included in this hearty boil-up, but the dish will be named after the vegetable used. A beef stew, served with potatoes, carrots and onions, is known as a *hutspot*.

In May, many restaurants of all types will offer fresh, locally-grown asparagus, served in various ways. However, the Dutch prefer the white variety, which is less flavoursome than the green. During autumn and most of the winter, fresh mussels are a delight; they are cultivated and reach a huge size with a delicate flavour. Not to be missed, the Dutch, like the French, appreciate them with chips, a combination that, to me, does not work. In general, Dutch home-produced meat is good – Texel Island lamb, and meat from a oneyear-old calf (fliandre) being exceptional. Dutch cheeses, due to their blandness, are mostly unexciting, but Leidse (Gouda with cumin seeds), the strong Oude Gouda, Maasdammer and the very pungent Limburger are exceptions. Remember the terms that refer to strength: jong (mild), belegen (medium) and oude (strong).

## Indonesian cuisine

Since the days of the British Raj ended, the English have become addicted to Indian food. Similarly, following the loss of their East Indian colonies, the Dutch have acquired a taste for Indonesian cuisine, and this now plays a major part in Amsterdam's restaurant scene, although the best examples are said to be found in the Hague. It is strange that whereas the English demand curries that are hotter than those found throughout much of India, most Dutch insist that Indonesian chefs reduce the chili content to such a degree that their dishes lack authenticity. In my experience, only Tempo Doeloe, in Amsterdam, offers the correct degree of fire. However, other restaurants also provide acceptable dishes of the more subtle variety. Lovers of coconut and peanut flavours will enjoy the food, which, apart from the satay, is very similar to Malaysian. I personally dislike the Indonesian method of preparing satay sauce; the result is much sweeter and darker, the finely ground peanuts producing a smooth sauce that is barely comparable with the Malaysian version.

No English-speaking visitor should ever have a language problem in Amsterdam restaurants and the following brief vocabulary concentrates on items that are difficult to translate. Most establishments will provide a menu in English.

| Dutch | English |
|-------|---------|
| Andijvie | Endive |
| Appelgepak | Apple strudel |
| Asperge | Asparagus |
| Bitterballen | Deep-fried meat balls (chicken and ham) moistened with béchamel sauce |
| Boerenkool | Casserole of kale, potatoes and smoked sausage |
| Bokking | Smoked herring |
| Broodjes | Soft roll sandwiches |
| Bruinebonensoep | Brown kidney bean and onion soup |
| Chocolade hagelslag | Pieces of chocolate on buttered bread |
| Erwtensoep | Dried pea soup, with smoked sausage |
| Fliandre | One-year-old calf |
| Fricandel | Minced meat and onion croquettes |
| Gerookte paling | Smoked eel |
| Hutspot | Beef stew with carrots, onions and potatoes |
| Lamsvlees Texel | Texel Island lamb |
| Lekkerbekjes | Fried fish fillets |
| Mosselen | Mussels |
| Oliebollen | Deep fried doughnut-style bun with currants, candied peel and apple |
| Pannekoeken | Pancake |
| Patatfrite | Chips (French fries) |
| Poffertjes | Small pancakes dusted with icing sugar and served with unsalted butter |
| Rodekool | Red cabbage |
| Speculaas | Crisp biscuits flavoured with herbs |
| Stamppot | Mashed potatoes with another vegetable, usually served with smoked sausage or bacon |
| Stroopwafels | Waffles with maple syrup |
| Worst | Sausage |
| Uitsmijters | Large open sandwich with ham, a fried egg, gherkins and cocktail onions |
| Zuurkool | Sauerkraut |

**Indonesian**

| | |
|-------|---------|
| Ajam | Chicken |
| Bami | Fried spicy noodles |
| Daging | Strips of marinated meat (usually beef) |
| Gado-gado | Salad of lightly stir-fried mixed vegetables with a hard-boiled egg, served with peanut sauce |

| | |
|---|---|
| Gulai ayam | Chicken curry |
| Ikan | Fish |
| Ikan padang | Fish curry |
| Kalio ayam | Chicken with curried coconut and peanut sauce |
| Ketuput | Sticky rice |
| Lontong | Steamed rice |
| Nasi | Rice |
| Nasi goreng | Fried rice with onions, chilis etc – usually served with meat or prawns and topped with a shredded omelette |
| Radang | Hot and dry sauce made with coconut milk |
| Rijsttafel | A Dutch Indonesian development, meaning rice table, that consists of a huge array of small dishes accompanied by rice; degrees of heat should vary for each dish |
| Sambal | Hot chili sauce, but hot side dishes are also called sambals |
| Satay | Beef or chicken cubes barbecued on skewers, served with peanut sauce, cucumber and bean curd |
| Soto ayam | Spicy chicken soup containing hard-boiled egg |
| Udang | Prawns |

## Drink

Serious drinking in Amsterdam takes place in the 'brown bars'. Most of these are ancient taverns, a few of which were originally added to an adjacent distillery as its tasting house (proeflokaal). The 'brown' referred to has been acquired by the walls and ceilings, mainly through nicotine in the tobacco smoke emitted by customers over the years. No-one would dream of cleaning or repainting these venerable establishments, most of which were founded in the 17th century. Thankfully, there is rarely a juke box and never a television. Beer, of course, is the most popular drink, normally taking the form of Dutch-brewed lager (pils). Heineken and Amstel are the best-known brands, but other ales, including foreign-brewed examples, are often available. Drinkers should bear in mind that in Holland, unlike England, lager is made the natural way and each glass should be topped with 'two-fingers' of froth – this is allowed for in the price.

If a small glass is required, ask for either a *kabouter* or a *lampie licht pils*. Larger glasses of beer are a *bakkie* or a *vaas*. Many will also wish to taste *genever* or *jenefer*, its name – meaning juniper – later being corrupted by the English to gin. The main differences between Dutch and London gin are that the former is sweetened and slightly less alcoholic. An *oud genever* is older and mellow, whilst a *jong* is a little rougher and stronger. A *borrel* is a standard glass of *genever*. When requiring a beer with a *genever* chaser a Dutchman asks for a *kopstoot* (knock on the head), or a *stelletje* (couple).

## Selected Restaurants

'**A**' indicates over £25, '**B**' £10-£25 and '**C**' under £10. De, Le and 't are ignored for alphabetical order.

Few of the grander restaurants open for lunch, as the business entertaining tradition is not strong in Holland and most prefer to eat their main meal early in the evening. For this reason, restaurants in Amsterdam generally take orders from 18.00 hours, or even earlier.

### An American Place   C

141 Utrechtsedwarsstraat (tel: 6207393). Open Wednesday – Sunday 17.00-23.30. American food includes regional US specialities, eg. Cajun rib-eye steak, New Orleans gambo.

### Beddingtons   A

6-8 Roelof Hartstraat (tel: 6765201). Open Monday – Saturday 18.00-22.00, Tuesday – Saturday 12.00-14.00. The English owner/ chef Jean Beddington offers a very international menu eg. monkfish tandoori, syllabub and Japanese specialities. Set menus for lunch and dinner.

### Bojo   C

51 Lange Leidsedwarsstraat (No bookings). Open daily until 04.00. Dull, Indonesian, food with virtually all the heat removed. Ideal for children and, so it seems, many Dutch. Bojo's main attraction is fast service and late closure.

### Bols Taverne   A

106-108 Rozengracht (tel: 6245152). Open Monday – Saturday 18.00-22.00. The delightful 17th-century building is, unusually, fronted by a courtyard. Fish dishes of a more exotic nature than usual are the speciality of this restaurant, owned by the famous Bols distillery family. Understandably, there is an unusually wide range of liqueurs and spirits.

### De Canova  A

9 Warmoestraat (tel: 6266725). Open Tuesday –Saturday 18.00-22.00. Warmoestraat's best and most expensive restaurant. Everything is home-made including, understandably, the pasta – but Italian dishes do not predominate.

### Centra  C

29 Lange Niezel (tel: 6223050). Open daily 13.00-23.00. Basic Spanish dishes include a good fabada (pork and bean casserole).

### Christophe  A

46 Leliegracht (tel: 6250807). Open Monday –Saturday 19.00-23.00. One of the city's finest restaurants: French cuisine with a delicate touch. Mediterranean specialities include authentic fish dishes.

### Taveerne Claes Claesz  C

24-26 Egelantiersstraat (tel: 6255306). Open Thursday – Sunday from 18.00. A popular Jordaan restaurant, concentrating on basic Dutch food. Live music adds to the friendly atmosphere most evenings.

### Edo  A

Grand Hotel Krasnapolsky, 9 De Dam (tel: 65549111). The city's smartest Japanese restaurant, located within the historic Grand Krasnapolsky hotel. Magnificently fresh sushi.

### Egg Cream  C

19 St. Jacobstraat (tel: 6230575). Open daily for lunch and dinner, but closes at 20.00. Famous for its economically priced vegetarian dishes, some meat is also available. Set meals are offered for lunch and dinner.

### De Gouden Real  B

14 Zandhoek (tel: 6233883). Open Monday –Saturday from 18.00. Basically French cuisine is featured. Good value for money.

### De Goudsbloem  A

Pulitzer Hotel, 8 Reestraat (tel: 6253288). Open daily 18.00-23.00. French Cuisine Nouvelle. Certainly one of Amsterdam's finest restaurants. Flavours are delicately combined.

**Haesje Claes   C**
273-75 Spuistraat (tel: 6249998). Open Monday – Saturday 12.00-
22.00. Good value Dutch food. Large, but often full due to popularity
with large groups. In many ways this is the ideal restaurant for those
in search of Dutch specialities.

**Keuken van 1870   C**
4 Spuistraat (tel: 6248965). Open Monday – Friday 11.30-20.00
(Wednesday 16.00-21.00). Probably the city's best-value Dutch
restaurant, there is always an economically-priced dish of the day.
NB open all afternoon but closes early in the evening.

**Lana Thai   B**
Warmoestraat (tel: 6242179). Open Wednesday – Monday 17.00-
22.30. Authentic Thai food here is rated the city's best. The dining
room overlooks Damrak's water.

**Lonny's   B**
6 Rozengracht (tel: 6238950). Open daily 18.00-23.00 (17.00-22.00
in winter). This small, very popular Jordaan restaurant is generally
full and booking is essential. The Indonesian food is not too watered
down.

**Lucius   A**
247 Spuistraat (tel: 6241831). Open daily 17.30-23.00. No longer an
economical restaurant, Lucius specialises in fish fresh from the North
Sea. A heavy hand with dill, tarragon etc. tends to disguise the
natural flavours to an unacceptable degree in some dishes.

**Maarakech   C**
134 N-Z Voorburgwal (tel: 6235003). Open Thursday   – Tuesday
17.00-22.30. Good quality and good value couscous, tajine (stew)
etc. is served in Amsterdam's only Moroccan restaurant. Lamb
dishes are much better than those usually provided in their country of
origin, due to the superior quality of the meat. Friendly service.

**(Opposite) Top:** *Canal-boat tours are a delightful way of exploring
Amsterdam.*
**(Opposite) Bottom:** *Diamond polishing (but not cutting) can be
observed in many establishments.*

**Moy Kong  C**
87 Zeedijk (tel: 6241906). Open Tuesday – Sunday 13.00-23.00.
Probably the best of several restaurants in this mini-
Chinatown.Authentic Cantonese food at very low prices.

**Café Pacifico  C**
31 Warmoestraat (tel: 6242911). Open daily 17.30-22.30. Mexican
food is served at the bar or in the rear restaurant of this sister to
similarly-named restaurants in London and Paris. As might be
expected, here, in Amsterdam, insufficient chilis deprive many dishes
of their authenticity. What is the point of a bland guacamole? Very
pleasant service and lethal Margaritas.

**Die Port van Cleve  B**   (see also page 86)
178-80 N-Z Voorburgwal (tel: 6244860). Open daily 12.30-22.30.
The Die Port restaurant, one of two within the hotel, has served
Dutch steaks since 1870, and each customer is given a card indicating
its number – now on the way to six million. There are several
combinations, however, the Steak Port van Cleve is cooked with
bacon, the strong flavour of which rather takes over – not
recommended. Pea soup, perhaps Holland's best known culinary
speciality, is served with smoked sausage, and accompanied by sweet
rye bread. A Dutch colleague tells me that in the home the soup is
usually much thicker. In winter, stamppots are available.

**Punjab  C**
7 Frederik Hendrikstraat (tel: 6866141). Open daily 17.30-23.30.
Amsterdam has far less Indian than Indonesian restaurants, but the
Punjab aims for a high standard. Tandoori's and north Indian breads
are authentic. Addicts of hot curries should clarify their tastes with
the waiter when ordering.

*The four types of 'Dutch' gable:*
**(Opposite) Top left:** *A step design was the first decorative form of
Dutch gable to evolve.*
**(Opposite) Top right:** *Trapezium gables were introduced by
Hendrick de Keyser, Amsterdam's most renowned 17th-century
architect.*
**(Opposite) Bottom left:** *Neck gables (left and middle houses) were
introduced by the Vingboons brothers.*
**(Opposite) Bottom right:** *Adjoining bell gable houses.*

### Le Reflet d'Or   A
Grand Hotel Krasnapolsky, 9 De Dam (tel: 65549111). Open daily from 18.00. This is the hotel's second restaurant. International cuisine, basically French, is served in a delightfully elegant dining room.

### De Roode Leeuw   B
93-94 Damrak (tel: 6240396). Open daily 12.00-22.00. Menus always include three typical Dutch dishes, prepared to a high standard. All served in this vintage hotel's large restaurant.

### Sama Sebo   B
27 P.C. Hooftstraat (tel: 6628146). Open Monday – Saturday for lunch and dinner. Famous Indonesian rijsttafels are served at a higher than usual price. The chef is willing to 'season it up' on request to the waiter; ingredients are always first-rate.

### Sea Palace   A
Oosterdokskade (tel: 6264777). Open daily 12.00-23.00. A long menu of Chinese dishes also includes Indonesian specialities but, as in most Chinese restaurants in the city, these are not remotely authentic. A large dining room can seat 700 at a time in this permanently moored 'pagoda boat'. The atmosphere is luxurious but the prices are high – incredibly high for ethnic food. Fish dishes are beautifully prepared.

### Semarang   C
15 Grote Geusplein (tel: 6134911). Open Tuesday – Sunday 16.00-22.00. A half-hour journey to the terminals of bus 21 or tram 13 is all it takes to reach this suburban Indonesian restaurant, rated by those in-the-know to be Amsterdam's finest. If ordered in advance, a rijsttafel for one can be prepared, otherwise two minimum. The range offered is tremendous and flavours most delicate, even though the absolutely authentic heat may be missing. All staff belong to the patron's family and a friendly atmosphere prevails. As the restaurant occupies a small, converted garage, booking is, in any case, advisable. Check the return bus or tram times to avoid a lengthy wait.

### De Silveren Spiegel   A   (see also page 128)
4-6 Kattengat (tel: 6246589). Open daily 18.00-22.00 also 12.00-14.00 Monday – Friday. Dutch/French cuisine is served in several delightful rooms occupying two step-gabled 17th-century houses. Flavours are not masked by the over-use of herbs, the plague of so many of the city's restaurants. Specialities generally available

include fresh shrimps in puff pastry with lobster sauce, poached turbot and Texel Island lamb (served a little too underdone for my taste). The wine list is phenomenal and includes items from the patron's own vineyards in southern France. Highly recommended for a special treat.

### Sluizer  B
45 Utrechtsestraat (tel: 6263557). Open Monday –Saturday for lunch and dinner (check times). Superb fresh fish with exceptional huge mussels in season (September – March).

### 't Swarte Schaap  A
24 Korte Leidsedwarsstraat (tel: 6223021). Open daily for lunch and dinner (check times). Facing Leidseplein, this restaurant is renowned for its intimate, 17th-century interiors. International cuisine is reliable without, perhaps, quite rating the high prices.

### Tango  C
49 Warmoestraat (tel: 6272467). Open daily 17.00-24.00. Argentinean food is served with the emphasis on grilled steaks. A pleasant atmosphere, where South American music prevails. Interesting desserts include *boudin de pan*, a heavy type of bread pudding, or *dulce de latte* – an unusual fudge-like dish made from condensed milk.

### Tempo Doeloe  B
75 Utrechtsestraat (tel: 6256718). Open daily 18.00-23.30. The only Indonesian meal that I had in Amsterdam to match the authentic heat of its native country was at this restaurant. Tempo Doeloe's rijsttafel comprises 24 dishes served as three courses, each of eight varieties. Waiters will point out the hottest –heed what they say. Plenty of rice, rather than liquid, is the antidote to the chilis.

### De Trechter  A
63 Hobbemakade (tel: 6711263). Open Tuesday – Friday 18.00-22.30. Patron/chef Jan de Wit is recognised as one of Holland's most innovative chefs. His international menu is short and ever-changing. Dishes follow nouvelle cuisine principles, with the emphasis on unusual, but generally successful, combinations.

### D'Vijff Vlieghen  A  (see also page 92)
294-302 Spuistraat (tel: 6248369). Open daily 17.30-23.00 (Lunch for large parties by arrangement).

Amsterdam's most famous, and probably its most expensive, restaurant, the 'Five Flies' has led the campaign in Holland to return to natural flavours. Intimate, 17th-century rooms retain an 'Old Amsterdam' flavour. Specialities generally include the newly fashionable rib of fliandre (one-year old calf), Texel Island lamb, home-made sausages and, in winter, game. Cinnamon ice cream and coffee mousse are unusual desserts. Order from the upstairs bar, taking the rare opportunity to sip a vintage (up to 19 years) *oude genever*.

## Selected Bars/Cafés

The words De, 't and Café are ignored for alphabetical order. Many bars do not open until mid-afternoon and only a few provide food. Those that do, tend to call themselves cafés, although they generally differ little from bars.

### Café Chris
42 Bloemstraat. Open from 14.00.
Amsterdam's oldest bar, built in 1624. Good 'woody' interior.

### De Doffer
12 Runstraat. Open from 20.00.
A brown bar with billiards and velvet curtains.

### De Drie Fleschjes   (see also page 85)
18 Gravenstraat. Monday – Saturday 12.00-20.30.
An atmospheric brown bar, one of Amsterdam's showpieces and not to be missed.

### De Druiff   (see also page 186)
83 Rappenburgerplein. Open from 11.00.
Founded in 1638 as an off-licence, De Druiff is an intimate local bar, off the usual tourist beat.

### Café Frascati   (see also page 89)
59 Nes. Open from 16.00.
An old theatre bar, with the usual mirrors and marble. Economical evening meals.

### Hoppe   (see also page 92)
18-20 Spui. Open 11.00-01.00 (02.00 Saturday and Sunday).

The city's most famous bar, Hoppe maintains much of its 17th-century appearance. Not to be confused with other bars displaying 'Hoppe' signs: these refer to a brand of spirits.

**Hegeraad** (see also page 171)
34 Noordermarkt
One of the Jordaan's most popular brown bars, formerly an off-licence.

**In de Lompen**  (see also page 106)
13 St. Olafspoort. Open from 16.00.
Built as a tasting house in 1618. In De Lompen specialises in liqueurs and venerable *genevers*.

**De Kalkhoven**
283 Prinsengracht. Open from 11.00.
An outstanding canal-side bar.

**Kokenbier**
51 Eerste van der Helststraat. Open from 11.00
A popular and friendly bar serving the Albert Cuypstraat street market: its interior is undistinguished.

**Papeneiland Café**  (see also page 170)
2-4 Prinsengracht. Open from late afternoon
Occupying Prinsengracht's oldest house, overlooking the picturesque Brouwersgracht junction, this bar sports an ancient stove and good Delft tiles.

**Café de Reiger**
34 Eerste Leliedwarsstraat. Open from 17.00.
Basically a Jordaan youngsters' bar; good home-made soups and sandwiches are served.

**Café 't Smalle**  (see also page 174)
12 Egelantiersgracht. Open from 10.00.
Founded in 1780, an ancient atmosphere prevails. Unusually good 'pub' food. Candle-lit at night.

**Café Schiller**
26 Rembrandtplein. Open from 11.00
Famous Art-Deco interior, but more a café than a bar.

**Twee Zwaantjes** (see also page 174)
114 Prinsengracht. Open from 19.00 (18.00 Sunday).
A small, 'sing-along' drinking venue, with accordion
accompaniment; this is a peculiarly Amsterdam institution.

**Café van Puffelen**
377 Prinsengracht. Open from 14.00 (16.00 in winter).
An attractive canal-side brown bar. Food is served from 18.00.

# Sightseeing

## Introduction

The city is divided into eight separate routes, which include the sights of major appeal. Although it is not expected that every visitor will wish to follow the routes slavishly, the great advantage of this method is that having visited a location of particular interest, it is immediately apparent what else is nearby, thus saving a great deal of tiring and time-consuming back-tracking.

Explicit directions throughout the book, combined with the large scale map, should ensure that visitors will not get lost, however, a city tour by coach or canal boat, taken at an early stage, will help to provide an early awareness of central Amsterdam's layout.

All the canals are narrow enough to permit property numbers to be read from the opposite side and it is usually irrelevant which of the canal's two thoroughfares are taken; where there is a special reason for selecting one side it is indicated in the directions. The most important factor of Amsterdam's layout to bear in mind is that the Canal Girdle: Herengracht, Keizersgracht and Prinsengracht, extends outward in that order, following the curve of Singel and Amstel in the city centre. Compass direction north and the core of the old city, therefore, lie within the curve. If this is remembered, inadvertently following the canals eastward instead of westward, or vice versa, should be avoided. Numbering of buildings begins at the north end, with even numbers on the west side and odd numbers on the east side.

Due to their ascetic nature, only a few consider Amsterdam's churches to be a major reason for visiting the city. However, the most historic provide much of interest. Some hold weekday services, but many are now little more than cultural centres with exhibition areas. Anglicans will find Sunday morning services at the English Reformed Church, in the centrally located Begijnhof, to be the most convenient. Visitors are permitted to attend Saturday services at the Portuguese Synagogue.

Museums and art galleries levy an entrance charge and many are closed on Mondays and Sunday mornings. A museum card, valid for one year, permits free entrance to all state and municipal museums in Holland and is incredibly good value if more than two are to be visited; some privately-run establishments do not accept the card.

As an aid to comprehension, names of buildings are given first in English, followed by the Dutch translation in brackets; names of thoroughfares appear first in Dutch.

## Summary of Museums and Art Galleries

All the following are discussed more fully on the pages indicated.

**Allard Pierson** (page 90). The archaeological collection of Amsterdam University; Egyptian, Greek, Etruscan and Coptic works are included.

**Amstelkring** (page 107). A 'hidden' Roman Catholic church, plus Amsterdam's finest 17th-century domestic interiors – Vermeer's paintings brought to life.

**Amsterdam's History (Amsterdams Historisch)** (page 99). Occupying a former nunnery, ideally, this museum should be seen first by visitors as it puts Amsterdam's development into perspective. Don't miss the original 17th-century Regent's Room.

**Amsterdam Water Level (Normaal Amsterdams Peil)** (page 147). Small, free display illustrates Holland's ever-continuing battle with the sea.

**The Anne Frank House** (Anne Frankhuis) (page 179). The museum is situated in the house where Anne Frank *(The Diary of Anne Frank)* and her Jewish family took refuge from the Germans until they were betrayed. Small details make a visit almost unbearably moving.

**Artis Zoo and Planetarium** (page 194). A wide variety of animals are kept in as natural a state as possible – there are few bars. Planetarium shows are given throughout the day.

**Biblical (Bijbels)** (page 156). Exhibits refer to historical aspects of the Bible, particularly life in Jerusalem at the time of Christ.

**Botanical Garden (Hortus Botanicus)** (page 195). Very small botanical gardens. Mainly for enthusiasts, but within the palm house grows a 400 year old fern – probably the world's oldest potted plant.

**Cannabis Information** (page 117). Advice is given on growing the weed – strictly, of course, of use to the Dutch only

**Electric Tramline** (page 219). Vintage trams, all of which have been restored to working order, transport visitors to Amsterdam Woods and beyond.

**Film (Nederlands Filmmuseum)** (page 208). Video presentation, early pieces of equipment and showings of historic films – never dubbed.

**Fodor** (page 162). Works by contemporary artists, changed regularly.

**Geological (Geologisch)** (page 193. Rock formations and gemstones. Only for enthusiasts.

**Heineken** (page 214). Visitors are shown around the former Heineken brewery for a small admission fee, but little of interest remains. There is a small museum. Sandwiches and beer are on the house but is it worth the two hours spent on a PR exercise?

**Jewish History (Joods Historisch)** (page 140. The history of the Jewish people is depicted, partly within Amsterdam's oldest synagogue, plus two others. Mementoes of the Holocaust are included.

**Madame Tussaud Scenerama** (page 68). The only overseas branch of London's waxworks museum. International in scope but naturally with a Dutch emphasis.

**Maritime (Nederlands Scheepvaart)** (page 187). This vast museum traces Amsterdam's naval history. A full-scale model of *Amsterdam*, an 18th-century merchant ship, is permanently moored as an exhibit.

**Moneybox (National Spaarpotten)** (page 130). Eclectic collection, ranging from piggybanks to African clay pots. Good for children.

**Multatuli** (page 151). Mementoes of Holland's best known 19th-century novelist are displayed in the house where he lived. Only really of interest to literary buffs or Dutch nationals.

**NINT Science and Technology** (page 216). Amsterdam's 'Science Museum'. Of main appeal to technically-minded, Dutch-speaking schoolboys. Not really for tourists.

**Rembrandt House** (het Rembrandthuis) (page 145). Although Rembrandt lived in the building for 21 years, virtually nothing internally survives from his time. Comprehensive displays of his etchings and a contemporary etching press are on view.

**Resistance (Verzetsmuseum)** (page 218). The Dutch resistance to the German occupation, 1940-1945, is recorded in a former synagogue.

**Rijksmuseum** (page 198). Holland's great artistic showpiece. Paintings from the Dutch Golden Age include Rembrandt's *The Night Watch*.

**Royal Palace (Koninklijk Paleis)** (page 69). Though not technically, of course, a museum, every effort should be made to enter this, Holland's most impressive civic edifice, originally built as Amsterdam's Town Hall. Within, there is a wealth of exceptional 17th-century carving by the Flemish sculptor Quellien.

**Script** (page 131). Ancient scripts from many countries are inscribed on various materials.

**Shipyard/Museum ('t Kromhout Museumwerf)** (page 191). Central Amsterdam's last remaining shipyard – now for repairs only. A small museum concentrates on engines developed by the company in the 19th century; primarily for small boat enthusiasts.

**Six Collection** (page 135). Works of art belonging to Amsterdam's patrician family Six are displayed in their present canal-side house. Rembrandt's portrait of Jan Six, which is never permitted to leave the building, is outstanding. Tickets (free) must be obtained in advance from the Rijksmuseum.

**Stedelijk** (page 206). Although this is a municipal museum, Holland's finest permanent collection of modern international master painters is displayed. Most space, however, is allocated to temporary exhibitions by contemporary artists.

**Taller Amsterdam** (page 162). Permanently displayed are works by members of the Foundation, which was created in Uruguay, plus temporary exhibitions. Some musical events are held.

**Theatre (Nederlands Theater)** (page 153). Items, displayed in 17th-century buildings, relate to the development of the Dutch theatre. The vintage model theatres are of historic interest.

**Tropics (Tropenmuseum)** (page 192). The way of life in much of the 'third world' is depicted. There is no emphasis on arts and crafts nor is there any connection with tropical plants.

**Van Loon** (page 160). This 17th-century mansion has been furnished and restored to reproduce its 18th-century appearance.

**Vincent van Gogh** (page 203). By far the world's largest van Gogh collection is exhibited, incorporating more than 200 paintings. Currently Amsterdam's top tourist attraction.

**Willet-Holthuysen** (page 137). Domestic interiors have been little altered since the late 19th century.

## Summary of selected religious buildings

Page numbers in brackets denote the fuller description.

**Begijnhof Chapel** (page 94). This 'hidden' church was created within two houses in 1680 for Roman Catholic worship, by the beguines, women who lived a nun-like existence.

**East Church (Oosterkerk)** (page 190). David Stalpaert, not de Keyser, designed this church, but followed the Greek Cross plan of the latter's North Church. It is now primarily a welfare centre; but after a long break, Sunday services are held once more. The pulpit is original, dating from 1669, when the church was built.

**English Reformed Church** (page 95). Standing in the centre of the Begijnhof, the church, consecrated in 1419, was originally built for

Roman Catholic worship. Its tower is the only medieval example to survive in Amsterdam. Within are an outstanding 17th-century Burgomaster's pew, a bronze section of the lectern presented by the joint English monarchs William and Mary, and a modern pulpit carved to designs by the youthful Piet Mondrian.

**Kritberg** (page 130). This late 19th-century Roman Catholic church, with Germanic flanking towers, retains a well-preserved, colourful interior.

**Moses and Aaron Church (Moses en Aäronkerk)** (page 143). This Neo-Baroque building was designed, under French influence, by T. F. Suys. It is Roman Catholic, therefore the church displays altarpieces, and the stages of the cross in bas-relief.

**The New Church (De Nieuwe Kerk)** (page 78). This, Amsterdam's second parish church to be built, was completed in Gothic style, between c.1385 and 1540. Following a fire, the interior detailing is mostly 17th-century work. The organ and pulpit are outstanding, and tomb monuments of leading naval heroes include that of Admiral de Ruyter. It is here that the inauguration of Holland's sovereign takes place. Unfortunately, visitors must generally pay to enter the church as it now serves primarily as an exhibition hall.

**North Church (Noorderkerk)** (page 171). This was de Keyser's last church, begun in 1620 for worship by the poor inhabitants of the Jordaan. Services held for the Bonders congregation on Sundays have a period quality that is unique in the city.

**Old Church (Oude Kerk)** (page 110). Dating from 1300, this is Amsterdam's oldest monument to survive. Remodelled throughout the centuries, medieval painting, stained glass and carved misericords are retained.

**Portuguese Synagogue (Portugees Israëlitische Synagoge)** (page 142). Constructed 1671-75, this is one of the largest synagogues ever built in Europe. A profusion of brass chandeliers and hardwoods are original features.

**Round Lutheran Church (Ronde Lutherse Kerk)** (page 128). Designed with a great dome, by Adriaan Dortsman 1668-71, the church was rebuilt, virtually as a replica, in 1823. It is now a conference centre but may be visited on Sunday mornings, when 'coffee' concerts are held.

**St. Nicolaas** (page 106). Built in 1887, this was the first Roman Catholic church to be erected after the Alteration.

**South Church (Zuiderkerk)** (page 122). South Church, completed in 1611, is the earliest known work by Holland's greatest architect, Hendrick de Keyser. It is a masterpiece of the Dutch Renaissance but now primarily given over to providing municipal housing information; displays conceal some internal features.

**West Church (Westerkerk)** (page 176). The tower of West Church has become Amsterdam's symbol. Completed in 1631, 10 years after the death of its architect, Hendrick de Keyser, a French influence is apparent throughout the building. The grand style of the church reflects the wealth of its parishioners, the wealthy merchants who had moved into the new Canal Ring mansions. Rembrandt and his son Titus are buried within. Oak furnishings are mostly original.

ROUTE 1

# Royal Palace and The New Church

The central area described follows a relatively short north/south route from the Central Station, tracing the course of the river Amstel as it enters the city. Four of Amsterdam's most interesting sights are inspected – the Royal Palace, The New Church, the Begijnhof (with its two churches) and Amsterdam's History Museum. However, to visit all of this route's locations on the same day will be difficult.

Most of the locations covered are on Nieuwezijds – the new side, west of the Amstel, with only a brief excursion being made to Oudezijds – the old side.

## Timing

- Guided tours of the former Trade Exchange must be arranged in advance.

- Apart from the summer months, when it is open daily from 12.30, the Royal Palace may only be entered on Wednesdays 13.45-14.45.

- The Allard Pierson Museum is shut Mondays and weekend mornings.

- The English Reformed Church is open only for Sunday services 10.00-11.30.

- Amsterdam's History Museum and Civic Guards Gallery do not open until 11.00.

## Locations for Route 1

1 Central Station
2. Damrak
3. Former Trade Exchange
4. De Dam
5. National Monument
6. Grand Hotel Krasnapolsky

## Start: Stationsplein

# 1. Central Station (Centraal Station)
P.J.H. Cuypers and A. L. van Gendt 1882-89

For most visitors, Central Station represents their introduction to Amsterdam, due to its direct link with Schiphol Airport. Outside, congregate buskers, beggars and hustlers, typical of those who haunt important rail terminals in many cities, some of them glazed-eyed, immediately emphasising that, in Holland, the taking of marijuana may be indulged in without fear of prosecution.

The station was built in the former harbour, thus blocking off the city's views of the IJ, a broad inlet of the former Zuider Zee, which served as Amsterdam's harbour. Three islands were created as a base for the great structure; partial subsidence occurred at one stage, necessitating additional lengthy and costly piling (there are 26,000 piles). Cuypers, who designed the overall scheme, was also responsible for the Gothic Revival Rijksmuseum, but here he favoured a basic Renaissance style, albeit incorporating pointed Gothic gables; the medallions, allegorical bas-reliefs and coats of arms are a good example of Renaissance-style decoration.

The centrally-placed municipal coat of arms is formed by ceramic tiles. In the 15th century, St. Andrew's crosses replaced, on these arms, the single-masted cog: the largest merchant ship in the Middle Ages and a popular emblem with many seafaring ports.

The gilded 'clock', left of the entrance, is, in fact, an indicator of wind direction, reflecting the dependence of Amsterdam's sailing ships on wind power.

Most of the station's interior has been modernised, but the central hall retains a great deal of its late 19th-century appearance. A return is worth making to visit the '1 Klas' restaurant on platform two. Originally the waiting room, its 'Arts and Crafts' décor has recently been restored. In addition to a restaurant, there is a coffee and snacks area. Huge Delft vases are an impressive decorative feature.

Facing the station is the **VVV Tourist Information Office**, where free maps and brochures are available. There is also a hotel booking service for those seeking accommodation.

Amsterdam's public transport office, to its right, straddling the corner with Damrak's bridge, will give advice on the most suitable tickets for your requirements.

Ahead stretches Damrak, both the canal and its street.

## 2. Damrak

Rak means a straight stretch of water – ie. a reach – in this case, of the Amstel river, Damrak marking its entry into the city. When modern Amsterdam was created, all of Damrak was open as far as De Dam, but, since the 19th century, more than half of its original length has flowed underground. Immediately left, on the east side of the water, may be seen the rear of houses in Warmoestraat, formerly Amsterdam's main shopping thoroughfare – as it backed directly on to the water, goods from boats in the harbour could be loaded easily into the storerooms.

Haringpakkerssteeg, first right, leads to the ultra-commercial Nieuwendijk, where cheap clothes shops, fast food and loud music rule the roost.

Immediately on the corner, however, at no. 75, stands **H.P. de Vreng**, one of the city's leading liqueur stores, specialising in very old genevers. At the time of writing, a mellow, 19-year-old cask-aged bottle cost 150 guilders. Around 9,000 miniature bottles of alcoholic drinks from around the world are suspended from the ceiling – they are not for sale.

*Return to Damrak and continue southward.*

**(Opposite)** *Old Church, dating from the 13th century, is Amsterdam's oldest building.*

**Numbers 28-30**, an American skyscraper in miniature, was built for the De Utrecht insurance company by J. F. Staal and J. Kropholler in 1905. The architects had returned from a visit to New York, impressed by the treatment then being given to the roof sections of the towering new buildings. Amusing sculptural embellishments are by J. Mendes da Costa.

*Continue eastward to Oude Brugsteeg, first left, which passes the north side of the Trade Exchange.*

At **no. 7**, on the Beursstraat corner, the building with pilasters was designed by Jacob van Campen in 1638; its attic was a later addition.

The Neo-Renaissance façade features busts of famous artists, and the old and new coats of arms of Amsterdam are depicted over the doors.

## 3. Former Trade Exchange (Koopmanbeurs)
Hendrick Berlage1898-1902

213 Damrak.

Open for concerts and exhibitions. Guided tours by arrangement (tel: 6258908). Admission free.

Built as an exchange, this great brick structure dominates much of Damrak. Generally known as Beurs van Berlage, its design initially aroused strong disapproval, but is now regarded as a major triumph, leading, as it did, to the Amsterdam School of Architecture. Both externally and internally, medieval themes are referred to - the flat-topped towers, for example, betraying an obvious Tuscan influence. Much of the building's success is undoubtedly due to the superb brickwork.

No longer an exchange, traders moved out during the 1980s and areas were gradually converted to concert halls and exhibition rooms. The Netherlands Philharmonic Orchestra are now based here and give 150 concerts each season.

**(Opposite) Top:** *The famous Skinny Bridge (Magere Brug), a modern facsimile of the 17th-century original.*
**(Opposite) Bottom:** *Converted warehouses provide sought-after canal-side apartments.*

Blue and gold gates, half way along the Damrak façade, provide the main entrance to the building.

Of major interest, internally, is the **Great Hall**, immediately right, with its glazed roof, supported by iron girders. On the ground floor, the former traders booths are lit by stained glass windows.

Medieval features are particularly prominent and the hall is known as the Knights' hall (Ridderzaal). The middle row of columns did not originally exist.

Decorative elements include the shields of leading trading centres, and a frieze depicting man's progression from Neanderthal to trader (wearing a hat). Above this frieze, a plaque commemorates Amsterdam's late liberation from the Nazi's, 4 May 1945.

Of great importance to conservationists is the treatment given to the **Agahall**, which has made it possible to hold concerts without altering the appearance of the walls for acoustic purposes. A frameless glass box has been erected, within which the musicians perform and the audience sits.

Number **5 Beursplein** was built by Jos Th. J. Cuypers in 1913 as the Effectenbeurs and still operates as Amsterdam's Stock Exchange.

Number 62**, Allert de Lange**, was built expressly as a bookshop, by J van Looy, in 1886, and this function continues. During the 1930s, the shop was renowned for stocking works in German that had been banned by the Nazis. A Neo-Renaissance façade features busts of famous artists.

On the corner of Damrak and Dam, no. 413, **De Bijenkorf**, is regarded as Amsterdam's leading department store, although window displays never match those of similar stores in London or Paris. It dates from 1913 and, like London's Selfridges, built five years earlier, was designed in Neo-Classical style (by J. A. van Straaten).

## 4. De Dam

Now a rectangular plaza, De Dam (The Dam) was created c. 1270 to dam the river Amstel and control its flow by means of a sluice. It provided the first link between Oudezijds (Old Side) to the east, where the original settlement probably began, and Nieuwezijds (New Side) to the west. An outer harbour, Damrak, and an inner harbour, Rokin, were formed on either side. De Dam, originally named the

Square (de Plaetse), covered approximately two-thirds of its present area until the mid-17th century.

From a civic aspect, De Dam is the most important square in Amsterdam, and the focal point of national rejoicing. Once the site of public executions and the assembly stage for medieval processions, the opening concert of Uitmarkt is held in De Dam, and the Aalsmeer flower parade ends here.

Towards the east end, the National Monument is believed to mark where the Amstel was first dammed.

## 5. National Monument, J. J. P. Oud 1956

De Dam

This monument commemorates Dutchmen who died in the Second World War. Built by public subscription, it was unveiled 4 May 1956, 11 years after Holland's liberation, in the presence of Queen Juliana. In the 17th century, Amsterdam's fish market had functioned at this point. An earlier national memorial that stood here was demolished in 1914. Holland, of course, remained neutral in the First World War.

The white, rounded obelisk is backed by a curved wall, bearing inscriptions. Sculptures are the work of John Rädecker.

Within the obelisk are 11 urns filled with earth from battlefields where Dutch soldiers died; a twelfth contains soil from Dutch military cemeteries in Indonesia.

Towering over the north-east corner of De Dam is the Grand Hotel Krasnapolsky.

## 6. Grand Hotel Krasnapolsky

9 De Dam

Amsterdam's oldest established hotel, the Krasnapolsky boasts 316 rooms and 14 suites. Its evolution began when a former tailor, Adolf Wilhelm Krasnapolsky, expanded his popular Warmoestraat coffee shop into a hotel to cater for visitors to the World Fair, held at Amsterdam in 1883. Following gradual expansion, the hotel now occupies the entire block bounded by De Dam/Warmoestraat, Sint

Annestraat, Oudezijds Voorburgwal and Pijlsteeg.

Part of the former coffee shop, its famous **Winter Garden**, added in 1879, survives as the hotel's breakfast room. Restoration of the iron-framed, glass-roofed building was completed in 1990. Tropical plants rival those in the Palm House of Kew Gardens. On Sundays, high tea is served here, but on summer Sundays there is also a splendid buffet brunch at lunchtime.

The hotel's restaurants include **Le Reflet d'Or**, dinner only, specialising in French cuisine, and the Japanese **Edo**, where lunch and dinner are served.

Now forming part of the complex, at no. 31 Pijlsteeg, is the famous **Wijnand Fockink** tasting bar, dating from the 17th century. Its reopening date has not yet been established.

## 7. Madame Tussaud Scenerama

20 De Dam

Open Daily 10.00-17.30 Admission charge.

Occupying the top three floors of Peek and Cloppenburg's clothing store since 1991, after 20 years in Kalverstraat, Madame Tussaud's waxworks exhibition has doubled its former size. This is the only overseas branch of Britain's top tourist attraction, and the entire presentation is completely new. Dutch history up to the 17th century 'Golden Age' incorporates many tableaux inspired by famous paintings.

A leap to modern times then follows, divided into varying themes: royal family – Queen Wilhelmina is shown broadcasting to Holland from London on radio 'Free Orange' during the Second World War; modern Dutch painters – Van Gogh and Piet Mondrian; Anne Frank; television, featuring Joan Collins and Tina Turner; and the Dome of Fame, in 32 parts, depicting celebrities who have shaped the history of the world. Whilst the show obviously has a Dutch emphasis, a major aim has been to provide international appeal.

*Exit left and proceed to the Royal Palace.*

The Royal Palace straddles the entire west side of De Dam.

## 8. Royal Palace (Koninklijk Paleis)

Jacob van Campen 1648-70

De Dam

Open early June – August (or early September) 12.30-17.00. At other times, Wednesdays only, 13.45-14.45 for guided tours. NB The palace is not open when a function of importance is being held or prepared. It is best to check first, particularly outside the summer months. Admission charge.

Externally, this grime-covered, bulky palace, built in the mid-17th century as Amsterdam's Town Hall, may not impress, but the interior boasts some of northern Europe's finest carving of the period: the work of Artus Quellien. Jacob van Campen was responsible, not only for designing the building, but also for selecting its decorative themes, many of which he sketched himself. Ancient Rome with a Baroque flourish was the inspiration throughout. Although technically a royal palace, Queen Beatrix, the present monarch, only visits it a few times each year and never stays the night.

### History

Amsterdam's medieval town hall comprised a picturesque group of buildings. Facing De Dam, on the corner of what is now Paleisstraat, was the arcaded Vierschaar (Courtroom); next to it stood the bell tower, with a pointed spire and, adjoining this, the 14th-century Gothic core of the complex, with an assembly hall on its upper floor and, after 1609, the city bank below. Adjacent properties were gradually purchased to provide additional accommodation, but Amsterdam's population expanded fourfold between 1600 and 1640, and the need for new, more extensive premises could no longer be ignored. Additionally, most of the ancient structures were by now dilapidated, the spire of the bell tower, for example, having been demolished in 1615, due to its dangerous state.

In 1640, the burgomasters agreed that a completely new town hall should be built. At the same time, they approved the westward extension of De Dam, to make room for the new building, which was to be half as wide and a great deal deeper than before. Demolition of buildings fronting Nieuwezijds Voorburgwal took place in 1643, and piles were sunk five years later. However, in 1648, the 80 Years War with Spain was officially terminated by the Treaty of Munster and, partly to celebrate this occasion, and partly because the city's heavy expenditure on the war would no longer be a burden, it was decided to double the proposed width of the Town Hall, extending it almost to the south-west corner of The New Church.

Several architects, including Philips Vingboons and Cornelis Dackerts de Rij, had submitted proposals at various times, but it was Jacob van Campen's, that was eventually selected, possibly because it was the most ambitious, and therefore suited the prevailing euphoric mood. More demolition followed, and a total of 13,659 piles of Norwegian pine were sunk for the great edifice, all driven in without mechanical assistance.

Van Campen was already an established architect, and his inspiration, ancient Rome, not only for the building itself but its allegorical sculptural embellishments throughout, was welcomed by the burgomasters, who saw Amsterdam as a latter-day Rome in its power and enlightenment. Costly stone, all of which had to be imported, was specified rather than local brick. Incredibly, within 20 years, the Town Hall, then the largest in the world, was virtually finished.

During the mid-17th century, Dutch sculpture, unlike Dutch painting, was at a low ebb, and it was decided to commission Artus Quellien from Antwerp to carve, with many assistants, the hundreds of embellishments specified by van Campen. The task took him almost 15 years and was executed during his prime; few other sculptors have devoted so much of their life to one project. It is probable that England's master sculptor, Grinling Gibbons, attended Quellien's studio, as he is reported to have left Amsterdam for England, aged 19, and certainly worked with Quellien's cousin at a later date, implying that the carvers knew each other. Four sons or nephews of the burgomasters laid the foundation stone in 1648, and the city architect Daniel Stalpaert then became responsible for the project, aided by master mason Willem de Keyser, son of the famous architect Hendrik.

Loss of income, due to the First Anglo-Dutch War of 1652-54, led the municipal authorities to scale down the plans, decreeing that, apart from the pedimented central area, the building should not exceed two floors in height. Not surprisingly, once the war ended this was revoked, it being said that the stone needed had already been purchased. Meanwhile, fire destroyed the old town hall, which was not due to have been demolished until the last moment, as it had continued to accommodate municipal offices. Arson was rumoured, although never proven. However, the conflagration certainly appears to have given impetus to the construction of the new building, and the city government was able to move in to the as yet incomplete structure on 29 July 1655.

A year before, van Campen had 'withdrawn' from the project, possibly in protest against the economies to his decorative scheme that were being enforced. However, the architect was not averse to a tipple, and it was said that drink had got the better of him, leading to ill-tempered disputes with the city architect and others in authority. Van Campen died in 1657.

As 'Felicitations to the Honourable Lords Regent of Amsterdam upon their new town hall', Constantijn Huygens wrote:

'Illustrious Founders of the World's Eighth Wonder
with so much stone raised high and so much timber under.'

(Wonder and under are similar words in Dutch and English – wonder and onder – which accounts for their rhyming in both languages.) Soon, the town hall was referred to by Amsterdammers as the eighth wonder of the world.

Following the French invasion of 1795, the Netherlands effectively lost its independent republic status and, in 1806, the 27 year-old Louis-Napoléon was appointed King, by his brother, the French Emperor. After residing at several addresses in Holland, he borrowed, on a temporary basis, the Town Hall, which was converted to a royal palace at his expense, in April 1808. Louis-Napoléon's queen, Hortense de Beauharnais, daughter of the Empress Joséphine by her first marriage, only spent a few weeks in Amsterdam with her husband, before returning to Paris with their son. Their always strained relationship was virtually over.

Within five months, in order to improve the view from his palace, the new king had angered Amsterdammers by ordering the demolition of the historic Waag (Weighhouse), sited on the north side of De Dam, near the present Damrak intersection. Built in 1565, the Waag was where heavy goods had to be weighed before they could be sold; it then stood a short distance from the open water of Damrak, where the merchant ships docked. In spite of this, Louis-Napoléon eventually proved to be a popular ruler, siding with the Dutch on many issues against his brother. In 1810, not unexpectedly, he was forced to abdicate and his son became king for a short time, until Napoléon incorporated the country officially into the French Empire, and the palace became an imperial residence. Only once, however, did Napoléon stay there: in October 1811 with his second wife Marie Louise. Louis-Napoléon's alterations have disappeared, due to remodelling, but his great legacy of Empire furniture can still be seen, most of it made for the palace, in Holland, to French designs.

After Holland regained its freedom, in 1813, Willem I officially returned the Town Hall to the city, but it was never again to resume its original function, permission being given to the sovereign to continue to use the building during visits to Amsterdam. In 1936, the City Council sold the building to the state and it is now officially the Royal Palace, although the building has been restored to its original 17th-century appearance, when it served as the town hall.

## Exterior

Apart from the balcony and cupola, the De Dam façade of the building remains exactly as van Campen intended. Unfortunately, however, the Bentheim stone, from Germany, although a delightful pale cream when first dressed, weathers to a dark grey, concealing detail and creating a gloomy appearance. As yet, nothing can apparently be done to clean it, because the water-resistant surface would be destroyed, revealing a porous base. An architectural criticism often levied is that the building appears to be at least one storey too high for its width, resulting in a dumpy appearance; a greater distance between the central and the corner pavilions would have overcome this problem.

Something also seems wrong with the plainness of the bell tower's cupola. Van Campen intended the pilasters supporting it to be surmounted by statues representing the eight winds; he designed them but they were never made, on the grounds of economy. Van Campen also planned that the cupola should be given three bands around its base. All this would have increased the Baroque appearance of the cupola, which would then have been more in tune with the façade.

No balcony was originally intended, but Louis-Napoléon commissioned one in 1809, so that he could speak from it to his subjects more easily. The present gilded balcony is a shorter version, added in modern times, but retaining the balustrade's design. It is alleged that in an early speech to Amsterdammers Louis-Napoléon aroused some mirth, when, in announcing 'I am your king', he pronounced the word koning (king) as konijn (rabbit).

Composite and Corinthian pilasters support cornices, which are carved with a pattern that is too detailed to appreciate from any distance.

Below the windows are swags, a very Baroque feature. The windows themselves were restored in 1936 to their original mullion and transome format, subdivided by small panes. Louis-Napoléon had replaced them, in Empire style, so that each window had either four or six panes.

The pediment's relief, of Carrara marble, represents the Homage of the Seven Seas to Amsterdam. Surmounting its apex, the figure of Peace probably alludes to the ending of the long war with Spain. On either side are the usual city hall figures of Prudence and Justice.

At first floor level, temporary scaffolds, on which those sentenced to death were executed, stood immediately below Justice.

The weather vane  – above the pineapple that surmounts the cupola of the bell turret – depicts the medieval cog ship, Amsterdam's earliest coat of arms.

At the ground floor level of the pedimented central section, the arches were originally open, forming an arcade. Through an iron grille behind them, the crowds could watch prisoners receive the death sentence. Louis-Napoléon had the openings filled, probably as a security measure.

The rear façade of the palace, in NZ Voorburgwal, is described when it is passed later (page 87.)

*Enter the palace from the pedimented section, by the door to the right.*

## Interior

Facing the cloakroom, a slide presentation describes the building and its history.

Throughout the complex, the genius of Artus Quellien (alternatively spelt Quellin, Quellijn or Quellinus), 1609-68, is apparent, much of the carving being his own work. Of course, many skilled craftsmen assisted, in particular Rombout Verhulst. Most of the sculptures are in white Carrara marble, which had been shipped from Italy.

*Visitors proceed to the De Dam side of the building.*

## High Court of Justice (Vierschaar)

Sited where a vestibule might be expected, this room was used solely for pronouncing the death sentence, the prisoner having previously been found guilty of a capital offence, usually confessing to it under torture in the Torture Chamber on the ground floor (not open).

Judges sat on cushions placed upon the marble bench. Behind them, wall reliefs symbolise Mercy, Wisdom and Righteousness. Van Campen's projected scheme for the upper part of this wall, which included paintings, was never executed.

The four caryatids represent Punishment.

At the far end of the room is the seat of the town clerk, who read the sentence. The front of this is carved to depict a woman with her finger against her lips, signifying the professional silence expected of the clerk.

In the wall-niches between the windows stand Justice and Prudence.

Originally, the windows were barred, not glazed, and a few members of the baying crowd were able to watch the ceremony.

Louis-Napoléon had the room adapted as a Royal Chapel.

*Ascend to the first floor.*

## Citizens Hall (Burgerzaal)

This is, undoubtedly, the most splendid room in Amsterdam, and forms the core of the building. Van Campen modelled its design on a public hall in ancient Rome. Decoration is based on the theme of a universe in miniature. The floor, for example, comprises maps, carved in marble, of both hemispheres (18th-century replacements) and the heavens (the 17th-century original).

Regarding these maps from her position enthroned above the entrance, Amsterdam, depicted as a virgin, is flanked by Strength and Wisdom.

At each end of the hall, arched entrances lead to the galleries. These surround the courtyards, which serve merely as light-wells, and therefore, unlike medieval examples, there is no access to them via steps. The spandrels of the arches display outstanding figures, representing Earth, Water, Air and Fire.

At the upper level, the six large figures in niches are the models from which the bronze statues on the external pediments were made. They were not intended for the hall, and their unsympathetic bulk introduces a jarring note. Van Campen had designed decorations more in scale with the remainder, but, presumably due to cost, they were never made.

The barrel-vaulted ceiling was not painted until the 18th century.

Crystal chandeliers from Louis-Napoléon's period were originally fitted with oil lamps.

Now used for important functions, the Citizens Hall was formerly regarded as an extension of De Dam: traders discussed business, friends chatted and children played.

*From the west end of the hall proceed to the Magistrates Court.*

### Magistrate's Court (Schepenzaal)
In this room, the magistrates and bailiff judged legal cases and established the city's regulations.

Ferdinand Bol painted the chimneypiece's scene of Moses descending from Mount Sinai bearing the Ten Commandments. Its marble frieze, depicting worship of the golden calf, was never completed.

Painted on the ceiling are the arms of the bailiff and magistrates who administered the first session here in 1655.

Turtle doves on the cornice reflect that marriage ceremonies once took place in this room.

### Chamber of Commissioners for Petty Affairs (Kamer van der Commissarissen van kleine zaken)
Approached from the Magistrates Court, it was here that less important cases were judged. Some of the Empire furniture of the Palace is displayed. Thomire, the renowned French caster, made the bronze clock, which first stood in the bedroom of Louis-Napoléon's young son, the Crown Prince.

Above the entrance to the court are carved fighting cocks.

### Galleries
High-relief figures, in the corners of the galleries, represent the planets known in the mid-17th century; they take the form of gods.

Paintings depict the Batavians fighting for independence with the Romans. The example at the east end of the south gallery, above the entrance to the Burgomasters Council Room, replaced a Rembrandt painting, *The Conspiracy of Claudius Civilis*, which was soon removed because it was considered to be too dark. It now hangs, in cut-down form, in the Swedish National Museum, Stockholm. Govert Flink, a former pupil of Rembrandt, had been commissioned to paint all the lunettes in the corridors, but died before this could be done. An existing watercolour by him on the same theme as Rembrandt's work was painted over in oils by the German Jurgen Ovens, as a replacement. Flink's commission was the largest ever awarded to a single artist in Holland; what a pity that it was not given to Rembrandt!

## Burgomasters Council Room (De Burgemeesters Raadzaal)

Paintings of Roman consuls resisting bribes are by Govert Flink and Ferdinand Bol.

Ceiling paintings are by Bronckhorst.

## Burgomasters Chamber (De Burgemeesterskamer)

Roman themes continue. The painting by Jan Lievens depicts Fabius Maximus, a general, dismounting in respect to his son's consular rank. Below, the frieze depicts Fabius Maximus's return to Rome in triumph following his defeat of the Spanish. A reference to the Netherlands' newly-won freedom from Spain is obviously intended.

Burgomasters watched the death sentence ceremony in the Vierschaar below from the window opposite the fireplace.

*Proceed through the room overlooking the balcony.*

## Balcony Room (De Pui)

Before the erection of the first balcony for Louis-Napoléon, important news was read out from behind the open window - citizens having been summoned to De Dam by the ringing of the Town Hall's bell.

Ceiling paintings refer to Good News, announced by Fame with one trumpet, and Bad News, with two trumpets, to indicate that bad news travels twice as fast.

## Chamber of Justice (Justitiekamer)

The prisoner sentenced to death was brought directly to this room from the Vierschaar below, and a minister prayed for his salvation. A wooden scaffold had been erected directly outside the room and there the victim was executed, usually by sword, if male, or by garotting, if female. The corpse was then taken to a field on the city outskirts, where it was displayed on a gibbet.

Justice is the central theme of the ceiling's painting, by Nicolas de Helt Stockade.

## City Council Room (Vroedschapskamer)
The 36 members of the council, the burgomasters' advisers, met in this room. Decorative themes throughout deal with the virtues of accepting advice.

*Choosing of the Seventy Elders*, the large painting, is by Jacob de Wit, who included himself in the top right corner, behind the man with folded arms. Grisailles above the doors are by the same artist, the developer of this type of grey painting.

## North Gallery (Noord Galerij)
More planets in the form of gods are depicted.

Above the sculptures, lunette paintings, by Jacob Jordaens, illustrate two further episodes in the Batavians' struggle with the Romans.

## Insurance Office (Assurantiekamer)
Disputes concerning insurance were adjudicated here. The chimney piece, by Willem Strijcker, illustrates Theseus returning to Ariadne the ball of thread that had guided him through the Minotaur's labyrinth.

Furniture assembled here comes from Louis-Napoléon's private rooms in the palace. The bed was made in Paris by Jacob-Desmalter.

## Bankruptcy Office (Desolate Boedelskamer)
Above the door, the relief illustrates the fall of Icarus, who flew too near the sun, thus melting the wax with which his wings were fixed so that he fell and drowned in the sea. The moral is don't 'fly' too high above your means.

Rembrandt was pronounced insolvent in this room in 1658 and had to sell his house, now the Rembrandt Museum.

*Exit from the palace and turn left.*

The splendid cast-iron lamp posts, painted bronze, are the work of Tétar van Elven, 1844.

Immediately ahead is The New Church.

## 9. The New Church (De Nieuwe Kerk)
c.1385-1540

De Dam

Open Monday–Saturday 11.00-16.00, Sundays 12.00-15.00. Evening concerts in Summer. Admission charge. (To enter it is generally necessary to pay to see the current exhibition.)

Holland's sovereigns are inaugurated in this former parish church; the last such event taking place for Queen Beatrix in 1980. The New Church is a Gothic structure, with an interior that mostly survives from the mid-17th century reconstruction that followed a disastrous fire. Of particular interest within are the tomb monuments of great 17th-century Dutch admirals, the painted organ, and an enormous, canopied pulpit, outstandingly carved.

### History
Building of The New Church is believed to have commenced c. 1385, but, as usual in Gothic churches, the architect is unknown. In 1408, the Bishop of Utrecht agreed that the new building would be granted parish church status, and the rivalry began with the other parish church that already existed in Amsterdam, now known as Old Church (Oude Kerk). Land for the building was donated by Willem Eggert, financial adviser to the Count of Holland and, at his request, the church was dedicated to St. Catherine, in addition to Our Lady, which had been the only dedication originally intended.

The normal building progression of churches from the east end westward was followed, and the chancel, with its ambulatory, and both transepts, was built by 1400. Probably due to Amsterdam's catastrophic fire in 1421, work on the nave did not begin until 1435. By the end of the 15th century, it was decided that the body of the church was insufficiently impressive, it was therefore heightened and a row of clerestory windows incorporated; the transepts were also extended from the nave/chancel building line, in the English rather than the French manner.

In order to match the recently erected spire of Old Church, it was decided to build a tower, but, although piles were sunk, work never progressed further, presumably due to religious and political unrest in the country.

The New Church escaped the damage inflicted by Protestants on other Amsterdam churches in 1566. However, after the Alteration of 1578, iconoclasts ripped out fittings considered to relate to Catholic worship, paintings were whitewashed over and the high altar and its reredos removed. As it happened, all this puritanical zeal proved unnecessary, as carelessness by plumbers working on the roof led to a catastrophic fire in 1645, which destroyed everything except the walls of the church.

Removal of houses in 1643, for construction of the new town hall, gave The New Church a direct frontage to De Dam for the first time, and construction of a west tower began once more. This was to be the highest tower in Amsterdam, and the first piles were sunk in 1646. However, work ceased seven years later and only a stump, representing part of its lower level, has survived.

Restoration, with the aim of reviving what was believed to be the pre-1648 appearance of the church, took place in 1892, and again from 1907-12, but the most far-reaching and costly scheme was that of 1959-80, directed by C. Wegener Steeswijk. The New Church was overhauled from top to bottom, reinforced concrete providing structural rigidity; few 19th-century additions were permitted to survive, but all the 17th-century furnishings and fittings were refurbished.

Holland's present constitution, agreed in 1814, established that the investiture of the sovereign should take place in Amsterdam, and The New Church was chosen as its venue, the largest hall in the palace proving to be too small. However, the investiture is a civic not a religious ceremony; the latter would not prove acceptable, due to Holland's mix of Protestants, Catholics and atheists. The following investitures have taken place here: Willem 1 1814, Willem II 1840, Willem III 1849, Wilhemına 1898, Juliana 1948 and Beatrix 1980.

Set up in 1979, the National Foundation of The New Church is responsible for the management of the building, promoting its use for exhibitions, conferences and concerts.

## Exterior

Facing De Dam, the protruding south transept is built of pale limestone, and dates from its extension around 1500. Most of the area is taken up by the great window, a common feature in Amsterdam churches of all periods, glass weighing much less heavily than stone or brick on the soft ground. Primarily due to the lighter loads, flying buttresses are rarely necessary in Amsterdam churches.

Built of similar limestone, the chancel was completed c. 1400, but heightened a century later, when the deep clerestory windows were incorporated. The east chapels were built c. 1500 of red brick interspersed with stone bands.

A painting of the church, contemporary with the building of its nave, illustrates eight windows, but, as can be seen, there are only five, presumably an indication that the original plans were scaled down. Although completed c.1500, the nave was then heightened in the same way as the chancel. Brickwork and stone banding is similar to that of the chapels, but the bricks are darker and, in fact, date from the 1907-12 restoration by Posthumus Meijjes.

The porch to the entrance from De Dam, in Neo-Gothic style, is entirely a 1907 fabrication.

Immediately right of this porch, the meeting hall, known as the Ministry, was built, also in Neo-Gothic style, at the same time, but replaced in 1980 by the present, lower building. An advantage is that the church windows behind it are no longer blocked, but the building has been much criticised for its 'non-Dutch' style.

*Return westward and follow Mozes en Aäronstraat.*

**Mozes en Aäronstraat** This street, that runs between the new town hall and The New Church, was laid out c. 1645, with houses and a row of shops fronting the church. Two graveyards had to be removed for its construction.

Posthumus Meijjes rebuilt the west façade in 1912, attempting to return it to the pre-1648 situation, when the tower at this end was begun. However, there were no illustrations of its appearance and most is guesswork. Turrets were built at the corners, and the same dark red bricks as had been used elsewhere were alternated with bands of sandstone. The window was rebuilt as a twin to the south transept's.

Forming a porch to the west door, the main entrance to the church, now only used for important events, is what survives of the tower of The New Church. Piles for this were sunk in 1646, three years after similar work had begun on the adjacent Town Hall. Several paintings illustrate how the great edifice might have appeared, and models survive; however, none of them exactly match what remains. There is no confirmation, but, on the evidence of a contemporary pamphlet, it appears that the design by the Town Hall's architect, van Campen, was eventually chosen. When the tower had reached half way up the nave, work was halted, and again there is a mystery, no records explaining why this occurred. Various suggestions are made: Willem Becker, mayor and an enthusiastic supporter of the project, was dead; the first naval war with England had begun the previous year, making great demands on the city's coffers; the less religious burgers objected to the tower overshadowing their new Town Hall; and structural problems, due to settlement, had already appeared.

In 1783, the part of the stump that protruded into NZ Voorburgwal was demolished, but the rest was spared because the organ's bellows had been built into it. A Gothic-style appendage was constructed above this, in 1847, to give the façade a more finished appearance, but it was removed during the 1912 remodelling.

Although Amsterdam never got what would have been its highest tower by far, this may have been all for the best, if the paintings of its excessively dominant projected appearance are anything like accurate.

*Return to De Dam and enter the church; the east and north façades are passed later. As is frequently the case, it is preferable to proceed directly ahead to the centre of the crossing.*

## Interior

The completely symmetrical plan of The New Church, less apparent externally because of extraneous structures, is immediately obvious from within. Rebuilding, necessitated by fires, and restoration, has always maintained the original Gothic plan, even though the building had been designed for celebrating the Mass, with the accent on the sanctuary at the east end, rather than Dutch Reformed Church services, focussed on a more centrally-placed pulpit.

Immediately left, against the west wall of the south transept, stands the 16th-century choir organ; this escaped the 1645 fire as it was under repair elsewhere at the time.

Large windows provide an exceptionally light interior, emphasised by the white walls and recently cleaned woodwork. Before the Alteration, paintings, wall hangings and a multitude of statues would have given a rather dimmer, although much more sumptuous appearance.

The fire of 1645 destroyed the internal fittings and roofs, most of which had been of timber. Rebuilding maintained timber for the barrel vaults of the nave and chancel, partly because stone might have placed too great a weight on the walls, but the aisles, ambulatory and chapels were all given stone vaults. The recent addition of braces between the walls has given the structure greater strength. Restorations have changed the interior remarkably little since 1645, and the 17th-century aspect of The New Church has therefore been retained.

The balustrade of the gallery is Gothic in style; above, the unusually deep clerestory windows are part of the late 15th-century raising of the nave and chancel.

In spite of its height, not many features of the building have a vertical emphasis; exceptions are the stone piers of the chancel, which reach up to the timber roof.

Gilded cupids, supporting the vault from the tops of the piers, have been given amusingly grumpy expressions, apparently reflecting the strain of bearing so much weight.

Decoration of the columns has provided a regular appearance to the jointing, which, in reality, is very irregular.

Chandeliers are modern, imitating those in Amsterdam's Portuguese Synagogue; earlier versions disappeared in the 19th century.

Underfloor heating necessitated the removal of the thick, deeply inscribed tombstones, which were formerly inserted in the pavement. To permit the passage of the heat they have been replaced by much thinner slabs of stone.

Looking back towards the window of the south transept, its stained glass depicts Dutch monarchs from Willem the Silent to Queen Wilhemina, and was made for Wilhemina's investiture in 1898. An earlier window, featuring the Emperor Maximilian of Austria, had been lost in 1750.

The north transept window's main section, by Gerrit Jansz van Bronchorst, 1650, illustrates Count Willem IV giving Amsterdam its coat of arms. Harry op den Laak made the upper section in 1977. This transept was the last part of the church to be completed structurally, its roof being raised to the level of the south transept's in 1540.

Immediately to the east of the crossing, the brass screen of the chancel was made by goldsmith Johannes Lutma in 1650, replacing an impressive piece lost in the 1645 fire. In front of this, facing the invited guests in the nave, the inauguration of each Dutch monarch takes place.

Following the Alteration, the Mass was no longer celebrated, but leading citizens continued to be buried beneath the chancel floor until 1865; after then no more burials took place within Amsterdam churches. Marriages were still solemnized, however, and it is also recorded that twice a year the 'Worst Grammar School Students' received their prizes behind the screen. It seems that the Amsterdammers unconventional quirkiness has a long history!

Dominating the former sanctuary, in the original position of the high altar, stands the tomb of Holland's greatest naval hero Michiel de Ruyter, 1607-76. Admiral de Ruyter was a thorn in the side of the English during all three of the Anglo-Dutch naval battles, covering the period 1652-74. A daring raid that he led up the Medway in 1667 virtually destroyed the English fleet, but his greatest triumphs were in the third war, when, greatly outnumbered on each occasion, he inflicted three successive defeats on the combined Anglo/French navies. De Ruyter was killed in action, aged 69, engaging the French fleet off Sicily, and lies in a vault beneath his monument. Rombout Verhulst, Quellien's chief assistant at the royal palace, carved the monument, the finest in the church, completing it in 1681.

*Return to the crossing and proceed westward through the centre of the nave.*

Ahead, occupying the entire west wall, stands the great organ, best viewed from some distance away. Although completed in 1655, due to puritanical Calvinist opposition to music during services, it was not played until 1680, when the authorities agreed that the instrument should accompany the singing of psalms.

It appears that van Campen designed the organ case, working, as at the Town Hall, with Artus Quellien. The painter of the closed side of the shutters was Gerrit van Bronchorst, who included himself – looking out from a window on the left side of the lower section.

The enormous canopied pulpit, the pride of The New Church, by its very size dominates the interior. However, in the Dutch Reformed Church, pulpits usually stand in the centre of the building, visible from all sides. Here, this was not possible, as the church had been designed for Roman Catholic worship, orientated to the high altar at the east end; rebuilding after the fire made no attempt to alter this basic configuration. Aelbert Vinckenbrink carved the piece, 1649-64, incorporating an unusual number of sculptures. Six corner figures represent the Virtues, and panels illustrate Charitable Acts, whilst the Evangelists stand in front, each with his traditional emblem.

Enclosing the area around the pulpit, which served as the baptistry, is a rail in the form of a balustrade.

Against the wall, in the south-east corner of the church, stands the tomb monument of Admiral van Speijk, who blew up his own boat in Antwerp harbour in 1830 to avoid its capture by the Belgians. Those killed included van Speijk and many of his crew, but his act was regarded as heroic, and what remained of him was buried in Amsterdam's East Church before being transferred here the following year.

In the opposite corner is the monument (c.1830) to another admiral, van Kinsbergen, who is buried in Apeldoorn.

Just before the north transept is reached stands the tomb of Admiral Jan van Galen, killed in battle against the English off Leghorn in 1653. Quellien designed the memorial to him the following year, but the work was carved by Verhulst and Willem de Keyser.

The windows above were commissioned by Amsterdammers in 1939 as a gift to Queen Wilhemina to mark her 40 years on the throne. They depict female members of the royal family, and were designed by Willem van Konijnenburg. Beatrix, the present monarch, is portrayed as an infant in the arms of her mother, Queen Juliana.

*Follow the ambulatory around the choir.*

The two north-east columns bear pre-1578 decoration, which had been whitewashed over before being revealed during the recent restoration. It is 16th-century work and indicative of the original appearance of the interior. Before the Alteration, the priest's vestry was sited between these columns.

During the Roman Catholic period, it was customary for trade guilds and wealthy families to sponsor apsidal chapels and altars in their names. After 1578, the chapels were abandoned. Most are now partitioned off and serve as offices. The north-east chapels are, clockwise, the Drapers and the Boelens. The Mason's Chapel (usually open) occupies the centre of the apse and, on the south side, are the Meeuws, Verbergen and Sills Chapels.

The ancient Eggert Chapel, which follows (generally partitioned off), was completed in 1417 to commemorate William Eggert, who died that year. Eggert had presented the land for the church and is buried within; his monument stands against a column. The chapel became the first vestry of The New Church.

At a later date, the Eggert Chapel was linked with the Sharpshooters Chapel to the west, which is left open.

Many samples of corbels remain within the church: in the Sharpshooters Chapel, several are carved to depict amply-proportioned monks. Its vaults are still decorated with the crossbows of the sharpshooters.

Windows in both the Eggert and Sharpshooters chapels depict the town fathers of 1645; 32 of them are originals by van Bronchorst, the other 14 are modern.

*Exit from the church, left, passing the south façade.*

First left, Gravenstraat skirts the apse of The New Church. Small houses and shops cling like limpets to the great building.

## 10. De Drie Fleschjes 1650

18 Gravenstraat.

Open Monday - Saturday 12.00-20.30.

One of Amsterdam's last remaining proeflokaal's (tasting houses), De Drie Fleschjes (The Three Bottles) is the quintessential 'old Amsterdam' bar. A beamed ceiling, 17th-century casks and a venerable atmosphere attract a professional clientele.

Sand covers the floor, not sawdust as in England, because the authorities consider this to be a fire hazard; the floor itself is replaced every 20 years.

There are no bar stools, but customers are welcome to sit on either of the benches. The one in the enclosed alcove was where buyers once negotiated after tasting; the man in the street was also served – as long as he brought his own bottle. Until 1960, there was an adjoining distillery; Bols had bought it from Bootz, the original owner.

Glasses are filled to the brim with the spirit selected, and the customer is expected, initially, to lean down and sip from the glass without touching it, otherwise, some will almost certainly be spilt. Beer is served in addition to a wide range of genevers and liqueurs, but the only bar food available is boiled eggs.

Externally, the original step gable was replaced by a bell gable in the 19th century.

Adjoining the tavern, **no. 20** displays a colourful carved 'gaper', the symbol of a chemists shop, which is frequently seen in the city, sometimes still denoting a pharmacy. The open mouth is presumably waiting to receive a spoonful of medicine.

Gravenstraat continues westward, passing the protruding Gothic Chapel of New Church, a modern and much criticised addition.

During the recent remodelling, the long deaconate, which extends to the north porch, lost its upper storey, which had been added in 1723, thereby revealing once more the three windows that it had blocked.

The north façade had been restored in 1892, but the brick and stone walls of the transept date from c. 1540, when it was made higher. Renaissance features are already apparent: shells, vases and triangular pediments intruding on the otherwise Gothic structure.

*At NZ Voorburgwal turn right and proceed ahead until reaching Nieuwe Nieuwstraat (fourth left).*

# 11. Nieuwezijds Voorburgwal

This major thoroughfare, now an important tram route, was a canal until filled in 1884. The long name, meaning 'new side before the borough wall', denotes that it was laid out to the west of the Amstel river. It is usually abbreviated to NZ Voorburgwal.

Number 75, on the north corner with Nieuwe Nieuwstraat, was built as the **Makelaarscomptoir** (Brokers' headquarters) in 1633. Due to its triangular site, the façade is asymmetrical. The porch and shell motif are Classical in style, and the half-orb decoration is reminiscent of contemporary Carolean work in England. Brokers continue to use the building as a 'guildhouse'.

Returning southward, the **Maarakech** restaurant, on the opposite side of the road, at no. 134, provides good value Moroccan food (also see restaurant listing).

# 12. Die Port Van Cleve 1870

178-80 NZ Voorburgwal

An Amsterdam landmark, remodelled in Neo-Renaissance style by I. Gosschalk in 1888, the original Die Port restaurant retains its 19th-century decor and much of its 19th-century menu, specialising in Dutch home cooking: brown bean soup, pea soup and stampots. Every steak has been numbered since the restaurant opened in 1870, and when I last dined here, in May 1991, number 5,632,503 was served to me.

The famous Bodega, on the opposite side of the hall, designed by A. le Comte in 1880, is similarly unaltered. However, it is no longer a wine bar but an international restaurant, named **De Blaue Parade**, the blue parade referred to being the great frieze of Delft tiles, depicting a children's procession.

The name Port van Cleeve was established when, during building work, an identity stone of one of the houses being demolished was discovered on which it was inscribed. Above the restaurants, the hotel was established after the Second World War.

At **no. 182**, the former main post office building (1885-89), is a spiky Gothic Revival pile, designed by C. H. Peters, who was evidently inspired by the late-Gothic Chancery in Leeuwarden. Its main hall was sensitively remodelled in 1991 to form a shopping mall.

The west end of The New Church is passed, followed by the rear of the **Royal Palace**. Carved on the pediment of the palace is the allegorical theme of the Four Continents (all that were then known) presenting Amsterdam with their treasures. Surmounting the apex, Atlas bears the Globe of the Heavens; Temperance and Vigilance stand on either side.

Further south, the street widens appreciably, and, at its broadest point, a coin and stamp market is held on Wednesday and Saturday afternoons.

Amsterdam's newspaper, *De Telegraaf*, commissioned the 1929 building at **no. 225**, now occupied by K. A. Associatie NV. Its brick tower is something of a landmark and certainly the most significant part of architect J. F. Staal's design. Staal was a member of the Amsterdam School, but Rationalism is ascendant here.

Stretching southward from Sint Luciënsteeg, first left, is the soberly Classical brick façade of Amsterdam's History Museum.

Number 15 Sint Luciënsteeg, **Posthumus**, is one of Amsterdam's many fascinating specialist shops. A wide range of stationery is sold, but the great joy of Posthumus is its collection of rubber stamps, around 5,000 patterns being kept in stock. Bespoke stamps can be made within eight days of supplying black and white artwork – at prices from 19 guilders' in 1991. Also on offer are bronze and wax seals and a blind embossing press for very stylish stationery headings – costing 90 guilders that includes an individual name and address plate. I also found the reels of shimmering metallic stickers, sold in one guilder sections, absolutely irresistible.

*Leave the shop and continue southward.*

Set in the wall of Amsterdam's History Museum are a series of carved and decorated identity stones collected from the façades of various demolished buildings; there was no house numbering in the city until the Napoléonic occupation. The stones were fixed here in 1927, the first of such displays in the city.

At no. 27, an impressive gateway of 1634 provides one of several entrances to the museum (location 22 on this itinerary).

*Cross Kalverstraat and follow Duiffjessteeg to Rokin, right.*

## 13. Rokin

Rokin, which follows the course of the Amstel southward from De Dam, accommodated Amsterdam's inner harbour and was originally called Rakin, meaning inward reach (of the Amstel). Much of the waterway was filled 1933-37.

A visual shock on the east side is provided by the Oudhof office building, at **no. 99**. Post-Modernist in style, not only the blue and pink colours are a surprise, but the oriel bow window reflects buildings opposite, evoking a distorted mural. Built in 1990, by van Schyudel of Utrecht, one will either love or loathe its boldness, but whatever view is taken, the respect shown for the scale of Amsterdam's domestic buildings is commendable. Apparently, nothing of value has been replaced.

Opposite, **P. G. C. Hajenius**, tobacconists founded in 1826, still occupy splendid Art-Deco premises, built to the company's specification in 1914. Even non-smokers will enjoy a browse inside, admiring the period fittings, superb carpentry and leather ceiling. Hajenius sells a vast range of cigarettes, including their own brand, but it is the cigar 'collection' that is exceptional. Knowledgeable assistants will guide you through the range, advising on how each cigar is produced and should be nurtured. You may select a Swiss-made Davidoff, the most expensive, at 82.50 guilders, produced from Cuban tobacco, or a Montecristo from Havana, the longest, at 30 centimetres.

Number 102 is the Amsterdam branch of London auctioneers **Sotheby's**.

Occupying the corner with Spui, and facing the bridge, no. 112**, Arti et Amicitae**, was built for Amsterdam's Artists' Association in 1885. Its architect, J. H. Leliman, designed the building in Neo-Classical style, being influenced by his studies in Paris. Sculptures are by F. Stracke.

On the corner of the bridge that crosses Rokin from Spui stands the recently erected equestrian **monument to Queen Wilhelmina,** 1880-1962, Holland's monarch who ruled in exile from London during the Second World War. Wilhemina relinquished the throne in 1948, 14 years before her death, to her daughter Juliana, who abdicated, in turn, for her daughter, Queen Beatrix, the present monarch.

The twirling blades of a miniature windmill, which faces the bridge on the east side, publicise the **Mill Diamond Factory**. It is one of the many Amsterdam factories that give a brief explanation of diamond-cutting to visitors, in the hope, of course, that they will make a purchase.

*To its left, follow Langebrugsteeg. First left Nes.*

At no. 59, **Café Frascati** is Amsterdam's most popular theatre bar: large mirrors, pink marble and a 'brown' ceiling; it is open from 16.00 and serves good-value meals.

*Return to Langebrugsteeg and turn left to Grimburgwal.*

An archway left leads to the strangely named **Gebed Zonder End** (Prayer Without End), the appellation being of 15th century origin, when the street lay between a series of monastic buildings.

**Kapitein Zeppos**, at no. 3, offers the best fish soup in the city, together with a wide range of beers, some of which are Belgian.

*Return towards Rokin and turn left just before the bridge, at Oude Turfmarkt.*

## **14. Allard Pierson Museum**, W. A. Froger 1865-69

127 Oude Turfmarkt

Open Tuesday – Friday 10.00-17.00. Saturdays and Sundays 13.00-17.00. The admission charge includes an information sheet in English.

This museum displays the archaeological collection of Amsterdam University; the national collection is at Leiden.

Rounded corners emphasise the curved building line of what was formerly the Nederlandse Bank.

Allard Pierson, (1864-1925), who the museum commemorates, was a distinguished professor of art history at the University of Amsterdam, but the nucleus of the collection belonged to C. W. Lusingh Scheurleer, the university acquiring it in 1934. Not until 1976, however, did the museum open in its present home.

Beside the stairs is a portrait of Allard Pierson, by Jan Veth. Particularly recommended are: the Coptic exhibits on the ground floor; the Egyptian section on the first floor, greatly expanded in 1991; and the Etruscan artefacts on the second floor. There are also, of course, Greek and Roman collections, also on the second floor.

*Continue eastward along Oude Turfmarkt.*

Numbers **141, 143 and 145 Oude Turfmarkt** all have neck gables.

**Number 145**, now part of the university, was built by Philips Vingboons in 1642, for the composer Jan Pieterszoon Sweelinck. Vingboons was a Roman Catholic and, due to this, never received any civic commissions. Three tiers of brick pilasters rise above the rusticated stone base, each one surmounted by Classical capitals, successively: Doric, Ionic and Doric. Originally, the gable was stepped.

**Number 147**, adjoining, was built identically, forming a pair, but remodelled in Neo-Renaissance style in the late 19th century.

All the period houses in Oude Turfmarkt had a narrow escape in 1953, when they were threatened with demolition by the iconoclastic Nederlandse Bank; conservationists battled to save them and won.

*Return northward and cross the bridge, left, to Spui.*

## 15. Spui

Although short, Spui is an important Amsterdam thoroughfare, with varied shopping. Foreigners trying to pronounce the name afford much amusement to the Dutch; it is very difficult – even after hearing the tram driver pronounce Spui several dozen times I still can't get the right vowel sound. However, it is definitely not 'spewy' – try saying a mixture of 'spy' and 'spow' without rounding the lips, for an approximation.

Number 10, **Esprit**, is a clothing shop, with the ground floor converted to expose its iron structure in High Tec style.

**Maagdenhuis** (Maiden's house), at no. 2, was built of brick (1783-87) in Classical style, by the city architect Abraham van der Hart. Now part of the university, the massive edifice originally served as an orphanage for Roman Catholic girls.

The pediment's sculpture, by Anthonie Ziesenis, is this rather arid building's only decorative feature.

On the Kalverstraat corner, **W.H. Smith**, at no. 152 Kalverstraat, is Amsterdam's foremost bookseller of English language editions. The building itself is architecturally important as it was the first major work by Berlage. Built in 1886, in Venetian Renaissance style, artists in glass and terracotta are depicted in the spandrels of the first floor windows: Palissy, Luca della Robbia, Wedgwood and the Crabeth brothers; these are a reminder that this was originally a china shop.

*Continue ahead passing, on the north side of Spui, the passageway leading to the Begijnhof (see location 18).*

Numbers 14-16, the **Athenaeum News Centre/Bookshop** permits free reading of Dutch newspapers.

Immediately outside stands the rather consciously 'cute' bronze statue of a schoolboy, known as **Het Lieverdje** (Little Darling), presented to the city in 1960 by a tobacco company, but not to universal applause.

*Continue westward to the Heisteeg corner.*

## 16. Hoppe 1670

18-20 Spui

Open 11.00-01.00 (until 02.00 Saturdays and Sundays).

Hoppe, Amsterdam's most famous brown bar, has changed little since the 17th century. Within, it is very brown, with dark wood and a painted ceiling. Due to the bar's central position and popularity, crowds drinking outside in summer can stand up to ten deep.

Freddy Heineken, of the brewing family, used to drink here regularly, but, since his kidnapping, has understandably kept a low profile. It is alleged that the millionaire never indulged in buying rounds. The opening time of 11.00 is unusually early for a brown bar in the city.

Adjacent, at no. 22, the **Luxembourg Café** is extremely popular.

*Proceed northward, following Spuistraat.*

## 17. D'Vijff Vlieghen Restaurant

294-302 Spuistraat (tel: 6248369)

Open daily 17.30-23.00.

This, Amsterdam's most famous restaurant, is housed in five 17th-century houses, which possess gables in varying styles. Many believe that Vijff Vlieghen (Five Flies) refers to these houses, but, in fact, the name commemorates the first proprietor, Jan Janszoon Vijff Vlieghen, who opened the restaurant in 1939. It was a later owner, the former antique dealer Nicolaas Kroese, however, who put the restaurant on the international map, chiefly through his talent for publicity stunts.

Spreading across the five properties, which all run back to Singel, the restaurant has seven public dining rooms, each furnished in Dutch Renaissance style and varying in size.

Many in the world of entertainment have dined at the 'Five Flies', including Danny Kaye and Bob Hope: every chair has a copper plate commemorating a celebrity who has sat on it. Whenever convenient, diners are shown the function rooms: the Rembrandt Room displays two of the artist's original etchings, the Glass Room hand-made glasses and the Print Room relates the history of Amsterdam since 1200. (Also see restaurant listing).

*Return to Spui, first left, and pass the NZ Voorburgwal intersection.*

Immediately left, a stone archway in the brick building leads to the Begijnhof.

## 18. Begijnhof

This traffic-free square of ancient houses and two churches is tucked away in the very centre of Amsterdam, and always surprises and delights strangers to the city. Founded in 1346, the Begijnhof, although not strictly monastic, catered for women who were attracted to a convent lifestyle, but preferred not to make a full commitment to it. The ladies, known as begijns, educated poor children and cared for the sick. Some took vows of chastity, but were allowed to leave and marry if they so wished. Until c. 1400, only the northern section as far as the church existed, but the Begijnhof was then extended southward to its present boundary. When monasteries were dissolved at the Alteration of 1578, although their church was closed, the beguines were not molested, nor did they lose their properties. The last died in 1971 and the houses are now occupied by single, retired women.

On the stone arch from Spui is inscribed 'Bagijnhof' and, in a niche, is set a bas-relief of **Saint Ursula**, the patron saint of the establishment.

*Follow the vaulted passage.*

**Number 35** is now an information centre and a café.

In the wall between nos. 35 and 34, house identification stones were set in 1961.

Number 34 is named on a brass plaque **Het Houten Huys** (The Wooden House). Built c. 1477, this spout-gabled house is the only timber-faced survivor in the Begijnhof. Other contemporary houses in Amsterdam were similar in appearance, although they would also have had an external staircase, giving access to the main living area on the first floor. Fires eventually led to brick or stone façades being favoured, but most houses in the Begijnhof retain their timber frames.

Proceeding clockwise, nos. 29-30 provide the Begijnhof's Roman Catholic chapel.

## 19. Begijnhof Chapel

29-30 Begijnhof.

Open throughout the day.

The beguine's church, now the English Reformed Church, was lost to them at the Alteration and, as elsewhere in Amsterdam, houses were secretly converted for Roman Catholic worship. Work took place remodelling these two dwellings from 1671-80, and the resulting church remained 'hidden' until 1795. At the time, there were 150 beguines and twelve single women living here, but up to 300 other Catholics in the city also attended services. The chapel was restored in 1950.

Four stained-glass windows in the entrance (east) wall depict the history of the Amsterdam Miracle. They are the work of Gisèle van Waterschoot van der Gracht (1951). During the night of 15 March each year, a 'Silent Procession' leaves the chapel, commemorating the miracle.

Proceed clockwise around the galleried interior to the south wall, where the 18th-century panel painting is by Jacob de Wit. A 16th-century carving of St. Ursula sheltering children is displayed above the second door, and a figure of St. Nicholas, with putti at his feet, stands between the arches.

The high altar's reredos incorporates paintings of scenes illustrating the Amsterdam Miracle.

A *Last Supper* bas-relief forms the altar frontal.

Immediately left of this altar is a 17th-century *Crucifixion* painting, by Nicolas Moijaert.

The pulpit is mid-18th century work.

Also by Moijaert, right of the altar, is a *Nativity* painting.

Stretching across the north wall, the painting of a medieval Amsterdam Miracle procession is by Antoon Derkinderen (1888).

*Return to the Begijnhof and continue clockwise.*

Number 26, **Bethany**, was where, in 1862, the remaining beguines decided to live in convent style. The last, Sister Antonia, died here on 26 May 1971, aged 84.

An outstanding identity stone, displayed at **no. 19**, depicts the Flight to Egypt. It is believed to have been made in the studio of the famous architect Hendrick de Keyser.

**Numbers 17-14** are two-storey, plus dormer windows.

*Return towards the north façade of the church.*

Fixed to the outside of the low garden wall is a small modern plaque, commemorating Cornelia Arens, a beguine, who died in 1654. Although no longer permitted to worship in the church, burial within was not refused the beguines, but Cornelia Arens, ashamed of her family's denial of the Roman Catholic faith, insisted on being interred outside the church 'in the gutter'. Flowers are laid at this spot every year on 2 May, the day that she died.

Standing in front of the church is a bronze figure of a beguine, clad in the simple dress and distinctive Flemish hat that they all wore. It is the modern work of M de Goede-Taal.

To the north of the church, the green is known as the **Grotehof** (Great Courtyard); it was used by the beguines as a 'bleaching field', ie. for laundry.

## 20. English Reformed Church

48 Begijnhof

Open for Sunday services at 10.30 and for occasional concerts.

The present church was consecrated in 1419, but there may well have been an earlier chapel on part of the site; this would have then marked the southern boundary of the establishment. Restoration, remodelling and extensions have taken place, but, surprisingly, the tower and its spire are original, and the only medieval examples to survive in Amsterdam. Until 1578, the beguines celebrated the Roman Catholic Mass in the church, but it was closed henceforth and served as a warehouse.

The Dutch Reformed Church granted the beguines' former building to the English and Scottish Presbyterians who had settled in Amsterdam, and the first sermon in English was preached on 5 February 1607. In 1974, a survey revealed the poor structural state of the building, its south wall being close to collapse. Restoration of the body of the church took place and was completed in 1975. It was marked by a rededication followed by a thanksgiving ceremony, which Elizabeth the Queen Mother (of England) and Princess Beatrix (the present Queen of the Netherlands) attended.

## Exterior

The tower was restored in 1976 and is perfectly safe, in spite of its rather alarming lean. In the north wall of the church, near the tower, the two Gothic windows were discovered and unblocked during the 1975 restoration. However, much of the north wall was rebuilt in 1727 and, shortly afterwards, the angled windows were inserted half way along.

Apart from the west tower, and the apse at the east end, the south side of the church dates from the extension of 1655, when a wide aisle was added with, at its west end, the Consistory Chamber and, at its east end, the narrow Deaconry. Fronting this façade is a small green called the **Kleine Hof** (Small Courtyard).

Above the west door is the date 1607 and, beside it, a bronze plaque presented by the American Reformed Church in 1927 to commemorate the Pilgrim Fathers, some of whom had lived in Amsterdam before joining others on the *Mayflower* at Plymouth in 1620.

*Proceed to the vestibule, which is lit by one of the restored Gothic windows.*

Within the nave, the second Gothic window, left, is followed by the two windows inserted in 1727. They are angled specifically to light the pulpit, which stood between them until moved to its present position in 1912.

Looking back from the chancel to the west end of the church, the organ case was carved by Jacob Hulstman in 1753.

In the east wall, the stained-glass window was presented in 1920 to mark the 300th anniversary of the departure of the Pilgrim Fathers, many of whom had worshipped here.

**(Opposite) Top:** *Houseboats relieve the shortage of city centre accommodation.*
**(Opposite) Bottom:** *Part of the façade of the Town Hall/Opera complex, unkindly, but understandably, known as 'the set of dentures'.*

The famous Dutch artist Piet Mondrian (or Mondriaan) designed four allegorical panels for the pulpit while still a promising young student, and has signed one of them; Edema van der Tuuk was the carver. These were commissioned to mark the accession to the throne of Queen Wilhelmina in 1898.

To commemorate their joint accession to the throne of England, William III (also Prince of Orange) and Mary II presented a bronze embellishment to the lectern, in the form of a lion and a lion's claw, bearing the monogram 'WMRR 1689' (William, Mary, Rex, Regina). This was later transferred from the lectern to the pulpit's desk.

During the Second World War, the swastika was hung in the chancel of the church, which the German occupying garrison used for their own Protestant services. Also displayed was a quotation from Saint Paul's first letter to the Corinthians: 'The kingdom of God is not in word, but in power', presumably accepted by the Nazis as proof of the Apostle's basic Hitlerian philosophy!

Against the south aisle's south wall, built in 1655, and representing the major extension to the church, is fixed the Burgomasters' pew, sited to face the pulpit, which had been moved to the wall opposite on completion of the extension. The pew was reserved for important visitors.

Several British parishioners are commemorated in the church, but the most famous person to be buried here was the Italian composer Pietro Antonio Locatelli, 1695-1764.

*Return to the north side of the Begijnhof and exit between nos. 17 and 14.*

Behind the east range of beguines' houses, running from Spui, is a narrow lane, **Gedempte Begijnensloot**. This follows the course of an odourous ditch (sloot), which was covered by a vaulted passage in 1745 and filled in 1865. Originally, the Begijnhof and the Convent of Saint Lucy (now Amsterdam's History Museum) stood on a triangular island bounded by the ditch and the canals of Spui and

**(Opposite)** *A concert in progress in the Citizens Hall of the Royal Palace, formerly the Town Hall.*
(Reproduced courtesy of the Amsterdam Tourist Office)

Nieuwezijds Voorburgwal; all three have been filled and are now thoroughfares.

The north section of Gedempte Begijnesloot has been remodelled and covered over to create the Civic Guards Gallery.

## 21. Civic Guards Gallery (Schuttersgallerij)
B van Kasteel and J. Schipper 1975

Automatic doors open to this air-conditioned gallery/thoroughfare, where group paintings of the Civic Guard companies, who protected Amsterdam from the late 14th century until the mid-17th century, are hung. The guards defended the city in a military fashion, but also kept the peace in the manner of modern-day policemen, and provided guards. At their headquarters, known as doelens, they practised with bows and arrows, later guns, and socialised. Gradually, the social activities predominated, culminating in great banquets. The guardsmen were originally grouped into quasi-religious guilds, but, at the Alteration of 1578, these were disbanded and replaced by Companies. However, the names of their patron saints continued to be used. Members had to supply their own clothing and equipment, which effectively meant that only the wealthier burghers could join. Group portraits of many societies became uniquely popular in the Netherlands in the 16th century; the first to be commissioned by members of a Civic Guard Company dates from c. 1529.

Exhibited in this gallery is the largest existing collection of Company paintings, spanning more than a century. Others are dispersed throughout various museums. The most famous of them all, Rembrandt's *The Nightwatch*, is permanently exhibited in the Rijksmuseum.

All such paintings were initially hung in the Companies halls, and every guardsman featured had to pay the painter; in course of time, the amount charged depended on the respective prominence given, those in the background or half-hidden paying less. The earliest works were very wooden, the guards usually set in two rows with doll-like faces that reveal little character. As Dutch painting progressed, however, the artists gradually overcame the problem of unnatural, posed groups and Franz Hals, as well as Rembrandt, painted several masterpieces in this genre.

When Amsterdam's History Museum moved to the adjacent premises, all the rooms proved too small to accommodate the huge works, and this part-thoroughfare/part-gallery answered the problem. It was opened, together with the museum, in 1975.

*At the end of the gallery turn left into the large courtyard.*

## 22. Amsterdam's History Museum (Amsterdams Historisch Museum)

92 Kalverstraat and 27 Sint Luciënsteeg

Open daily 11.00-17.00 (18.00 in summer). Admission charge, with an additional admission charge to some major temporary exhibitions optional.

This large and splendid museum, most of it occupying the buildings of a former orphanage, originally a monastery, traces the history of the city from its beginnings in the 13th century to the Second World War.

### History

The courtyard was formerly the cloister of the Convent of St. Lucy, established in 1414. It was confiscated by the city in 1578 and sold to the Burgher Orphanage. Children who lived here were required to be the orphans of parents who were born in, and sworn citizens of, Amsterdam. The orphanage had been founded in a house in Kalverstraat c.1520 and moved here in 1580. Remodelling took place the following year, supervised by Bilhamer, who is also believed to have been responsible for designing the Kalverstraat entrance, described later.

The present appearance of the courtyard was established by Jacob van Campen, architect of the Royal Palace, who rebuilt the north and west façades in his favoured Classical style. He also built the completely new, but matching, south range, which divided the original cloister in two. Colossal pilasters create an air of grandeur.

Hendrick de Keyser designed a Dutch Renaissance building for the east side, 1691-96, but this fell into disrepair and was rebuilt 1745-50, to match the other buildings, which then formed the girls' courtyard; the boys had been moved to accommodation on the other side of the Begijnensloot, acquired in 1631.

Amsterdam's History Museum opened in the Weighhouse, at Nieuwmarkt in 1926, but the building was never large enough to display the entire collection, much of it being dispersed among other buildings. In 1960, the orphanage was relocated and conversion of the complex for the museum's use began. Exteriors were restored to their original appearance, but the interiors were completely remodelled, with the exception of the Regents' Chamber. The museum opened on 27 October 1975, precisely 700 years after the earliest recorded reference to Amsterdam. Work had taken 12 years, under the supervision of the architects, B. van Kasteel and J. Schipper, whose responsibilities included the Civic Guards Gallery.

Visitors are given a plan with a suggested route and a brief summary of each room's theme. A complete guide to the museum in English may be hired or purchased. Most captions throughout are in Dutch only. Entered from the west wing, the vestibule displays the original relief by Bilhamer (1581) from the Kalverstraat entrance to the orphanage, where it has been replaced by a replica.

**Room 1** A steel column, with illustrated numbers, indicates the growth of the city's population; not until 1300 were there 1,000 inhabitants.

The oldest known document alluding to Amsterdam is the toll privilege granted by Floris V in 1275, but a copy, not the irreplaceable original, is displayed.

A tunnel connects the west with the east wing after **room 3** has been seen.

**Room 4** Here is displayed the earliest plan of the city, a birds-eye view of 1538, by Cornelis Anthonisz. It can be seen that Amsterdam was then bisected by the Amstel, with De Dam blocking it at the halfway point. West of the Amstel runs Nieuwendijk, passing The New Church and changing its name south of Dam to Kalverstraat, a route still recognisable. However, to its west the two canals have been filled and are now the main roads NZ Voorburgwal and Spuistraat. The Singel, still open water, marks the outer limits of the city, following the line of its defensive wall. From the opposite bank stretch open fields.

East of the Amstel, as now, Warmoestraat passes Old Church, becoming Nes. The two canals, OZ Voorburgwal and OZ Achterburgwal, remain unfilled. Gelderskade, also still unfilled, now ends at the Weigh house (Waag) in Nieuwmarkt, which continues as Kloveniersburgwal. Its route follows the eastern section of the city wall.

Montelbaanstoren (tower) marks the entrance to Oude Schans; behind it stretch the shipyards. Land has since been reclaimed for laying out Prins Hendrikkade, and the tower, therefore, no longer directly faces the harbour.

**Room 5**   Explorers routes may be illuminated on the map displayed by pressing buttons.

**Room 6**   Items relating to the development of the Town Hall (now the Royal Palace) include a painting, by Cornelis de Bie, of the burning of the old Town Hall, terracottas, by Quellien, of his sculptural decorations, a model of the completed building, made in 1648, and one of several paintings of the pristine Town Hall, by Gerrit Berckheyde (1638-98).

*From Room 7 ascend to the first floor.*

From **Rooms 8, 9 and 10**, there are views through large windows of the Civic Guards Gallery.

**Room 8**   Paintings of the proposed tower of The New Church that was never completed, and the Old Exchange.

**Room 9**   Model of the Trippenhuis, the great 17th-century mansion restored in 1991.

**Room 10**   Two models of The New Church tower and a painting that depicts a design matching neither. Other paintings depict interiors of Old Church and The New Church.

*From Room 10 ascend the spiral staircase to the Bells Room.* By pressing buttons, the 17th-century carillons of West Church, the Royal Palace, Old Church and South Church may be played.

A bridge leads to **Room 11**, where group paintings of various 'Regents' (governors) of charitable institutions, both male and female, are displayed. Outstanding, is the work facing the entrance, *Regents of the Leper House*, by Ferdinand Bol (1649).

*Return over the bridge.* The throne and stool of Willem IV from the Royal Palace are exhibited in **Room 12**.

**Room 13** displays a model of Maagdenhuis 1783.

**Rooms 14-17** depict life in Amsterdam from the 18th to the 20th centuries.

**Room 18** houses selected prints from the museum's large collection.

**Room 20**, on the second floor, depicts crafts in the 17th and 18th centuries, whilst **Room 21** deals with archaeology.

*Return to the ground floor vestibule and proceed to the Regents Room, which faces the reception desk.*

**The Regents Room (Regentkamer)**, where the governors met, is the only one in the complex to have been restored to its 17th century appearance. Paintings feature regents from several periods. The ceiling was painted in 1656, symbolising Charity, Love and Generosity.

Adjoining, the **Van Speyk (or Speijck) Room** displays paintings of orphans, including Jan van Speyk, who became a national hero by setting fire to his ship rather than let it be captured by the Belgians.

*Exit from the museum left. Immediately left pass through the gateway to Sint Luciënsteeg.*

This entrance to the orphanage was created when the boys' section was separated from the girls. The gate, made in the 16th century for the Town Carpenter's Yard in Oude Turfmarkt, was brought here in 1634, the date carved on its face.

*Return to the courtyard and turn left.*

The **boys' courtyard** had not been monastic, its west block, a 16th-century building, formerly provided accommodation for elderly men and women. This was acquired by the orphanage in 1631 and given its present façade in 1735; it now houses major temporary exhibitions. Facing this range, the east wall incorporates lockers in which boys kept their personal possessions.

A Doric arcade, with schoolroom above, on the north side, was added, probably by Pieter de Keyser, in 1632. From the arcade, the museum's restaurant, **David and Goliath**, may be approached. This was formerly the orphan's carpentry shop, and originally the cow-barn of the convent. Its impressive tie-beam roof has been restored, and the former dimensions of the room reverted to.

The colossal figure of Goliath and the smaller one of David, together with the shield bearer, are attributed to Albert Jansz Vinckenbrinck c. 1650. They were made for a Prinsengracht pleasure garden, Oude Doolhof (Old Maze), where they remained from 1650-1862, afterwards standing in an alleyway in the Jordaan. Goliath's head can be mechanically turned and his eyes made to roll.

*Exit from the restaurant left and proceed ahead, following the arcade to Kalverstraat.*

The gateway to **no. 92** incorporates a copy of the relief displayed in the museum's vestibule. Dated 1581, it depicts orphan boys in red and blue uniforms surrounding a dove, representing the Holy Ghost. A Baroque piece, the entire gate was allegedly designed by Joost Janszoon Bilhamer.

## 23. Kalverstraat

Never a canal, the pedestrianised Kalverstraat has been Amsterdam 'New Side's' most important shopping street for many years, although clothing establishments are now in the ascendancy. In spite of its ancient roots, however, little of architectural interest has survived. Kalver means calves, probably indicating a cattle market origin.

Immediately ahead, the block between Wijdekapelsteeg and Engekapelsteeg accommodated, for more than 500 years, the chapel once known as the **Heilige Stede** (Holy Place), until it was demolished in 1908. This was built on the site of the house where, on 15 March 1345, the 'Amsterdam Miracle' had occurred. A dying man regurgitated a consecrated wafer that he had been given by the priest, which was then thrown on the fire but would not burn. Within two years the house had been replaced by the chapel, and a formal, commemorative procession to it is recorded as early as 1360. In 1489, the Holy Roman Emperor Maximilian took part, seeking a cure for an ailment; his health was restored and, in thanks, he gave the city permission to incorporate the imperial crown in its arms.

Following the Alteration of 1578, the processions were ended, and the chapel adopted by the Dutch Reformed Church, which renamed it the Nieuwezijds Kapel (Newside Chapel). The Gothic building was an important architectural monument, but, in spite of conservationists' protests, it was demolished in 1908. Redevelopment included a much smaller, and undistinguished, chapel designed by C. B. Posthumus Meyjes senior. Fortunately, two distinguished porches from the chapel were spared and have been incorporated within Old Church.

Roman Catholic processions began again in the late 19th century, and take place every year on the Sunday closest to 15 March. It is known as the Stille Omgang (Silent Procession).

Northward, nos. 48-52, **De Slegte**, stocks one of the best selections of second-hand books in the city.

Number 58 is a Roman Catholic church, **Sants Petrus en Paulus**, built in Gothic Revival style by G. Moele, in 1848. It's site is often wrongly confused with that of the former Nieuwezijds Chapel.

Kalverstraat ends at De Dam. Behind the Royal Palace, NZ Voorburgwal is followed by tram routes 1, 2, 5, 13 and 17 and Raadhuisstraat by 21, 67, 170 and 171. Tram routes 4, 9, 16, 24 and 25 follow Damrak to the north and 9, 14, 16, 24 and 25 follow Rokin to the south.

ROUTE 2

# Old Church and the Red Light District

Old Church, Amsterdam's most historic building, was founded at a very early stage in the city's development. It stands in surrealist juxtaposition with the famous red light district, where porn and drugs go hand in hand. In spite of the vice, the picturesque, treelined canals give an aura of respectability, and sightseers are perfectly safe. South Church, a Dutch Renaissance masterpiece, by Hendrick de Keyser, was the first building in Amsterdam specifically designed for Protestant worship. Of outstanding interest is the Museum Amstelkring, which preserves a 17th-century 'hidden' church and the finest domestic interiors of the period in the city.

## Timing
• The Museum Amstelkring is open on weekdays from 10.00-17.00, but only in the afternoon on Sundays.

• Although Old Church is open daily (not Sunday afternoon) its tower may be ascended only in summer, Mondays and Thursdays 14.00-17.00, Tuesdays and Wednesdays 11.00-14.00.

• South Church is open Monday to Wednesday and Fridays 12.30-16.30 and Thursdays 18.00-21.00. Its tower is open in summer on Wednesdays 14.00-17.00, Thursdays and Fridays 11.00-14.00 and Saturdays 11.00-16.00. There is a carillon concert on Thursdays 12.00-13.00.

## Locations for Route 2
1. St. Nicolaas
2. Zeedijk
3. Oudezijds Voorburgwal
4. Museum Amstelkring
5. Old Church
6. Warmoestraat
7. Oudezijds Achterburgwal
8. Koestraat
9. Kloveniersburgwal
10. Trippenhuis

| | | | |
|---|---|---|---|
| 11. | Oudemanshuispoort | 14. | Nieuwmarkt |
| 12. | Sint Antoniesbreestraat | 15. | St Antony's Gate |
| 13. | South Church | | |

**Start:   Stationsplein** *From Stationsplein cross the bridge towards Damrak. First left, Prins Hendrikkade follows the water. Continue to the domed church of St. Nicolaas.*

## 1. St. Nicolaas, A.C. Bleys 1885-87

76 Prins Hendrikkade

This was the first Roman Catholic church to be built in the city after freedom of worship was again permitted, and its Neo-Baroque cupola serves as a landmark for the northern sector of Amsterdam. Unfortunately, the brickwork has become very blackened and grim; cleaning is under consideration.

Internally, everything is well-preserved, with the polychrome but dull colouring enlivened by columns of black marble and the paintings on the side walls, which depict the stages of the cross. The nave is barrel vaulted, but the sanctuary has been given a rib vault.

A.C. Bleys, the architect of St. Nicolaas, designed the reredos of the high altar, which was carved by E. van den Bossche.

*Return southward. First left, Zeedijk leads to, first right, Sint Olofspoort.*

On the Nieuwebrugsteeg corner, right, no. 13, **In de Lompen**, was built in 1618 as a shop with living area above. It is a former 'tasting house' offering a wide selection of Amsterdam distillery spirits; open evenings only.

Renaissance stepped gables are designed in the style of Lieven de Key.

Keystones on the first floor take the form of human heads; on the second floor, lions heads.

## 2. Zeedijk

In spite of cleaning up efforts, this is still Amsterdam's most notorious street. It does border the red light area, but most of the solitary 'gentlemen' propping up doorways are concerned not with the prostitutes, but with drugs; their trade soon becomes apparent.

**Number 1** is one of only two houses retaining timber façades in Amsterdam (the other is in the Begijnhof). Although the woodwork is not original and the side and rear walls are of brick, the appearance is typical of Amsterdam houses in the Middle Ages.

Towards the central section of the road are found a group of economically-priced Chinese restaurants. Particularly recommended, at no. 87, is **Moy Kong** (also see restaurant listing).

*Sint Olofsteeg, first right, leads to OZ Voorburgwal.*

## 3. Oudezijds Voorburgwal

So many wealthy citizens lived overlooking this waterway in the 17th-century that it was called the 'velvet' canal.

Step-gabled, no. 14, built by Burcht van Leiden in 1605, was known as **Leuwenburg**, due to the lion's head masks, which form the corner stones above the lower wooden frontage.

A centrally-placed stone tablet is carved with the coat of arms of Riga, the home town of the client who commissioned the house. Unusual in Amsterdam, there is a slight overhang of the upper storeys on the side of the house.

**Numbers 18-18B**, apart from the modern spout gable, was built early in the 17th-century and is attributed to Hendrick de Keyser.

A central stone tablet illustrates Egmont Castle and is inscribed with its name, Int Slode van Egmondt.

Huge dolphins support the neck gable of **no. 19**.

## 4. Museum Amstelkring 1661-63

40 Oudezijds Voorburgwal

Open Monday – Saturday 10.00-17.00. Sundays and holidays 13.00-17.00. Admission charge.

Not to be missed, this is the only complete example of the many 'hidden' Roman Catholic churches in Amsterdam to survive. It also incorporates, in the living room, a 17th-century domestic interior that is, again, unique in the city.

## History

Jan Hartman built this house for his own accommodation, together with two attached residences for letting purposes along the adjoining side street, Heintje Hoeckssteeg. A church for Roman Catholic worship was created within the second and third storeys, plus the attic of all three properties. Entrance to the church was gained from Heintje Hoeckssteeg only and, because of this, it was frequently referred to as Het Haentje. The more common name, however, was Het Hart, after the owner, Jan Hartman. At the Alteration of 1578, all Catholic worship was proscribed and those wishing to celebrate Mass had to do so in secret. By the mid-17th century, hidden churches were under construction and, in 1680, as many as 30 were operating in the city. Although fondly believed to be clandestine, most were known to the authorities, but the Dutch law enforcement officers, unlike those in some other countries that readers may be familiar with, have generally been loath to persecute on matters concerning personal freedom. In other words, a blind eye was turned, as it is today to soft drugs and prostitution, both still technically illegal.

The church was extended towards the canal frontage and a second staircase built c. 1735.

With the arrival of the French occupying forces in 1795, religious freedom was established in Amsterdam and the hidden churches were replaced, initially with buildings financed by the Ministry of Inland Waterways, and known as Waterstaatskerken (the state's water churches). However, worship continued in the building, the church then being known as 'Our Dear Lord in the Attic', and dedicated to St. Nicholas. It had become the only church of this type to survive in its former condition, when, in 1887, its parish was transferred to the Roman Catholic church of St. Nicolaas, which had just been built. Threatened with destruction, the 'attic' church was purchased by the Stichting Amstelkring, a Catholic history society, in 1887, and opened the following year as a museum. Although several other buildings in the city retain traces of clandestine churches, this is the only complete example to survive.

The exterior is typical of its period, with a timbered ground-floor and cross windows.

*Enter from the canal frontage.*

## Interior

An excellent guide book in English has been updated to incorporate alterations made in 1991 to the items displayed, most of which relate to Catholic life in Holland after 1578. Originally the entrance hall, the **front room** was remodelled in Dutch Louis XV style in the 18th-century.

From the **back room**, which retains much of its 17th-century appearance, the **stairs** are approached via an opening made after the museum was created.

Ascend the stairs and turn right to the **living room** (de Sael), now said to be the only complete 17th-century domestic interior surviving in Amsterdam. The emphasis on symmetry evokes a Vermeer painting.

*The Presentation in the Temple* was painted specifically for its position above the walnut chimney piece. Below it are carved the hart arms of Jan Hartman, and a compass: the arms of his second wife, Lysbeth Jans, whose father was a compass maker.

The walnut cupboard doubles as a bed.

Stairs lead up to the small, **first floor front room**, containing another cupboard bed.

*Descend to the landing and ascend the stairs to the former church.*

The **chaplain's room** may be viewed through a window en route.

Around 1735, radical alterations took place to the **church**: the altar was renewed and moved forward, behind it, a second stairway was built, the area was extended to the frontage, and galleries were created.

Forming the reredos to the altar are three paintings by Jacob de Wit, 1736, which can be alternated; generally displayed is the *Baptism of Christ*.

The altar rail is 19th-century and the silver sanctuary lamp was made by Cornelis Bogaert in 1656. Most other items are 18th century work.

Within the altar is stored an unusual, revolving pulpit.

Stairs lead to the **first gallery**, from where there is a good view of the organ, made in 1794. The space behind the altarpiece was allocated for peat storage.

Rear stairs descend to the **sacristy**, **confessional**, and other small rooms, which display silverware and paintings.

At the rear of the ground floor, the **kitchen** retains its 19th-century fittings.

*Exit from the museum right and proceed to Old Church.*

Facing the church, **no. 57** was built by Hendrick de Keyser in 1615. Busts, cornices and double pilasters provide a highly decorative exterior.

## 5. Old Church (Oudekerk)

23 Oude Kerksplein

Open Monday – Saturday 11.00-17.00. Admission charge. Sunday service 11.00. Tower open for guided tours June – September on the hour, Mondays and Thursdays 14.00-17.00, Tuesdays and Wednesdays 11.00-14.00.

Dating from 1300, Old Church is Amsterdam's most historic building, and refreshingly maintains the appearance of a church that is still in use. Its confusing extensions and remodellings throughout eight centuries are reminiscent of many Gothic churches in England, but unique in Amsterdam. Of particular interest, internally, are the painted vaults, stained glass windows and misericords of the choir stalls.

### History

The core of the tower, believed to be 13th-century, is the most venerable part of Old Church to survive. Nothing remains of the body of the first building, which was completed as Amsterdam's earliest church, probably c.1300. It appears that this was lengthened within a short space of time and, by 1340, the nave had been completely rebuilt to a much greater width, the rapid growth of Amsterdam's population urgently necessitating expansion.

Between 1380 and 1412, the north transept was constructed and the chancel rebuilt once more, this time with an ambulatory so that it matched the width of the nave.

Possibly due to the city's destructive fires in 1421 and 1452, a south transept was not added until 1462; it replaced a mid-14th-century chapel. The south portal and baptistry were also constructed at this time.

Chapels were built against the north and south aisles c.1500, and, by 1512, the nave had been heightened by a clerestory. A similar raising of the chancel did not take place until 1560, thus marking the final major alteration to the body of the church. However, in 1566, a steeple was added to the tower.

In 1566, also, the first wave of Calvinist iconoclasm struck Dutch churches, and Old Church was invaded, most carvings and fittings being destroyed. High level murals were spared, simply because they could not be reached easily; after the Alteration these were white-washed over.

Limited repair work took place from 1912-14, but complete restoration was effected between 1955 and 1979.

Concerts and other cultural events are held in the building, which is now administered by the Stichting de Oudekerk foundation.

## Exterior

Houses clinging to the walls were built in the 17th and 18th centuries for leasing purposes to supplement the income of the church.

The pitch-roofed south porch was built in Gothic style in 1462. Carved in stone above its entrance are the arms of the Emperor Maximillian and his son Philip the Handsome, c. 1500.

Forming the corbel to the window, right, an ape with a skull records that the south door was the entrance used for funerals.

Immediately left of the porch, the church warden's room dates from 1611, although its windows are 18th-century.

Proceeding clockwise, the steeply-pitched gables of the 14th-century south aisle mostly comprise huge windows displaying Gothic tracery.

On the west side, the polygonal baptistry (c. 1462) protrudes from the wall of the nave, which dates from rebuilding in 1334.

The west tower was encased in 1747, but its 13th-century core survives within. Set out strangely at an angle to the nave, and containing pre-1300 masonry, it has been surmised that the tower may originally have been an appendage to an earlier chapel. Its splendid Renaissance steeple was designed in 1566, probably by Bilhamer. Four pealing bells date from 1659, but, above them survives a bell made c. 1450. This bell tower, like others in Holland, has been acquired, primarily for security reasons, by the State, which is responsible for maintenance and opening facilities. Views from the top (summer only) are exceptional.

Much of the north-west corner of the church was heavily restored in 1914, but the fabric of all the north chapels of the nave dates from c. 1500.

The north porch was built in 1520 and, attached to it, the Holy Sepulchre Chapel in 1530. Classical pilasters and an arch, at the top of the chapel, denote the coming of the Renaissance and are in unusual juxtaposition with the remainder of the design, which is entirely Gothic.

The north transept, completed in 1412, marks the end of the longest stretch of the church to remain uncluttered by extraneous buildings; from here on, many will find it difficult to avert their eyes from the succession of brightly-lit picture windows that ring the chancel of Old Church like an additional set of chapels. Instead of displaying figures of saints, however, they are occupied by scantily-dressed ladies of varying age, build and race. Apparently this has been a brothel area since the 17th century. Enthusiastic photographers may be tempted to capture the scene, but be warned, most girls in the Red Light district strongly object to being photographed, and their minders have a reputation for 'accidentally knocking' the cameras of offenders into a canal. The police evidently show scant sympathy when this occurs.

Mostly hidden by houses, the Lady Chapel, which follows, was built in 1555. Behind this is the wall of the chancel, built 1370-82. Its continuation, the polygonal apse, at the east end of the church, was completed c. 1380.

*Continue around the apse to the south side of the church.*

Fronting the south façade of the apse is the early 16th-century sacristy.

Brick-built, but with bands of stone, the south transept's gabled façade was completed c.1462.

*Enter the church from the south porch.*

**(Opposite)** *Vintage street-organs maintain their colourful decoration. City venues constantly change.*

(Reproduced courtesy of the Amsterdam Tourist Office)

## Interior

As in most large churches, the best overall impression is gained by proceeding directly to the crossing. From here, looking westward, may be seen the great organ, its case made by J. Westerman in 1724.

Private pews are built around the south-west pier of the crossing and the south columns of the nave. The second of these columns bears traces of painting that imitates brocade, probably 15th-century work.

On the north side of the nave, the wooden pulpit was made by Jan Pietersz in 1642; its brass handrail is the work of J. G. Geelgieter. The entire area is screened by a wooden balustrade c.1664. It was customary in the Dutch Reformed Church to hold baptism services within a screened area in front of the pulpit.

Box pews on both sides, at the west end, were reserved for important members of the congregation. Some of them have survived from the 17th century but most are 19th-century replacements.

*Return to the crossing and proceed through the chancel screen.* This screen was designed by A. Cuyper in 1681, with brasswork by G. Wijbrants. The choir's pulpit, left, is of wood decorated to simulate marble. Choir stalls are fitted with 15th-century misericords, which are designed in an unusually bold style.

Brocade paintings have been revealed on the 12 chancel columns, each of which represents an Apostle. Their figures originally stood on brackets facing inward, but all were destroyed in the 16th century. On the north side, the first angled arch, painted green, formed the canopy above the Tabernacle. It is flanked by gilded censing angels.

*Return again to the crossing and proceed to the south transept.* This transept is separated from the aisle by an early 17th-century screen, decorated with strapwork. Immediately left, the Red Door was the entrance to the sacristy, later the Bridal Chamber. The inscription above it translates 'Marry in haste, repent at leisure'. Vaults within were painted with different themes c. 1517.

Few of the chapels may be entered, as most are now used as offices. However, it is often possible to look over a partition to admire the painted vaults, many of which date from the 15th-century, and

**(Opposite)** *The steeple of West Church has become Amsterdam's symbol. Anne Frank refers to its bells in her famous diary.*

sections of the stained glass windows. A free brochure, available in Dutch but with an accompanying English translation, details each of the vaults and windows.

Chapels passed westward are the Smidskapel and the Huiszittenkapel, the latter displaying engravings, and views of Old Church.

Outstanding 15th-century painted vaults have been revealed in the south aisle.

The name of the most westerly of the south chapels commemorates its founder, Elizabeth Gaven. Against this chapel's east wall is the large Baroque monument to Vice-Admiral Abraham van der Hulst, by Artus de Wit, 1666. Like the other naval heroes buried in the church, he was killed in action. The monument to Admiral Isaac Sweers, 1622-73, by Verhulst, stands against the west wall.

The next portal, in the west wall of the church, leads to the former baptistry and was allegedly designed by Quellien some time after 1651.

Just north of the organ, against the west wall, stands the Renaissance inner porch of the Nieuwezijds (Miracle) Chapel, demolished in 1908. Made c.1621, with barley sugar columns, the porch appears rather incongruous as it leads nowhere of importance.

Set in the floor, against the wall, are the tomb slabs of Field Marshal Paulus Wirtz (1612-75).

A wall tablet commemorates two poets, husband and wife, N.S. van Winter and L. van Merken. It was erected in 1828 by Amsterdam's Society for Eloquence.

The Baroque wall monument to Rear-Admiral W. van der Zaan, in the Hamburger Chapel (north-west corner), was made by Verhulst in 1670. Also standing in this chapel is a 15 feet high, painted wooden model c. 1700 of a church that was planned to occupy the site of the former Butter Market, now Rembrandtsplein, but never built.

The next two north chapels are the Binnenland and the Weitkopers. From the latter, one row of floor slabs in from its east wall, may be found the tomb slab of Rembrandt's wife, who lies below. Its inscription, 'Saskia 19 Juni 1642', was commissioned by the Amstelodamum Historical Society in 1953. Rembrandt himself lies in an unmarked (and unknown) grave in West Church.

Built around the column of the north transept's protruding west wall is the choir organ of 1658; its shutters were decorated by C. Brizé. The beams in the north transept (St. Joriskapel) are of interest. One is decorated, and another, facing the window, bears an inscription recording that the chapel was completed in 1412.

The large Lady Chapel (Mariakapel), which follows, was added to the church in 1555. Its north-west *Annunciation* window is original although somewhat restored. Below are depicted the donor, J. K. Hoppen, and his family. Also original, but renovated, are the chapel's north-east, *Adoration of the Shepherd's* window and the east, *Death of the Virgin* window, again depicting its donors, the Brant family.

The next window, in the east wall of the chancel's north aisle, was begun by De Angelis in 1758 and illustrates coats of arms of the burgomasters and aldermen who served 1758-1867.

Against the chancel's second column from the west (after the crossing's north-east pier), facing north, is the memorial to Admiral Jacob van Heemskerck, 1567-1607.

Follow the ambulatory clockwise to the second bay of the apse, where has been erected a second inner porch from the Nieuwezijds Chapel, also made in 1621. However, the design of this example is much less exuberant. Neither porch now leads anywhere of importance and, whilst their preservation is to be commended, one hopes that a more relevant location may eventually be found.

In the last bay of the apse, the window, designed by Pieter Jansz in 1655, commemorates the Treaty of Munster. For some reason it was not installed until 1911.

From the south wall hangs the funeral hatchment of Hendrick Gerritsz Zeehelm, a Swedish admiral, who died in 1688. This is one of several examples in Old Church. A hatchment, painted with the coat of arms of the deceased, was displayed outside his residence and then borne in the funeral procession. As in England, those of the more famous were later exhibited in a church.

*Exit from the church.*

Immediately opposite, **no. 57 OZ Voorburgwal** is a very decorative, step-gabled example of Hendrick de Keyser's work, built in 1615. Forming the window piers are double pilasters linked by escutcheons.

*From the west end of Old Church, Wijdekerksteeg leads to Warmoestraat. Turn left and proceed to the half way point of the Stock Exchange's rear façade, which takes up much of the west side of the street.*

## 6. Warmoestraat

Originally, this was Amsterdam's principal shopping street, but now the north section is mainly devoted to restaurants in the medium price range: Thai, Mexican, Italian and Argentinian cuisines are represented, all within close proximity of each other.

Set against the Stock Exchange wall is a statue of **Joost van den Vondel** (1587-1679) Holland's 'Shakespeare', who ran a hosiery business from no. 101, now lost. He wrote official verses in the manner of a poet laureate, but his most popular work was 'Gijsbrecht van Amstel'. Following the Dutch tradition, Vondel ended his life in poverty, working as doorman to a pawnbroker. He died, aged 92, of hypothermia.

Further south, no. 141 is another shop that illustrates the popularity of specialisation in Amsterdam: **Condomerie Het Gulden Vlies** (the Golden Sheath Condomery), open daily 10.00-12.00. Run by its charming proprietress, with female assistants, the shop offers condoms in a wide variety. Ingenious disguises include boiled sweet wrappers. Some are even reputed to play tunes when put to their intended use!

*Sint Jansstraat, first left, crosses OZ Voorburgwal, where it becomes Stoofsteeg. First right OZ Achterburgwal.*

## 7. Oudezijds Achterburgwal

Achter means behind, therefore OZ Achterburgwal indicates that the canal ran behind the town wall, on the 'old' side. In spite of this ancient lineage, there is little of great architectural interest, partly because, as neon signs indicate, this is the centre of the red light district's porn industry. Locally, the district is known as the **Welletjes** (Little Walls), referring to the relatively narrow width of OZ Voorburgwal and OZ Achterburgwal where the girls congregate. Cinemas, live shows and sex shops in profusion are what quite a high percentage of visitors to Amsterdam primarily come to see. Elegant trees also line this canal, partly obscuring some of the glitz: green leaves provide a bucolic contrast that is unusual in such districts.

Freedom to partake of cannabis in Holland without risking prosecution attracts yet another group of visitors and, at no. 148, the **Cannabis Information Museum**, together with the adjacent Cannabis Connoisseurs Club, at no. 50, provides advice and products to would-be horticulturists (for interest only to law-abiding foreigners). Those with research inclinations should be warned that the hash-filled 'space cakes', sold in many cafés, vary tremendously in strength; some will give a mild buzz, others can incapacitate.

*Return northward to Koestraat, first right.*

## 8. Koestraat

A short street, but with a great deal of interest. Koe, meaning cow, may indicate the former existence of a dairy.

A plaque on **no. 5** indicates that Jan van der Heyden, the great painter of detailed city scapes, lived here from 1681 until his death in 1712. He is also credited with inventing the fireman's hose.

**Numbers 7, 9 and 11** are delicately carved in Rococo style. Between the doors and fanlights are depicted Faith, Hope and Charity.

A stone Bacchus on the portal is a reminder that **no. 10** was once the Wine Merchants Guildhouse.

Number 20, **Vergulde Leeuwshooft**, was built by Hendrick Gerritsz in 1611. In 1633, this also served as the Guildhouse for the Wine Merchants and, set in the pediment of the entrance, is a statue of their patron, St Urbanus, designed by Pieter de Keyser. The building has the oldest known example of a neck gable to survive in the city.

*First left, follow Kloveniersburgwal northward.*

## 9. Kloveniersburgwal

One of Amsterdam's most picturesque ancient shops is the herbalist's, **Jacob Hooey**, at no. 12. Founded in 1743, more than 400 herbs and spices are stocked for both culinary and medical applications. The wooden interior is original.

**Numbers 6 and 8**, built in 1722, are known as 'Abraham and Isaac' due to the biblical names that they bear. Previously, **no. 4**, adjoining, possessed a neck gable inscribed 'Jacob' but this has been lost.

*Return southward.*

Number 26, **Klein Trippenhuis** (1696) was built of sandstone, with a frontage just seven feet wide. Allegedly, the house was built for the coachman of the wealthy Tripp brothers who, with great humility, told his employers that a house no wider than their front door would meet his needs. The stone used is supposed to have been left over from the Tripp mansion, Trippenhuis, which is situated on the opposite side of the canal. A frieze, below the circular window, incorporates an hour-glass, whilst sphinxes decorate the gable.

## 10. Trippenhuis Justus Vingboons, 1622

29 Klovenlersburgwal

One of the most splendid Baroque mansions in Amsterdam, this building was commissioned by the Tripp brothers, Louis and Hendrik, as two separate residences behind one grand façade; false middle windows mask the dividing wall. The Tripp's were one of the city's four most powerful families, known as the 'Magnificat'; the others were the Six, the Hooft and the Pauw. In 1815, the houses were linked internally and the building accommodated the Rijksmuseum from then until 1885. Complete restoration took place in 1991. Chimneys in the shape of mortars reflect the pofessional interest of the Tripps in arms dealing.

The central pediment was carved by Jan Gleslingh de Oude. Below this, the frieze of putti and arabesques incorporates the completion date, 1662. The second and sixth bays of the mansion are wider and more richly decorated, emphasising the two entrances.

*Continue southward to Oude Hoogstraat, first right.*

(Hoog means High, not Hog, and is not, therefore, another of the farm animal appellations that are common in Amsterdam.)

Approached through its courtyard, and occupying the south range ahead, no. 24 Oude Hoogstract was built as **Oostindisch Huis** for the Dutch East Indies Company, probably by Hendrick de Keyser, in 1606. The complex now forms part of Amsterdam University. The north, entrance range and the west range were added, in matching style, in 1664, and the east range in the 19th century.

The highly decorative gable of the original building is crowned, unusually, with a short balustrade. Cushion blocks of stone around its doorway, and volutes and masks to the ground floor windows' tympanums will remind many English visitors of their contemporary Jacobean buildings.

*First left, OZ Achterburgwal.*

Lying back, in Walenpleintje, at nos. 157-9 is **Waalsekerk**, (Waloon Church), built for Amsterdam's French-speaking Waloon population. This was under restoration in 1991.

*Return northward. First left, Oude Doelenstraat leads to OZ Voorburgwal, left.*

**Number 187**, built in 1663, is decorated with festoons and cartouches around the windows. Of greatest interest, however, are the carvings of Africans and Indians transporting bales of tobacco.

Opposite, at no. 244, **Bredero** is renowned for its large pancakes: closed on Mondays and Tuesdays.

**Number 274** has been mostly rebuilt, but retains its original cattle-head decoration to the gable, from the period when the building accommodated a butcher's premises.

**Number 300** was built in 1550 as a warehouse; the first two gables are early examples of the spout variety. In 1660, Hendrick de Keyser converted the block to a pawnbrokers, known as 'Uncle Jan's', and it was here that the poet Vondel was employed as a doorman to keep out money-lenders.

A southward extension, in 1669, proved to be an austere building for the period – although the height of modernity at the time. Further conversion took place in 1991 and the complex is now occupied by a bank.

The entrance to the original building, in the style of Hendrick de Keyser, incorporates the city's coat of arms.

Opposite, **nos. 215-17**, with a decorative centrepiece, cornice and corbels, retain two hoists.

Number 316, **De Mayer Huis**, was built by Philips Vingboons in 1655 and is typical of a mid-17th century patrician's house. A stone tablet illustrates resting pilgrims accompanied by angels.

The gateway of no. 231, opposite, was built as the entrance to the **Sisters of St. Agnes Convent**. It displays strapwork, half orbs and masks, once more evoking Jacobean architecture in England. In 1632, the convent was remodelled for the Athenaeum Illustre, precursor of Amsterdam University. Now the University's museum, the building is open Monday – Friday 09.00-13.00 and 14.00-17.00. Admission free.

On the Grimsburgwal corner, **no. 249** has step gables on all three façades. It was built by Claes Adriaensz in 1610 and known, not surprisingly, as 'The House on Three Canals'. Now a bookshop, some features were lost in the 1910 restoration, but the general horizontal appearance, created by strips of sandstone, survives.

*Turn left, following Grimburgwal to OZ Achterburgwal, left.*

**Number 201** is a neck-gabled house, built in 1673. A cooper is depicted on its tablet.

*Return southward to Oudemanhuispoort, left.*

# 11. Oudemanhuispoort

The stone archway, with its pediment illustrating a pair of spectacles representing old age, provided access to almshouses for both men and women, although its name means Old Men's House Gate. The entire complex, including its gateway, was rebuilt in 1754. Since 1876, everything has belonged to the University.

A covered arcade, ahead left, serves as a second-hand book market, open Monday to Saturday, 11.00-16.00. Stalls are set into the brick walls.

Accommodation for the old people was provided in the four pedimented ranges built around the courtyard. Decorating the north pediment is the Amsterdam coat of arms.

*At the end of the passage turn right into Kloveniersburgwal.*

Here, the gateway from Oudemanhuispoort was built in 1786. Surmounting this is a carving by Ziesenis depicting a young woman proferring a cornucopia to an elderly couple.

*First left Staalstraat. First left Groenburgwal.*

Number 42 is the **English Episcopal Church**, converted from the Drapers Hall by J. Jansen, 1827-29, as an early Amsterdam example of the Gothic Revival style. Hendrick de Keyser, the architect (1565-1621) lived in what is now the vicarage, which fronts the church; this has been given a new façade, also Gothic Revival and is possibly, it has been suggested, the work of an unknown Englishman.

From Groenburgwal may be obtained the best view of the clock tower of South Church (see next page).

*Return to Staalstraat and turn left.*

Approached from a picturesque iron drawbridge, **no. 7ab**, the work of Hendrick de Keyser, 1646, was built as the Drapers Hall; appropriately, draped sheets carved in stone form the roof cornice of this trapezium-gabled house.

Above the date tablet is the city's coat of arms.

*At the end of Staalstraat follow Zwanenburgwal northward.*

On the opposite side of this relatively wide canal, the unremarkable west façade of the modern Town Hall is passed.

*Continue ahead, up steps, to Jodenbreestraat.*

Immediately right, in the centre of the street, stands the figure of a turtle bearing a truncated column on its back. This symbolises that time has gradually removed most traces of the old buildings that once stood here. Amsterdam's Jewish quarter was formerly located in this area, but little now predates the Second World War.

From the west side of the bridge, Sint Antoniesbreestraat curves north-westward.

## 12. Sint Antoniesbreestraat

Formerly an unexceptional thoroughfare in the Jewish quarter, Sint Antoniesbreestraat is now lined with boutiques and cafés, most of them very fashionable due to the proximity of the Town Hall/Opera complex. Only five buildings in the street survived the reconstruction that followed the laying out of the Metro line below, and it cannot be said that the new architectural standard was high.

Number 126, **Roxanne**, a more interesting than usual shoe shop, includes hand-painted examples by Roudenberg in its range.

Number 69, **De Pintohuis**, is by far the most important building in the street. Built by Elias Bouman in 1671, Isaac de Pinto, of Portuguese-Jewish extraction, and a founder of the East India

Company, remodelled the mansion, which thereby became one of the most splendid in Amsterdam. Conservationists battled successfully to save the house in 1975 and, for a while it stood isolated while buildings around it were demolished. De Pintohuis is now a public library: open weekday afternoons.

Cream paintwork emphasises the Italian nature of the façade, with great buttresses, which double as pilasters, giving a strong vertical emphasis. A parapet conceals the roof, and attractive ironwork forms the curved grilles to the ground-floor windows. Some painted ceilings survive internally.

Directly opposite, a gateway decorated with skulls provides the entrance to South Church.

## 13. South Church (Zuiderkerk) Hendrick de Keyser
1603-1611

17 Zandstraat/72 Zuiderkerkhof

Church open Monday – Wednesday and Fridays 12.30-16.30. Thursdays 18.00-21.00. Admission free. Tower open 1 June - 15 October: Wednesdays 14.00-17.00; Thursdays and Fridays 11.00-14.00; Saturdays 11.00-16.00. Admission charge. Carillon concert Thursdays 12.00-13.00.

Historically important, South Church is not only the first building in Amsterdam to have been specifically designed for Protestant services, it is also the first known work of Hendrick de Keyser, and regarded as a masterpiece of the Dutch Renaissance. No services have been held here since before the Second World War, the building serving as an information centre for the municipal housing and town planning authorities.

South Church established the style of Amsterdam's post-Gothic churches, all the most important of which, apart from East Church, were also designed by Hendrick de Keyser.

Externally, the clock tower is the building's most impressive feature. Completed in 1614, its steeple surmounts a brick tower decorated with quoin stones. The grey-painted clock stage is made of wood clad in lead, whilst the octagonal sandstone section above incorporates Ionic columns at the corners.

Immediately right of the entrance to the church, a plaque commemorates that, from February to August 1945, this building housed the municipal registry of death, and served as a morgue for the victims of malnutrition and German violence, who were so numerous in the last stages of the war that they could not be interred quickly enough.

Within the building, exhibition displays tend to conceal the layout, but the Tuscan columns and timber barrel vault may be observed.

Collected in the centre of the floor are deeply-carved 17th-century tombstones.

*Return to Sint Antoniesbreestraat and continue northward.*

**Numbers 72 and 64** are two more of the five houses that were permitted to remain. Both are late 18th-century examples and possess bell gables.

*First left, Nieuwe Hoogstraat.*

**'t Klompenhuisje**, at no. 9A, is Amsterdam's most famous klompen shop, all types of which are known in English as clogs. Presumably, the admonition to 'stop clomping about' has some connection with the Dutch word. There is a 600 year-old tradition of wearing wooden shoes in Holland: they were economical to make, due to the many trees once available, and proved ideal for the country's frequently waterlogged ground and muddy paths. During the Second World War, wooden shoes became popular again because of their cheapness. Formerly, the wood used was willow, as it was so tough, but now most shoes are carved from poplar.

The proprietress stresses that this is not a souvenir shop, the clogs are made for wearing and have the essential internal shaping. They are still popular for fishing (combined with leather), gardening and farming and, of course, as gifts for children, who delight in clomping about.

Evidently, wooden shoes help strengthen the feet, as the muscles must be continuously clenched to keep them on – the shoes must not be a tight fit because they will never stretch and would soon prove too uncomfortable to wear. A wide variety, plain or decorated, are displayed. In 1991, clogs for children cost 19 guilders plain, or 30 guilders decorated.

On returning to Sint Antoniesbreestraat, **Willem van Eijk's Brood Banket** occupies the corner building, at no. 1 Snoekjesteeg. A popular baker, his almond cakes are renowned.

**Numbers 10** and **6** are the two other houses that survive from the street's past.

Opposite, the perplexingly numbered **Pyramid**, at 3 LM, specialises in all types of leatherware, except clothes. Everything is made on the premises, much of it, particularly belts, to individual specification.

The north end of the street enters Nieuwmarkt.

## 14. Nieuwmarkt

An ancient square, originally occupied by a fish market, later a cloth market for Jewish merchants, Nieuwmarkt (New Market) provides an open space of great character, surrounded by houses that are mostly of ancient lineage and crowned with gables in varying styles. On summer Sundays, an antique market is held from 10.00-17.00. Still dominant is the central, late 15th-century Sint Antonieswaag, now in an advanced state of dilapidation. During the Second World War, the entire square was surrounded with barbed wire, forming a pen for Jews about to be deported.

To the south, municipal housing, predominantly occupied by low-income groups, has created a somewhat run-down ambience, and the open nature of the square is an encouragement to itinerant alcoholics and drug addicts, which does nothing to improve the situation.

Those with nostalgic tendencies will delight in Nieuwmarkt's two aromatic pissières, now no longer a feature of the Paris scene but, in Amsterdam, fighting successfully against modern plastic WC units. On the west side, **nos. 20-22**, built in 1605, incorporate decorative blocks of stone in otherwise brick façades. Their timber ground floors are not original.

## 15. St Anthony's Gate (Sint Antoniespoort)

4 Nieuwmarkt

This large, turreted building, with conical roofs, is one of the most picturesque in Amsterdam and a rare survivor from the Gothic period. When built, in 1488, this was the most important gate in the city wall. Alterations were made to it by Alexander Pasqualini and Willem Dirksz in 1545 and, in 1617, the building was converted to a public weigh house (De Waag). Amsterdam had three, but the others, in De Dam, and what is now Rembrandtsplein, have long been demolished. This weigh house was earmarked for exceptionally heavy objects, such as cannon and anchors. Eventually, the upper floor was used by the Guild of Bricklayers as their meeting room, and the Guild of Surgeons as a dissecting room. It was in the latter that Rembrandt's two anatomy lecture paintings hung from 1690-1841.

The building's functions as a weigh house and guild rooms ended in the 19th-century, and it became, successively: a furniture store, a fencing academy and a fire station. Until 1986, the Jewish Historical Museum was sited here in two of its rooms, but plans were then made to accommodate a luxurious restaurant, Philippe Stark being commissioned for its décor. However, the restaurant never opened and the building rather forlornly awaits restoration and a useful purpose.

From most viewpoints, everything seems to be a medieval jumble of octagonal and circular towers, but when the Metro station is reached, in the south-east corner of Nieuwmarkt, the elements resolve in a surprisingly symmetrical fashion.

*Descend to Nieuwmarkt Metro Station.*

ROUTE 3

# Singel, Amstel, former Jewish Quarter and Rembrandt House Museum

Singel marked the limit of pre-17th century Amsterdam, having been laid out to serve as the moat around the city's defensive wall. Its entire length is explored, from north to south, ending at the Mint Tower.

The central stretch of the Amstel River, which gave the city its name, is seen before crossing to the former Jewish Quarter, most of which has been rebuilt since the Second World War. Poignant reminders of the Holocaust, particularly in the Jewish Historical Museum, much of which is housed in western Europe's oldest synagogue, are countered by the hope expressed in the newly restored Portuguese Synagogue, when built, the largest in the world. Rembrandt's House and the modern Town Hall/Opera House complex end the route.

### Timing
- The Six Collection may only be viewed after a ticket (complimentary) has been obtained from within the Rijksmuseum. It is open Monday, Wednesday and Friday 10.00-11.00.
- The Portuguese Synagogue, due to services, cannot be toured on Saturdays.
- The Round Lutheran Church may only be entered for 'coffee' concerts on Sunday mornings at 11.00.
- Cat lovers may board the Cat Boat daily 13.00-14.00.
- The Moneybox Museum is open Monday – Friday 13.00-16.00
- The Rembrandt House Museum is closed on Sunday mornings.

### Locations for Route 3
1. Corn Measure House
2. De Silveren Spiegel
3. Round Lutheran Church
4. Singel

## Start: Stationsplein.

*Cross the bridge to Damrak. Immediately ahead is the Scandic Crown Hotel, occupying the west corner of Damrak and Prins Hendrikkade.*

The hotel building is interrupted by two small houses, **nos. 46/47,** now a souvenir shop. Apparently, the owners refused to sell the properties to the developer of what was originally called the Victoria Hotel, which therefore had to be constructed around them.

*Follow Damrak southward to Oude Brugsteeg, third right, which becomes Kolksteeg and NZ Kolk.*

## 1. Corn Measure House (Kornmetershuis) 1620

28 Nieuwezijds Kolk

Now the offices of Bond Heemschut, the present building, isolated in the centre of a small square, replaced an earlier Corn Measure House, which is known to have been in existence by 1558. Above the central window on the south side, a stone tablet illustrates the corn measurer's tools.

On the same façade, the Amsterdam coat of arms surmounts the central gable. Painted wooden shutters enliven the brickwork.

Entrances, on the north and south sides, are approached by steps.

*Continue ahead, branching right, to NZ Voorburgwal and turn right. First right Sint Jacobstraat.*

At no. 19, **Egg Cream** is one of Amsterdam's most popular vegetarian restaurants (also see restaurant listing).

*Return to NZ Voorburgwal and cross to Korte Kolksteeg, immediately ahead. Proceed ahead to Spuistraat, first right.*

Number 4, **Keuken van 1870**, serves economically priced traditional Dutch food and is a popular lunch-time venue (also see restaurant listing).

*First left Kattengat.*

## 2. De Silveren Spiegel
4-6 Kattengat

Both houses were built in 1614, but linked internally to form the present 'Silver Mirror' restaurant in 1950. There has been a restaurant in one of the buildings since 1880 and it is recorded that Queen Wilhelmina dined here.

The step gables incorporate pilasters in their upper sections. Unusually, the keystones and string courses are of yellow brick rather than sandstone.

Internally, rooms display much of their 17th-century character (also see restaurant listing).

*Continue northward.*

## 3. Round Lutheran Church (Ronde Lutherse Kerk) 1823
1 Kattengat

'Coffee' concerts Sundays at 11.00 (tel: 6239896). Admission free.

No longer a church, this building now accommodates the Sonesta Conference Centre, operated by the Sonesta Hotel opposite. Designed by Adriaan Dortsman, the original church was completed in 1671, but a conflagration in 1882, due to carelessness by plumbers, led to it being rebuilt the following year by T. F. Sluys and J. de Greef. Virtually a replica, the only major alteration was the coffering of the vault, which originally had been ribbed.

The area around the church is known as the Koepelkwartier (Dome Quarter), due to the prominence of the building's green copper dome. If attending a Sunday morning 'coffee' concert it is advisable to arrive by 10.30 to reserve a seat.

*Continue northward, following Stromarkt. Second left Singel.*

## 4. Singel

Singel, meaning moat in Dutch, was created, in 1425, around the western perimeter of the new city wall. Contemporary with this, and for the first time, Amsterdam's wall was built of brick, rather than timber. Its position had been moved westward from the former moat at Nieuwezijds Voorburgwal, to allow for the expansion of the city. The earliest map of Amsterdam (1538), which is displayed in Amsterdam's History Museum, shows that apart from a few windmills, only fields then lay to the west of Singel.

Facing Stromarkt is one of the most picturesque lock gates in the city. Singel's odd-numbering commences south of Stromarkt. **Number 7** is claimed to be the smallest house in Amsterdam: its overall width being little greater than that of the front door.

Permanently moored outside no. 40 is **De Poezenboot** (Cat Boat), providing temporary shelter for some of the city's 50,000 stray cats. The animals are neutered and, if possible, found a home. Visitors are admitted 13.00-14.00 and donations appreciated. A heron frequently struts on the cabin, presumably unaware of the feline danger below.

Outside no. 146, I witnessed a whole pig being barbecued on the pavement, apparently to feed squatters, but I cannot guarantee that this is a regular occurrence.

On the opposite side of the canal, at the Lijnbaansteeg junction, **nos. 83-5**, built in 1652, displays three façades; festoons and date plaques alternate below the windows, and Ionic pilasters support the roof cornice.

**Numbers 140-42** was built by Hendrick de Keyser in 1600. It was the residence of Frans Banningh Cocq, the Civic Guard Company commander immortalised by Rembrandt in his painting *The Night Watch*. The two double step gables are linked and vivacious sandstone detailing includes busts between the first and second floors.

The next stone bridge is exceptionally wide, because a tower, built in 1648, formerly stood in its centre. Part of the tower served as a prison, but all was demolished in 1829. The bridge itself is built of brick and stone, with a prison cell incorporated at basement level, now an art gallery. Barred windows on both sides may still be seen from the wooden steps.

A bust of **Multatuli** (1820-87) commemorates the Dutch novelist.

*Continue southward. First right Raadhuisstraat. Just past the bridge, on the north side, lies one of Amsterdam's most engaging museums.*

## 5. Moneybox Museum (Spaarpotten Museum)

20 Raadhuisstraat

Open Monday - Friday 13.00-16.00. Admission charge.

Whilst there are over 12,000 piggy banks in the collection, the museum is eclectic and includes African clay pots and plastic souvenir boxes of excruciating kitsch. Amongst the 19th-century mechanical toys are American examples that would certainly be banned now, due to their racist connotations.

*Return to the east side of Singel and continue southward.*

**Number 233**, built in 1790, is typical of the Louis XVI period, particularly its lower floor. The door is original but balconies are later additions.

## 6. Kritberg   A. Tepe 1881

446 Singel

Open throughout every day.

Built expressly for Roman Catholic worship, this aisled church, with its colourful interior, is exceptionally well preserved. Towers, surmounted by slender spires, flank the east façade, giving a Germanic appearance; the Gothic Revival style has been followed throughout.

Within, the aisled church is entirely rib-vaulted; brightly-coloured stained glass and painted walls contributing to the polychrome effect.

The pulpit, rood screen and an unusual baldachino above the high altar are good examples of Gothic Revival fittings.

It will be noted that the west (chancel) end of the church is wider than the east end.

*Exit from the church, return westward and cross the bridge to the north side of Singel.*

Immediately opposite Kritberg, on the Spui corner, at no. 411 Singel, the **Old Lutheran Church** (Oude Lutherse Kerk), is now the Assembly Hall of Amsterdam University. It was built in 1633, and is attributed to Hendrick de Keyser.

Two great brick gables, lit by Neo Gothic windows, indicate a nave with a side aisle, but the church is, in fact, aisleless. The original tiered galleries remain within.

*Continue along Singel, which now curves eastward.*

Housed within the modern university library (an architectural blot), at no. 425, is the **Script Museum**. Displayed within are scripts from many countries throughout the world, inscribed on various materials, including animal skins and the bark of trees. Some of the alphabets are works of art in themselves. (Open Monday – Friday 10.00-13.00 and 14.00-16.30. Admission free.)

**Number 423** was built by Hendrick de Keyser and is dated 1606. Arms and gunpowder were once stored within, however, the building is now owned by Amsterdam University. Its unusual trapezium gable incorporates pilasters, lions heads and scrolls. The straight roof cornice is decorated with pointed orbs.

A modern feature for the time is the lack of sandstone string courses.

Almost opposite, best viewed from the north side, **no. 460** was built by Philips Vingboons for a wealthy merchant, on the site of a brewery, in 1622.

Garlands decorate the supports of the neck gable, and festoons are placed beneath the windows. The hoisting beam is set within a cartouche.

At the rear, on the first floor, is a small concert hall, built by Tétar van Elven in 1837, and known as the **Concertzaal Odeon**. Van Elven was a devotee of the Classical Style, but, although regarded as one of the leading architects of the time in Amsterdam, he unfortunately gained few commissions. His paraboloid auditorium was acoustically designed to the calculations of a mathematician.

Complete restoration of the building began in 1991.

*Continue eastward. First left Heiligeweg.*

## 7. Heiligeweg

The name of this street, meaning Holy Way, commemorates that it marked the last stage of the processional route to Kalverstraat in connection with the Amsterdam Miracle.

**Number 42**, neck-gabled, is dated 1651. It accommodates a chemist's shop, which is possibly of long standing, as a colourful 'gaper' still decorates the façade.

Number 35, **D. W. Kinebanian**, a carpet store, retains its delicately carved front of 1890. A brass column and a marble pilaster are unusually combined to flank the doors.

Facing Voetboogstraat is a 17th-century portal, all that survives of a small prison known as the **Rasphuis**. Petty criminals were held within and, as part of their punishment, forced to rasp Brazil wood to make a dye – hence the prison's name. Above the arch, a frieze depicts lions pulling a cartload of logs, encouraged by the driver's whip. Surmounting the portal is the allegorical figure of Amsterdam Justice and the word Castigatio (Punishment).

Kalverstraat, first right, leads to **Muntplein** (Mint Square), which was formerly the site of Amsterdam's sheep market.

The façades of **no. 2**, the multi-storey brick building on the Rokin corner, were remodelled by Berlage in 1911. Typical of his style is the vaguely medieval roof line, with its strange balustrade, and the heavy flatness of the wall treatment.

## 8. Mint Tower (Munttoren)

Muntplein

Originally, this tower formed part of Regulierspoort, a gate in the medieval wall, which overlooked Singel.

Built in 1490, Hendrick de Keyser added its steeple in 1619. This is made of timber, clad with lead, and stands on a brick base, which is circular at its lower level but octagonal at the second stage. Now primarily a clock tower, the building housed a mint only in 1672 and 1673, when the French occupied Utrecht, where the coinage was normally minted.

This was the first important building to be restored after the Second World War, and its remodelled archway cannot be claimed to have proved successful architecturally. A currency exchange and a souvenir shop specialising in kitsch occupy the ground floor units.

*Follow Reguliersbreestraat due eastward from Muntplein.*

## 9. Cannon Tuschinski Cinema, H. L. de Jong 1921.

26 Reguliersbreestraat

Tours: July and August, Sundays and Mondays 10.30. Otherwise by appointment. Admission charge.

This Art-Deco cinema retains much of its original appearance. It was built for a Jewish immigrant from Poland, Abram Tuschinski, who, initially planning to settle in America and continue his trade of waistcoat maker, stopped en route at Rotterdam, where he opened his first cinema in 1909. Enough money was made to commission a building in Amsterdam and the Theatre Tuschinski was the result.

An exuberant exterior features twin cupolas, and alligators flanking both bronze side doors.

Internally, Art Deco lamps, Chinese silk and a Moroccan carpet, a 1984 reproduction of the original, give a sumptuous appearance.

The Tuschinski has been extended at the rear and now provides six separate cinemas. Cine 1 possesses the most attractive auditorium, and it is here, that the main film, usually in English and never dubbed, is shown. Cine 3 is a completely modern structure.

*Exit and follow Reguliersbreestraat eastward to Rembrandtplein.*

## 10. Rembrandtplein

Now the hub of Amsterdam's café life, this square was a butter market until the mid-19th century. In the medieval period, a weigh house stood here, but, like the weigh house in De Dam, nothing has survived. The central garden was laid out when the butter market ceased to function.

At its western extremity, the large **statue of Rembrandt**, by Louis Royer, was erected in 1847.

In the north-east corner, **L'Opera** café, with its south-facing, well-protected terrace, is a popular sun trap.

Number 26, **Café Schiller**, on the south side, retains original Art Deco decor.

## 11. Thorbeckeplein

Lying immediately to the south-west of Rembrandtplein, this rectangular plaza is named to commemorate the liberal statesman, three times prime minister, Johan Rudolf Thorbecke (1798-1877), whose statue, by F. C. Leeuhoff, 1874, looks over the Reguliersgracht/ Herengracht confluence at the south end.

From this point, the view over Reguliersgracht and its picturesque bridges is popular with photographers. An open-air crafts market is held in the square on Saturdays 12.00-18.00, but, unfortunately, performances in the central bandstand are now a rare event.

*Return to Rembrandtplein and follow Halvemaansteeg, directly ahead, to Amstel, right.*

Number 56, **De Kleine Komedie Theatre**, was built by Abraham van der Hart as the French Theatre (Franse Schouwburg), in 1785. A cornice and small pediment over the single dormer window are the only ornamentation.

With this building the architect introduced the French style of larger-pane windows to Amsterdam.

*Continue eastward.*

From here, the best views are obtained of the modern Town Hall/ Opera complex, approached from Blauwbrug.

Obviously inspired by the Alexander III bridge in Paris, W. Springer and B. de Graf built **Blauwbrug** of stone and cast iron in 1884.

The balustrade on each side is punctuated by four pedestals, which support columns of red Swedish granite. These are surmounted by pairs of bronze lanterns, decorated with the imperial crown.

The piers of the bridge are carved with prows of medieval rowing boats and dolphins.

## 12. Amstel

It was, of course, the Amstel river that provided Amsterdam with the first part of its name. Until dammed c. 1270, the Amstel followed an uninterrupted course from the IJ estuary through the then small fishing settlement. The western stretch of the river is known firstly as Rokin and then as Damrak, but, as has been seen, much of this is now covered. Odd-numbering of houses begins east of Blauwbrug, but the buildings of greatest interest are all wide-fronted and best appreciated by remaining on the south side of Amstel.

Opposite, east of Nieuwe Herengracht, at 51 Amstel, stretches the widest domestic façade in Amsterdam, built as an old people's home **Diaconie Oude Mannen en Vrouwenhuis**, by Hans Petersom in 1683. Thirty-one bays face the Amstel. Austerely Classical, a pediment with Ionic pilasters indicates the central entrance, whilst Doric pilasters denote the side entrances.

**Number 216**, built by Adriaan Dortsman in 1671, displays a leaf coat of arms and, above its entrance, a balustraded stone balcony.

*Proceed to no. 218, adjoining and, if a ticket has already been obtained, wait beside the steps for the guide to the Six Collection.*

## 13. Six Collection

218 Amstel

Open for guided tours (limited to 15 visitors), Mondays, Wednesdays and Fridays 10.00-11.00, on presentation of a card previously obtained from the Rijksmuseum's information desk (a passport must have been presented to obtain the card). Admission free. Photography is not permitted.

The house is the property of the Six family, who acquired it in 1915. Early 17th-century Huguenot refugees from France, the Six family soon became one of the most powerful in Amsterdam and occupied several other important residences before moving here from Vijzelgracht. Rembrandt's famous painting of *Jan Six* (1654), who lived in Herengracht, not, of course, this house, is never permitted to leave the building.

The guided tour consists of the entrance floor only as members of the family still live above. In addition to the paintings, look out for Roman glassware, family jewellery, and, according to *The Guiness Book of Records*, the world's smallest tea set, all displayed in cabinets.

Works by Cuyp, van Ruysdael, Jacob de Wit (grisailles brought from the family's Vijzelgracht house) and Ter Bosch (miniatures) are included in the collection, but *The Kitchen Maid*, by Vermeer, is now in the Rijksmuseum.

Although Doctor Nicolaas Tulp is featured in Rembrandt's earliest *Anatomy Lesson* painting, of 1632, the portrait of him here was painted not by Rembrandt, but by Franz Hals. Tulp's daughter married Jan Six in 1655.

The two great Rembrandts, in the front room and seen last, are, understandably, the pride of the collection, although, unusually, neither are signed. Their most striking feature is the difference in style: *Anna Wijmer*, the mother of Jan Six, is portrayed with great accuracy of detail, whereas her son, opposite, painted 10 years later, is given a much freer treatment, almost verging on Impressionism.

Jan Six, who was elected a burgomaster in 1691, collected works of art. He lent money to Rembrandt in 1653 and the portrait may have been considered as part-payment by the artist, although not commissioned. He never did repay Jan Six and their relationship ended on a sour note.

*On leaving the house, continue eastward.*

Ahead, the modern **Magere Brug** (Skinny Bridge) is a replica of the 17th-century original. Next to this rises the domed Royal Theatre Carré.


## 14. Royal Theatre Carré (Koninklijk Theater Carré) J.P.F. van Rossen and W.J. Vuyk 1887

115-125 Amstel

Built as the Oscar Carré Circus, the theatre now stages large musical productions. It was apparently built in a few months, being a virtual copy of an existing structure in Cologne. Although basically Classical, a balcony, pilasters, columns and a cornice are lively features. Theatrical embellishments: masks, grimacing clowns, jesters and dancers' heads, are by E. van den Bossche and G. Crevels. Internally, the great roof of the amphitheatre appears to be unsupported.

From this point, on the south bank of the Amstel, the **Amstel Hotel** can be seen immediately east of the next bridge, at no. 1 Prof. Tulpplein. An extra storey was subsequently added to the wings, which significantly altered the original proportions. Built by C.

Outschoorn, 1863-67, the hotel was for some time closed for internal remodelling, before reopening in 1992.

*Continue south-eastward, remaining on the south side of Amstel. First right Achtergracht.*

On the south side, nos. 26-2 Achtergracht front the **Nederlandse Bank**, their 13 modern façades reproducing the 15th-century warehouses that they replaced. Each one, in splendid old Dutch calligraphy, bears the name of a month, apart from the last, which displays 'De Zon' (The Sun). Exhibited in the central lobby are iron fittings from the original buildings.

Ahead, Frederiksplein formerly accommodated the 'Crystal Palace' of Amsterdam, the **Palace of Industry** (Paleis voor Volksvlijt), an immense, 19th-century iron and glass structure that burnt down in 1929.

Dr. Samuel Sarphati (1813-66), 'the father of modern Amsterdam', planned the public and commercial buildings around the square expressly to create employment.

Second right, **Reguliersgracht** is an attractive canal, although lacking individual buildings of outstanding importance. At one point, it was proposed that the canal should be filled in; fortunately, the scheme was defeated.

Parallel streets on either side, Utrechtsestraat and Vijzelstraat are now almost entirely modern and of little interest.

*Sixth right Herengracht. Take the north thoroughfare.*

**Number 554** presents a 1716 remodelling of the 17th-century house that originally stood on the site. It has been given an attic, with Baroque swags, and two central figures decorate the roof balustrade.

East of Utrechtsestraat, the last section of Herengracht to be built reaches Amstel. However, it continues north of the river as Nieuwe Herengracht.

## 15. Willet-Holthuysen Museum

605 Herengracht

Open daily 11.00-17.00. Admission charge.

Internally, this house gives a good impression of late 19th-century life in Amsterdam, due to its complete preservation since 1895. Long rear gardens were a feature of all the city's 17th-century Canal Ring houses, but the example here is one of the few that may be glimpsed, yet alone visited.

Sandra Holthuysen inherited the house in 1858 and married Abraham Willet three years later, both of them living here for the remainder of their lives. Willet had been an enthusiastic collector of objets d'art and books and, when his widow died heirless, she left the house and its contents to the city, with the proviso that it should be preserved, opened to the public and named the Museum Willet-Holthuysen. Immediately following its opening, in 1896, few visitors came, as little existed within that was out of the ordinary and could not be seen in many houses at the time. Of course, things have changed, and the interiors are now very much out of the ordinary. A contemporary London example is Linley Sambourne House in Kensington, where a similar situation has occurred, although due to preservation by the occupants, rather than, as here, by the trustees of a museum.

Visitors are admitted at the ground floor, former tradesman's entrance. Captions are in Dutch only but the names of rooms are also translated into English. At the end of the corridor, film shows in Dutch and in English trace the history of the building and its contents.

Immediately right, after tickets have been purchased, the 18th-century **kitchen** is entered. Two of its walls are clad with Delft tiles and the ceiling is beamed. Most period utensils displayed are from the 19th century.

Opposite the kitchen entrance, a door leads to the **garden**, which stretches back to the busy Amstelstraat. Remodelling in 1972, with box hedges, restored this to its formal 18th-century appearance. When the three great canals, Herengracht, Keizersgracht and Prinsengracht were laid out in the 17th century, each plot's long rear garden proved to be an important selling point. Many backed onto a subsidiary street, where coach houses could be built, with accommodation above for the coachman.

*Return to the house, ascend the stairs to the main floor and proceed towards the front door.*

The **canal-facing room**, right of the door, is decorated in Louis XVI style.

Double doors to the interconnecting **Ballroom** are left open; a painting of it in 1882, displayed on an easel, shows how little has changed in the interim.

On the other side of the hall is the **Smoking Room**. Its ceiling, by Jacob de Wit, was transferred here from no. 250 Herengracht. The painting above the fireplace is also by de Wit. Blue velvet on the walls is known as velours d'Utrecht.

An interesting long-case clock, made by Albert Vreehuis of Amsterdam, stands in the **hall**. The season, date and moon phase are indicated whilst, below the face, ships ride the waves.

From the end of the hall, right, is approached the **Dining Room**, decorated in Louis XV style. Its furniture was purchased by the Willets soon after their marriage.

The **Garden Room**, virtually a conservatory, displays porcelain.

Stairs lead to the **first floor**, originally accommodating bedrooms, but no beds are now to be seen. Instead, items from the Willet collection are exhibited in cabinets, including paintings, flasks, glass and silver boxes.

*Exit, right and continue eastward from the house.*

A plaque at **no. 619** records that this was the residence of Jan Six, 1618-1700, whose portrait, by Rembrandt, has already been described.

*At Amstel, cross to the north side by means of Blauwbrug, and follow Nieuwe Herengracht.*

## 16. Nieuwe Herengracht

Laid out in the 18th century as an extension to Herengracht, Nieuwe Herengracht continues much further north than the other 'new' streets but, like them, numbering begins at the south end.

Numbers 6-18, with its great segmental pediment, supported by Ionic pilasters, is known as **Corverhof**, after its architect J. Corver, who, together with S. Trip, designed the building to house poor elderly couples. Carved on the pediment is an allegory of Charity, and an eagle bearing the coat of arms of the establishment.

**Number 20**, a detached Classical structure of 1790, displays the words of a poem between the central first and second floor windows.

This relates that a legacy of Johanna van Mekeren-Bontekoning paid for the building.

*At the main road, Weesperstraat, turn left and continue to J. D. Meijerplein.*

## 17. Jewish Historical Museum (Joods Historisch Museum)

2-4 Jonas Daniël Meijerplein

Open daily 11.00-17.00. Admission charge, but free on 3, 4 and 5 May.

The museum, which describes 400 years of Jewish culture in Amsterdam, is housed in a group of former synagogues, one of which is western Europe's oldest.

Persecution of the Jews in central Europe and the Iberian peninsula led to a mass migration to tolerant Amsterdam in the late 16th century. Partly due to this, a fourth expansion of the city took place c. 1600, creating the quarter of Vlooyenburg, and it was almost immediately adopted by minority groups, particularly the Jews. Those from central Europe were known as Ashkenazic, and their 'High German' or Great Synagogue, completed in 1671, is the oldest public example in Western Europe. This soon became too small, and a second synagogue was built at the rear, above a Kosher butcher's shop, called the Obbene (Upstairs) Shul. Another synagogue, Dritt (Third) Shul, was added within a short time and, in 1752, the last synagogue, Neie (New) Shul, completed the group of four.

Deportation of Jews in the Second World War led to the closure and decay of the complex, which the greatly reduced orthodox Jewish community could not afford to restore; the municipal authorities acquired it in 1955. Almost 20 years later, the decision was made to adapt the former synagogues to house the Jewish Historical Museum, then inadequately accommodated in two rooms in Sint Antoniespoort (De Waag), and this was opened in 1987. Its architects, Abel Cahen and Premsela Vonk, were awarded the international museum prize for their work.

The first synagogue passed, facing J. D. Miejerplein, is the **New Synagogue**, the last of the four to be built. Completed in 1752, probably by the City Architect, G. F. Maybaum, this had been closed since 1936. A roof-line balustrade and a Baroque centrepiece, at cornice level, are the features of greatest interest on the façade. The small glass dome may be seen from the opposite side of the road. A modern extension now links the building to the Great Synagogue.

Built in 1671, the **Great Synagogue** has been attributed to Elias Bouman, who was responsible for the Portuguese Synagogue, on the opposite side of the road. However, similarities with Protestant churches designed by the City Architect, Daniel Stampaert, have been noted. More austere than the New Synagogue, pilasters divide this façade into three distinct sections. The main frontage, however, is on Nieuwe Amstelstraat, where there is a central pediment.

Visitors enter the museum at 3 Nieuwe Amstelstraat. A suggested route is provided with the entry ticket. Almost 1,000 worshippers could be accommodated within the **New Synagogue**, where the route begins. Unfortunately, its splendid Ark was lost in the Second World War.

Here, the museum's theme is Jewish identity, exhibits connected with the Holocaust arousing sadness and uncomprehending disgust, which are likely to be compounded by visits to the Anne Frank House, the Resistance Museum and various other monuments within the city. Rightly, Amsterdammers do not intend to let anyone forget this black moment in the history of mankind – be prepared for intense disquiet.

Glass passageways and galleries link the four synagogues in an ingenious manner. The **Great Synagogue** retains much of its early 17th-century appearance, original features including the marble Ark and the ritual bath, which was rediscovered during building work. Themes depicted are Jewish Festivals, the Jewish Community and the Jewish Life Cycle.

Separate galleries in the Great Synagogue, for men and for women, have been restored, and here the social history of Dutch Jews is described. A bridge links these areas with the newly created gallery in the New Synagogue, where temporary exhibitions are held.

The museum's shop, and a coffee shop offering many kosher specialities, now occupy the **second synagogue**, which was built over the butcher's premises. It evokes the 'secret' attic churches, where Roman Catholics worshipped during the proscribed period.

The butcher's shop, initially retained below, was later converted to a ritual bath.

*From the museum return to Jonas Daniël, Meijerplein.*

On the north side, in front of the Portuguese Synagogue's south wall, stands the **Dock Worker Monument** (Dokwerker), a bronze, by Mari Andriessen, 1951. This commemorates Amsterdam's general strike, led by dockers 25 February 1941, in protest against Nazi anti-semitism. Also, until recently, it served as a reminder of the plight of the Jews who were forbidden to leave Russia.

On 23 February 1941, as a reprisal for the killing of a Dutch Nazi sympathiser in a brawl, 425 young Jewish men were assembled in the square by the German chief of police and transported in trucks to Mauthausen concentration camp, where all of them are believed to have died. The general strike that followed two days later, organised by Communists, was the first example of mass-protest by a German-occupied country in the Second World War. However, wholesale arrests ended the strike in two days. A commemorative march-past takes place on 25 February each year and flags are lowered to half mast.

## 18. Portuguese Synagogue (Portuguees Israëlitische Synagoge) Elias Bouman, 1671-75

1-3 Mr Visserplein

Open Sunday - Friday 11.00-16.00. Admission free with guide, but donations welcome. Saturday: services only.

Amsterdam's largest synagogue ever built was begun just after the Great Synagogue, opposite, was completed. Its interior is exceptionally well preserved.

Not until the 17th century were Jews permitted to build synagogues in Amsterdam: by then, their wealth and influence had become so great that the burgomasters at last gave permission. Previously, a blind eye had been turned to the conversion of private houses for Jewish worship, in the manner of the Roman Catholic 'hidden' churches. This synagogue was commissioned by Amsterdam's Sephardic Jews, who fled to the city from the Iberian peninsula. Like the 17th-century building, which survives in the City of London, this should have been called the Spanish and Portuguese Synagogue, but Holland's long war with Spain precluded this. A similar example exists in Curaçao, a former Dutch colony in the West Indies.

Before the Second World War, there were 7,000 members of the congregation; although there are now less than 600, Amsterdam's Jewish population is increasing steadily (from 10,000 in 1945 to almost 22,000 now).

## Exterior

Under restoration in 1991 (but remaining open), the long, J. D. Meijerplein elevation is subdivided by pilasters. Extremely tall windows, even for Amsterdam, are an important feature. The synagogue's only decorative element is its balustrade. Small houses form a courtyard around the building.

Approached from the Mr Visserplein façade, visitors must ring the bell beside the door to gain entry. Gentlemen are required to wear a skull cap (provided) on entering the synagogue with the guide.

## Interior

A high barrel vault immediately emphasises the great size of the synagogue, which, on completion, was the world's largest.

Four great chandeliers are suspended from the centre, whilst 22 others provide additional lighting. All are of brass and still provide illumination by means of candles. The use of expensive oak and jacaranda wood for the fixtures is a reminder of the first congregation's great wealth.

Stretching directly ahead from the synagogue's entrance, behind the rear of the new town hall, is the north section of Waterlooplein.

## 19. Moses and Aaron Church (Mozes en Aäronkerk) T.F. Suys/J. van Straaten 1837-41

205 Waterlooplein

Open at most times for exhibitions. Admission free. Some services.

Moses and Aaron Church originated in the 17th century as a 'secret' Roman Catholic church in a house on Jodenbreestraat, the thoroughfare that runs behind the building. The chief architect, Suys, was Flemish, but had studied in Paris under Napoléon's favourite architect Charles Percier, winning the Prix de Rome. Restoration took place in 1969.

The renowned philosopher, Benedict de Spinoza, a Portuguese Jew, was born in a house on the site in 1632. Excommunicated from the synagogue in 1656 for his Rationalist views, and his doubts on the authenticity of sections of the Old Testament, Spinoza was banished from Amsterdam and moved to The Hague, where he died in 1677.

Entirely Neo-Classical, the depth of the portico of the church had to be reduced to comply with planning regulations: what should have been columns at each end are set as pilasters. Before street widening, the church was flanked by buildings on both sides.

Twin towers, made of wood, have been likened to those of St. Sulpice in Paris, with which they are contemporary. However, unlike the Paris examples, both of these have been completed.

Within, the interior is a good example of the Baroque revival. Aisle columns and wall pilasters are Corinthian, whilst bas-reliefs depict the Stages of the Cross.

The high altar's reredos, made in Italy, covers the entire east wall.

It was built to accommodate three existing paintings by Jacob de Wit, which can be alternated. Side reredoses are in matching style.

Mass is still held, at irregular intervals, but now the church also serves as an adult education centre and exhibitions are frequently presented.

On leaving Moses and Aaron Church, glance left to the two buildings that make up the north-east section of **Waterlooplein**, both designed by Willem de Keyser, but with 44 years between them.

**Number 211**, built in 1654, is Classically austere, with a central pedimented section. It is now an architectural academy but retains a grand first floor 'Governor's Room', with 17th-century decor that includes the fireplace.

**Numbers 213-219**, adjoining to the south, was built in 1610. With its trapezoid gable, flanked by spout gables, stone string courses, and keystones, all of which create a horizontal emphasis, the house is much more typical of Dutch Renaissance architecture than its neighbour.

*Continue eastward following Waterlooplein.* A long-established flea market, specialising in second-hand clothes, occupies much of the area. *First right, Houtkopersdwarsstraat leads to Jodenbreestraat, left.*

## 20. Rembrandt House Museum (Het Rembrandthuis)

4-6 Jodenbreestraat

Open Monday–Saturday 10.00–17.00, Sundays 13.00-17.00. Admission charge.

Rembrandt lived in this house for 21 years. Examples of most of his 280 etchings are displayed throughout the ground and first floors.

Built in 1606, as a two-storey, step-gabled residence, with basement and attic; an additional storey and a Classical pediment were added by Jacob van Campen in 1633, six years before Rembrandt purchased the building.

### History

Rembrandt Harmenszoon van Rhijn was born at Leiden in 1606, coincidentally, the year that this house was erected, moving permanently to Amsterdam in 1631. Three years later, he married Saskia van Uylenburgh and, by 1639, as a successful and relatively wealthy artist, Rembrandt was able to place a deposit on nos. 4-6 Jodenbreestraat. In 1641, his son Titus was born; Saskia died the following year. Rembrandt's expenditure on furnishing and the repayments on his house, combined with dwindling commissions, led to the artist's insolvency in 1656, and Rembrandt was forced to sell practically everything he owned in order to pay his creditors.

The artist was permitted to remain in the house until 1660, when he moved to Rozengracht. Titus and his former nurse Hendrickje Stoffels, who had become Rembrandt's mistress, opened an art gallery, primarily to sell Rembrandt's work, but Hendrickje died in 1662 and Titus died six years later, in the year of his marriage. Heartbroken, Rembrandt died in 1669 and, like Titus, was buried in West Church. Penniless, out of fashion, and disregarded by most, the burial place of Holland's greatest old master painter was unrecorded.

After Rembrandt vacated it, the house was subdivided vertically to provide two dwellings, but, in 1906, the city of Amsterdam purchased the building to mark the 300th anniversary of the artist's birth, and it was restored by K.P.C. de Bazel to match its 17th-century appearance as closely as possible. The museum was opened by Queen Wilhelmina in 1911.

Externally, Van Campen's roof pediment is believed to be the first to have graced the façade of an Amsterdam house. According to a map of 1625, the original doorway occupied the bay immediately left of its present position. The existing, pedimented version dates from the 1911 remodelling of de Bazel.

## Interior

An inventory, made at the time of Rembrandt's insolvency, gives an indication of the use of some of the rooms. The basement was for servants. Main living quarters were on the ground floor where, it is recorded, over 100 paintings, almost half of them by Rembrandt, were kept. On the ground floor, there was a main room and a side room facing the street; at the rear, there were two rooms, the larger of which was apparently used as a bedroom. Four first floor rooms included both a large and a small studio and an 'art' room with its antechamber.

Only the beamed ceilings survive from the time of Rembrandt's occupancy; the present stairwell replaced a 'small office' and part of the antechamber to the art room on the first floor.

Displayed by theme, rather than chronologically, are 245 of Rembrandt's 280 etchings.

The second room exhibits a contemporary press and explains the 17th-century method of preparing etchings. Also on display are some of Rembrandt's drawings, and paintings by his teacher Pieter Lastman, and one of his many pupils, Jan Pijnas.

A 10-minute slide show in the basement traces, in English, Rembrandt's life and work.

*Exit left and left again, proceeding to the esplanade that fronts the Town Hall/Opera House.*

# 21. Town Hall/Opera House (Stadhuis/Muziektheater) Wilhelm Holzbauer and Cees Dam 1988

22 Waterlooplein

Generally referred to as the Stopera, the first two letters coming from Stadhuis (Town Hall), this controversial juxtaposition of civic centre and opera/ballet venue is Amsterdam's most significant postwar architectural project. The theatre is the home of the Nederlands Opera and The National Ballet companies.

On grounds of economy, it was decided to merge schemes for a new town hall and a new opera house. Wilhelm Holzbauer, an Austrian-born Amsterdammer, won the competition for the town hall and Cees Dam took over the opera house project on the death of its original architect, Berhard Bijvoet, in 1979. The opera house is fronted to its north and west by the L-shaped town hall.

The long-established Waterlooplein market provided the site, its popularity being one of the reasons for the strength of a campaign organised by opponents of the scheme. However, squatters in the dilapidated houses provided the major resistance. Although now accepted, it cannot be said that the immense building has done much to enhance the urban scene. It hardly blends in, but then, Amsterdam is a city of narrow-fronted buildings, and any centrally located project on this scale would have great difficulty in not calling excessive attention to itself.

The west façade of the Town Hall is of brick, and lacks architectural pretensions until the Amstel corner is reached, where a glass box surmounts the roof line and blocks of white marble begin to appear. These continue along the Amstel façade in a regular manner and have been referred to cynically as 'the set of dentures'. As has been said already, the building is best viewed from the opposite side of the Amstel, from where it does present a lively spectacle when illuminated during the evening.

The main approach is from the Amstel esplanade, but, and this is surely an architectural deficiency, an intensive search must be made to locate the entrances.

Within, a grand foyer and an impressive flight of steps are preliminaries to the 1,689 capacity auditorium, which was built to Bijvoet's design.

Another entrance, on the east side, just before the Metro station is reached, gives access to all parts of the building via a wide hall, (Lange Houtgang), in which a permanent exhibition, **Amsterdam Water Level** (Normaal Amsterdams Peil), is devoted to Holland's perpetual battle with the sea (Admission free).

Water levels were systematically established by the Dutch in the 17th century, based on the average depth, known as zero, of the sea at high tide in the Zuider Zee (now IJselmeer). On learning that 60 per cent of Dutchmen live below sea level (some East Amsterdammers 18 feet below) and Schiphol Airport's runway lies 15 feet below, nervously inclined visitors may wonder if they have time to leave the country before global warming melts the polar ice caps and the dykes are breached. No doubt, however, data collected here will provide sufficient warning for Holland to increase the height of its 1,864 miles of sea defences in time to stave off disaster. Not without reason are Holland and Belgium known as the Low Countries!

The tall glass columns left, indicate, respectively: high or low (if descending) tide at IJmuiden on the North Sea, high or low tide at Flushing and, usually after waiting a few minutes, the maximum sealevel reached at Zeeland during the 1953 floods – 15 feet above zero.

By descending the steps to the base of the columns, visitors may touch the bronze knob that indicates the precise level of zero.

*Ascend the stairs and continue ahead.*

On the wall, left, the geological substrata of Holland is indicated in natural stone sections. It is interesting to observe that the upper layer of sand provided the foundations for houses in the medieval period, round, wooden piles being driven manually into it. Square, concrete piles are now driven mechanically into a lower, and much harder, level of sand.

*Exit from the hall to the Waterlooplein Metro, left.*

ROUTE 4

# Herengracht and Keizersgracht

This itinerary comprises most of the lengths of these two important 17th-century canals, linking them with the streets of greatest interest as they are reached. By this means, a more varied route is explored than if both canals were followed from end to end.

## Timing

• The Theatre Museum is closed Sundays and Mondays.
• The Biblical Museum is closed Sunday mornings and Mondays.
• The Museum Van Loon is open Mondays and Sunday afternoons only.

## Locations for Route 4

1. Herengracht
2. Keizersgracht
3. Raadhuisstraat
4. Theatre Museum

5. Wolvenstraat
6. Shaffy Theatre
7. Biblical Museum
8. Museum Van Loon

## Start: Stationsplein.

*Proceed southward to Prins Hendrikkade, right. Second left Singel (west thoroughfare). Second right Brouwersgracht (south thoroughfare). Second left, cross the bow-shaped bridge, known as Melkmeisjebrug (Milkmaid's bridge), to the east thoroughfare of Herengracht.*

## 1. Herengracht

Between 1570 and 1640, Amsterdam's population increased from 30,000 to 139,000. The Spanish Occupation of Antwerp, in 1585, had led many Protestants to leave that city for Amsterdam, which had turned Protestant at the Alteration of 1578. Amongst them were merchants, whose experience promoted Amsterdam's rapid growth as a trading city. Wealthy Jews fleeing the Inquisition, many of them Portuguese, added to the immigrants, putting a great strain on the resources of what was still a relatively small city. In 1609, a significant expansion of Amsterdam was agreed, which was begun by filling in plots that remained vacant, and building on all the former monastic land, recently seized by the state. The city walls were then moved westward from Singel the former moat, and three new canals – the Canal Girdle – were excavated from 1613: Herengracht, Keizersgracht and Prinsengracht. It has been suggested that Hendrick Staets, the municipal carpenter, was responsible for this great project.

As usual in European cities, fashionable society moved westward, and the wealthy residents of Warmoestraat acquired most of the plots in the first stage of the scheme, which had reached its planned southern terminus, at Leidsegracht, by 1625. The three canals ran concentrically, following the line already established by the Amstel river, and continued by Singel.

Existing fields, paths and ditches were disregarded when the plots were laid out. Although these plots were narrow in width, developers could purchase more than one if they required wider frontages. However, properties were taxed according to their widths and most owners were satisfied, therefore, with a single plot. Space was allocated for churches and public buildings, but none was fronted by a great avenue or square, which is why Amsterdam lacks the open spaces and vistas that were the pride of 17th-century Paris. Amsterdam's fourth planned expansion began in 1658, when the Canal Girdle was extended to the Amstel.

Virtually all the buildings in Herengracht (Gentlemen's Canal) were originally domestic, although some merchants stored goods in their semi-basements and multi-storey attics. Every property had a rear garden and the most important rooms overlooked this, rather than the picturesque, but then smelly, canals, which, moreover, resounded to the sound of carriages rumbling over the cobblestones of their narrow thoroughfares. Today, only a few buildings in Herengracht are still entirely residential.

Mid-18th century Herengracht warehouses, nos. 37 and 39, are timbered on the lower part of their façades, indicating use as offices.

**Numbers 43-5**, c. 1600, are spout-gabled and inscribed, respectively, Fortuin (Fortune) and d'Arke Noach (Noah's Ark).

*First left, Korsjespoortsteeg boasts a mini red light area.*

The **Multatuli Museum**, at no. 20, open Tuesday 10.00-17.00, exhibits, in one large room, mementoes of Holland's great 19th century novelist, including some of his furniture. For obvious reasons, it is of greater interest to Dutch-speaking visitors. Multatuli, the Latin pen-name of Edward Douwes Dekker, spent his last years in the house. He achieved notoriety with *Max Havelaar*, which subtly derides the arrogance of Dutch colonisers in Indonesia – it is now regarded as a classic.

*Return to Herengracht and continue southward.*

Built in 1791, and attributed to Jacob Otten Husley, the wide, stonefaced house, at **no. 40**, is a rare example, on this canal, of an 18th-century domestic building.

Fanlights above the ground floor windows are an unusual feature.

**Number 81**, by Hendrick de Keyser (dated 1590) is a step-gabled warehouse, built in Flemish Mannerist style.

On the corner, left, at no. **22 Blauwburgwal**, the upper floors protrude slightly, a rare example of a jetty in Amsterdam.

**Number 115** is a sauna (mixed sexes) with, internally, exceptional 1920's Art Deco work, transported lock stock and barrel from Paris: visitors are welcome.

*First right, cross the bridge to Leliegracht. First right Keizersgracht; follow its east thoroughfare.*

## 2. Keizersgracht

Construction of this, the Emperor's Canal, named in honour of the Holy Roman Emperor, to whom, technically, the Dutch owed allegiance, ran parallel with Herengracht. However, it is slightly wider, the present trees are younger, and the mix of art galleries, bars, restaurants and apartments adds a lively note. The northernmost sector is more conveniently viewed in combination with Prinsengracht, therefore, nos. 8, 40-44 and 58 are described in the next chapter.

One of the widest-fronted buildings of its period, no. 123, **The House with the Heads**, is the premises of the Municipal Bureau for the Conservation of Monuments. It was built in 1622 and historians believe that the mansion was the work of Hendrick de Keyser, rather than his brother Pieter, as was once thought. Huge busts, representing, from left to right: Apollo, Ceres, Mars, Pallas Athene, Bacchus and Diana gave the house its name.

Single Doric pilasters, flanking the ground floor windows, are extended on the second floor as double pilasters.

The Bureau is responsible for Amsterdam's 7,000 listed buildings. Under its auspices, on the second Saturday in September each year, various private buildings in a selected area of the city are opened to the public.

Visitors to this house are always welcome and may be shown, if convenient, the two rear salons, with their original fireplaces.

*Return southward, crossing Leliegracht.*

Numbers **174-6 Keizersgracht** is the headquarters of Green Peace. Claimed by many to be the only genuine example of Art Nouveau (Nieuwe Kunst) in Amsterdam, it must still be said that most of the decoration is less-flowing and more in the Arts and Crafts tradition than true Art Nouveau. The main building was completed by G van Arkel in 1906; both side extensions are by C Wegener Sleeswijk, 1969. It is generally possible to enter the building to view the outstanding staircase.

Palladian influenced, **no. 177**, Jacob van Campen's first known architectural work, constructed in 1624, is an eight bay house with Ionic below Composite pilasters.

*First left Raadhuisstraat.*

## 3. Raadhuisstraat

Raadhuisstraat was laid out from 1894-96, cutting through rows of ancient houses. At its curve, nos. 25-53, **Winkelgalerij Utrecht**, incorporates a long shopping arcade. The block was designed in 1899 by the architect of the Concertgebouw, A. L. van Gendt, for an insurance company. Predatory beasts of stone on the roof line, and the balustrade of the central balcony, are presumably a warning of life's hazards.

It is possible that the arcade of London's Regent Street, which fronted its curved Quadrant until 1848, was the inspiration for this example.

The façade bears traces of Art Nouveau work, particularly in the flowing curves of its central stone front, but everything remains symmetrical.

*First left Herengracht; take the west thoroughfare.*

Number 182, by Ludwig Friedrich Druck (1772) **De Zonnewijser** (Sundial), is so-named from the previous house on the site, which displayed a sundial on its façade. With its severe roof balustrade, the building was restored in 1972; the double entrance steps date from this time.

**Bartolotti House**, at no. 170-72, is an important Dutch Renaissance work, designed by Hendrick de Keyser in 1617. It was commissioned by a brewer, Willem van den Heuvel, who, in the then fashionable mania for everything Italian, changed his name to Guglielmo Bartolloti, hence the name of the house. With its angled wings, the elevation subtly reflects the bend in the canal at this point. A split pediment and its supporting columns are Italian-inspired elements on the step gable's middle stage. The building may be entered via no. 168 as it forms part of the Theatre Museum.

## 4. Theatre Museum (Nederlands Theater Instituut)

168 Herengracht

Open Tuesday – Sunday 10.00-17.00. Admission charge.

The museum is operated by the Netherland's Theatre Institute, the offices of which are accommodated at nos. 166-68. Items relevant to the history of the Dutch theatre are displayed and supplemented each year.

**Number 168**, from where the museum is entered, was built as a confectionery, but remodelled in 1638 by Philips Vingboons for its new owner, Michael de Paun, a city magistrate. He was a member of the Knights of St. Mark, hence two lions (St. Mark's emblem) support his coat of arms on the gable.

Vingboons added the white sandstone façade, and this led to the building being called The White House.

Internally, modernisation took place in late-Louis XIV style, 1728-33. A master plasterer, Jan van Logteren, was responsible for the

**hall**. With matching doors on both sides all seems symmetrical, but those on the left (from the entrance) lead nowhere - visual trickery in the French manner. Huge canvases depicting Arcadian landscapes, by Isaac de Moucheron, are the main feature of the **front room**. Dampness, due to the canals and the maritime situation, made wall painting in either fresco or mural form impossible in Amsterdam. Above the doors are grisailles by Jacob de Wit, who also painted the ceiling.

In other rooms – both houses are interlinked – are displayed models of 18th-century theatres; Commedia del arte figures, in Nymphenburg porcelain; and theatrical costumes. To the rear, a large cafeteria overlooks the garden.

**Number 164**, built 1750-75, has an elegant sandstone façade. The Ionic door surround is original. An unusual curved centre to the roof's cornice frames an attic window.

*Return southward, to Raadhuisstraat, first right. First left Keizersgracht.*

**Number 224**, now part of the Pulitzer Hotel, was built in 1765. Its façade betrays French influence and incorporates a decorative treatment to the attic storey, with vases and a raised centrepiece.

**Number 238**, due to subsidence, evokes a drunkard supported on both sides by caring friends.

*Continue southward, crossing Hartenstraat.*

The lion's head, in the roof cornice of **no. 235**, built in 1735, originally supported a hoist.

*Return to Hartenstraat, first right. First right Herengracht; take the west thoroughfare.*

Four adjacent houses, **nos. 265, 267, 269 and 271** are untypically varied for Herengracht: no. 265 was built in 1882, but in pastiche 17th-century style, no. 267 dates from 1900. Number 269, a genuine 17th-century house of 1656, has a stepped gable, and no. 271 is unusually tiny, even though it is gabled and comprises three storeys.

Almost entirely glass-fronted, **no. 284** is a 17th-century house that was rebuilt in 1728. The exuberant attic parapet incorporates a central crest, and the bands of stonework framing the central range of windows are richly carved.

This is the headquarters of the Hendrick de Keyser Society, which purchases and restores important buildings in the city.

*First right Wolvenstraat.*

## 5. Wolvenstraat

Not to be missed are three specialist shops: Number 7, **Laura Dols**, sells 'vintage' clothes – ladies only. Number 9, **Kerkhof**, specialises in braid. Number 14, **Knopen Winkel**, stocks buttons in literally thousands of styles – all displayed and graded.

*First left Keizersgracht. Follow the east thoroughfare.*

## 6. Shaffy Theatre  Jacob Otten Husly, 1788

324 Keizersgracht

The reason for recommending the east thoroughfare of Keizersgracht at this point is that the theatre's Palladian front, overlooking the west thoroughfare, is better appreciated from some distance.

Four great pilasters, virtually columns, support the wooden pediment, which is inscribed 'Felix Meritis' (Happiness through Achievement), the motto of the Fellowship that commissioned the building. Its height and imposing nature rather overpower the neighbouring houses.

When built, during the Louis XVI period, this was Amsterdam's cultural centre. It is said that a reception was arranged for Napoléon in 1811, during his only visit to the city, but, complaining of the smell of tobacco, the Emperor would not remain. For a period, Holland's Communist party was established in the building. Now the Shaffy Theatre, its concert room, on which the Concertgebouw's acoustic design was apparently based, has been restored, like most of the interior, following a fire in 1932.

**Number 319,** a narrow-fronted house, was built by Philips Vingboons in 1639. Two pairs of Doric pilasters support second floor pediments, while scrolls, garlands and vases provide decoration.

The **British Council** occupies no. 343.

*First right Runstraat*

**WTW, de Witte Tandenwinkel** (White Teeth Shop), at no. 5, is another of Amsterdam's extraordinary specialist shops. A toy fairground wheel rotates in the window, loaded with the establishment's stock in trade – toothbrushes. Every conceivable type, from electric to hand-made with the finest bristles, is to be found. A psychedelic Alan Stuart one-off, from Los Angeles, costs 11 guilders, while a gimmicky, banana specimen, presumably a help in encouraging young children to brush regularly, will set you back 20 guilders. Good investments for brightening up what can hardly be called an exciting daily chore. The shop is closed on Monday mornings.

Number 12, **De Doffer**, a famous brown café, opens at 20.00. Velvet curtains and bar billiards are unusual features.

Towards the Prinsengracht end of Runstraat are several antique shops.

*Return eastward, crossing Keizersgracht, to Huidenstraat.*

In the middle, at no. 12, **Pâtisserie Pompadour**, occupying a Louis XVI period building, is renowned for its gateaux, chocolates and glacé fruits – all home made. The shop is closed on Mondays. Teas are served at the rear but as there are only four tables a wait may be necessary at popular times.

*First right Herengracht; take the west thoroughfare.*

**Number 319**, a 17th-century style, spout-gabled tasting house, was built in 1889. A painted figure of an admiral who, surprisingly, appears to be Lord Nelson, adorns the central arch.

## 7. Biblical Museum (Bijbels Museum)

366 Herengracht

Open Tuesday–Saturday 10.00-17.00. Sundays 13.00-17.00. Admission charge.

This fascinating museum is concerned with proven historical aspects of the Bible, concentrating mainly on events referred to in the Old Testament. The museum is one of Amsterdam's oldest, being founded c.1850, when the Reverend Leendert Schouten began to open his personal collection for viewing.

**Numbers 364-70** Herengracht were commissioned by Jacob Cromhout, a wealthy merchant, from Philips Vingboons in 1662. All are sandstone-faced, with pedimented neck gables and oeil de boeuf windows in their attics; there is much Baroque carving.

**Numbers 364** and **366**, the two most northerly of the buildings, are noticeably wider fronted, higher gables. Above the first floor window, right of the door of no. 366, where Cromhout lived himself, is the merchants' punning emblem, a crooked piece of wood (crom hout, in Dutch).

Internal remodelling in 1717 included an outstanding painted ceiling in the rear gallery, by Jacob de Wit, depicting Classical mythological themes, and an unusual spiral staircase to provide a link between the two houses. Further remodelling took place prior to the opening of the museum in 1975. At the time of writing, only exhibits on the upper floor were identified in English. Temporary exhibitions are held from time to time.

Of particular interest are: a mummified head from the Exodus period, a reconstructed Israelite house, ritual objects, and models that include the Temple and the city of Jerusalem as Christ would have known it.

Reproduced from the Dead Sea Scrolls is the oldest known manuscript of the Book of Isaiah, dating from 200BC.

What resembles a French château combined with a New York mansion stands at **nos. 380-82**. Built by A. Salm in 1890, its carved exterior is the most extravagant 19th-century example on the canals. Filigree work incorporates fleurs de lys, emphasising the French influence. The interior is not original.

**Number 388**, built of stone in 1665, is exceptionally elegant, with Ionic pilasters to the ground floor and Corinthian above.

On the Leidsegracht corner, **no. 394**, built in 1672, is neck-gabled, with a segmental pediment. A stone tablet depicts a medieval Dutch legend, illustrating the four Heems children on the horse Begaart.

*At this point, Herengracht bends sharply to the east, but follow Leidsegracht, first right. First right Keizersgracht.*

**Number 452**, an enormous white mansion, received its present Baroque façade in 1860, when C. Outschoorn remodelled the original 17th-century building. Outschoorn was the last Classicist, ending a 200-year tradition of Palladian and Baroque architecture on

Amsterdam's canals. It must be said, however, that this example is demonstrably mid-19th century work.

Comprising two buildings, **nos. 444-46** were constructed in 1725 as separate residences, but combined 33 years later. An unusual 'wedding-cake' façade reflects several subsequent remodellings. The doorway is not placed symmetrically, and its appearance has been spoiled by removing the original double steps that led up to it. Similarly placed off centre is the decorative focal point of the parapet.

The building is now primarily a public library, but **no. 446** also accommodates the municipal town-planning authority.

*Return southward, crossing Leidsegracht.*

Leidsegracht marked the end of the first stage in creating the Canal Girdle, completed in 1625; the extension towards Amstel began in 1658.

In its shop front, **Café Walem**, no. 449 Keizersgracht, boasts a rare example of De Stijl architecture, by Gerrit Rietveld, 1938. An 18th-century summerhouse survives in the rear garden.

Cor, uncle of Vincent van Gogh, sold books and works of art at **no. 453**.

**Number 508**, on the south-west Leidsestraat corner, by A. C. Bleys, (1888) is an eclectic Neo-Renaissance building. It presents a wedge-shaped corner, this treatment often being preferred in the 19th century to the earlier juxtaposition of two angled façades. Above the door is a bust of the Dutch dramatist and poet Pieter Corneliszoon Hooft (1581-1647).

Occupying the north-west corner with Leidsestraat, at no. 455, Keizersgracht, **Metz & Co**., an important department store, was originally built for the New York Life Assurance Corporation by J. van Looy in 1891. It is an example of the Baroque Revival.

Rietveld added the steel and glass structure above the roof, known as the Rietveld Koepel, in 1933.

The store is entered from Leidsestraat, and visitors to the sixth floor, restaurant, created below Rietveld's structure in 1986, have superb views over the canals. Until 14.00, the popular Inter Metzo brunch – a typical Dutch breakfast, including waffles – is available at 17.50 guilders.

*Follow Leidsestraat northward.*

The travel industry and fast food shops have taken over much of Leidsestraat but, at no. 48, **Eichholt** is an exceptional delicatessen and, adjoining it, the **Berkhoff Tea Rooms** are renowned for their biscuits and chocolates.

*First right Herengracht.*

Between Leidsestraat and Vijzelstraat, Herengracht bends northward, the size of its houses, all of which originally belonged to wealthy burgomasters and bankers, earning this stretch the appellation 'Golden Bend'. Many of the buildings stretch to five bays, with a centrally-positioned door. All are of stone, either rusticated or ashlar. In spite of their grandeur, however, few can be said to be architecturally distinguished.

Philips Vingboons was responsible for **no. 450**, built in 1663, but it has no features of great interest; the attic floor is a 1922 addition.

**Number 475**, with its Louis XIV sandstone façade, was built in 1730 and is attributed to Hans Jacob Husley. Carved females flank the central first floor window. Internally, original plasterwork and sculptures of a high standard have survived.

Adriaan Dortsman designed **no. 462** in 1670. A splendid front door and allegorical roof sculptures of Welfare and Trade are the chief features.

*At Nieuwe Spiegelstraat the direction of the canal turns sharply northward. Continue ahead.*

**Number 493** is a 1770 remodelling, in Louis XV style, of a 17th-century house.

Adjoining, no. 495 was also remodelled, by J. Coulon, in 1739, for a member of the Six dynasty. Balconies are a feature that is untypical of Amsterdam.

**Vijzelstraat**, first right, has lost almost all its early houses and is now one of the central areas most charmless thoroughfares, dominated by undistinguished banks and offices.

*First right Keizersgracht.*

**Numbers 606-08**, built in 1730, have two of the most pronounced neck gables in Amsterdam: both are profusely decorated.

To the south, **no. 610** had a façade that matched those of its adjacent neighbours until it was remodelled in 1790.

*Return southward. First right Vijzelstraat. First right, Kerkstraat.*

The street passes through the hideous **ABN-AMRO Bank** block, the extension of which conservationists tried, unsuccessfully, to stop being built in the 1950s.

**Kerkstraat** (Church Street) was laid out to provide mews for the grand houses in Keizersgracht and Prinsengracht, and follows their routes. It begins at Leidsegracht, continuing to the Amstel river. The church referred to in its name is Amstelkerk, built by Stalpaert in 1668.

Straddling the Leidsestraat junction are a group of bars and hotels that are frequented by gay men, mostly of mature years. Further east is a concentration of antique shops.

**Smit Volendammer Vishandel**, a wet fish shop, on the south-west corner of Nieuwe Spiegelstraat (no. 54), is an economical source for smoked eels. Nothing in the street, however, particularly warrants a detour from an architectural or historic viewpoint.

*Return northward to Keizersgracht, first right, taking its south thoroughfare.*

## 8. Museum Van Loon

672 Keizersgracht

Open Mondays 10.00-17.00 and Sundays 13.00-17.00. Admission charge.

The interior of this 17th-century mansion has been restored to its 18th-century appearance, although some of the furnishings and objets d'art are 19th century. An unusually attractive feature is that the areas are not roped off, thus giving the impression that one is visiting a private home.

Adriaan Dortsman designed nos. 672 and 674, which were completed as a matching pair in 1672, soon after Keizersgracht had been laid

**(Opposite)** *In summer, patrons of popular bars encroach on the pavements creating a vivacious atmosphere.*

out. Painter Ferdinand Bol was the first occupant of no. 672, renting it from the owner, Jeremias van Raey. However, the house was not finished, and Bol sued Raey, who soon went bankrupt.

Hendrick van Loon purchased no. 674, next door, in 1889, and much of the existing collection is based on his family's possessions. Restoration to a late 18th-century appearance was commissioned by the Van Loon Foundation in 1964, and the museum opened nine years later. Apart from balconies above the entrances, and the roof balustrade with its statues, the two stone-clad houses are extremely plain. Within, a quiet, genteel atmosphere prevails, as the museum is rarely crowded, in spite of its restricted opening times (these are due to the mansion's popularity with large corporations as a hospitality venue).

The collection includes a large number of Van Loon family portraits.

Amstel porcelain, laid for dinner in the Dining Room, is just part of a 240-piece service.

Most of the balustrade of the staircase is of brass, made in the mid-18th century; iron infills were added later, because it was feared that the wide gaps would prove a danger to children. The 18th-century Rococo plasterwork is exceptional.

From the rear room, with its peacock decoration, visitors are permitted to view the formal garden. The rear façade of the house dates from 1775.

A coach house/summer pavilion backs on to Kerkstraat; its upper windows are fake. The inability to complete this was one of Ferdinand Bol's main grievances against Raey as, by the terms of their agreement, it was included in the rental.

**(Opposite) Top left:** *Corner towers and superb brickwork are features of the Amsterdam School of Architecture.*
**(Opposite) Top right:** *Post-Modernism, squeezed sympathetically betweeen period neighbours.*
**(Opposite) Bottom left:** *St Anthony's Gate, a picturesque former gateway in the city's medieval defensive wall.*
**(Opposite) Bottom right:** *All Amsterdam houses were once timber-faced, with spout gables; this example, in the Begijnhof, is one of only two that have survived.*

On the first floor of the house, a refreshing feature is that the bedrooms actually have beds in them. Wall-hangings, printed in Nîmes from 18th-century plates, feature sheep in one room and birds in another. The 'Sheep' bedroom is furnished with chairs and an 18th-century bed from Portugal. In the main bedroom, the 'HS' monogram of Hendrik Sanders, for whom the room was designed in 1771, may be seen in several locations.

*Exit from the museum right.*

Built for worship by the French-speaking Walloon community, at no. 676 Keizersgracht, **Nieuwe Walenkerk**, by A. N. Godefroy (1856) unusually blends a rusticated Classicism, on the ground floor, with Romanesque Revival work above. Lamps flank the entrances to the sandstone-faced church. Within, galleries are supported by cast-iron columns.

*Return westward. First right Vijzelstraat. First right Keizersgracht; take its north thoroughfare.*

**Taller Amsterdam**, promoters of avant garde art, has its premises at no. 607. Created in Montevideo ('taller' is Spanish for studio) by Armando Bergallo and Hector Vilche, the foundation stages art exhibitions and musical events. A permanent exhibition of works by members of the foundation is held on the ground floor. (Open Tuesday -Saturday 13.00-17.00. Admission charge.)

Next door, at no. 609, **Museum Fodor** occupies a former warehouse, remodelled and faced in sandstone by C. Outschoorn in 1863. It is open daily 11.00-17.00 for a small entrance charge, and works by contemporary artists are changed at intervals. The collection of C. J. Fodor, originally exhibited here, was incorporated in the Stedelijk Museum in 1948.

*Return to Vijzelstraat, right. First right Herengracht.*

Since 1927, no. 502, **Deutzhuis**, has been the official residence of Amsterdam's mayor. The house is named from its owner C. Deutz van Assendelft, who commissioned Abraham van Hart to remodel an existing 17th-century building in 1792. A marble balcony is supported by Doric columns.

Opposite, **no. 527** has an early-Louis XIV façade of 1770 (windows altered c. 1800). Surviving from the original house is the 17th-century hipped roof. An eagle decorates the pediment.

The neck gables of **nos. 504-10**, a 17th-century group, are embellished with various figures, mostly nautical, which possibly indicates ownership by merchants.

**Number 520** displays the coat of arms of the Alliance on its remodelled façade of 1727. Below the windows is a Baroque shell pattern.

*First right Reguliersgracht. Continue ahead to Amstel left. From Rokin trams 4, 9, 14, 16, 24 and 25 proceed northward and, from Vijzelstraat, trams 16, 24 and 25 proceed southward.*

ROUTE 5

# Prinsengracht, the Jordaan and The Anne Frank House

This route weaves between Prinsengracht, perhaps the serenest of Amsterdam's great waterways, and the intimate streets of the Jordaan, with their many bars and restaurants. Much dates from the 17th century, including the last two churches to be built by Hendrick de Keyser. The Anne Frank House, Holland's most visited dwelling, evokes the horrors of the German occupation, when a dreaded knock on the door by the Gestapo usually meant transportation to a concentration camp.

## Timing

- North Church may be visited on Saturday mornings, but a visit during a Sunday service (at 10.00 or 19.00) is highly recommended, due to its period quality.

- Whilst the church itself is generally open, the tower of West Church – for Amsterdam's finest views – may only be ascended from June until mid-September, Tuesdays, Wednesdays, Fridays and Saturdays, by joining guided tours on the hour, 14.00-17.00.

- At The Anne Frank House, although now open Monday – Saturday from 09.00 (Sundays from 10.00), there are always queues, and a very early arrival is necessary to avoid the crowds; they can be claustrophobic.

## Locations for Route 5

1. West Indies House
2. Haarlemmerdijk
3. The Jordaan
4. Lindengracht
5. Prinsengracht
6. Noordermarkt
7. North Church
8. Bloemgracht
9. West Church
10. The Anne Frank House

## Start: Stationsplein

*Cross to the south side of Prins Hendrikkade. First left Martelaarsgracht. First right Nieuwendijk.*

Nieuwendijk is believed to be the oldest street on the New Side, but few early houses remain. The best example is **no. 30**, built in 1630. A central indentation from the second to the top floor emphasises the narrow, vertical nature of this step-gabled building.

*Continue ahead, crossing Singel to Haarlemmerstraat.* At the Herenmarkt junction, second left, stands a building of great historic interest to New Yorkers.

## 1. West Indies House (West-Indisch Huis)

75 Haarlemmerstraat

Courtyard open Monday - Friday.

Constructed in 1615, as the Kleine Vleeshal (Small Meat Market), the West Indies Company rented the building for its offices in 1623, and it was here, two years later, that the decision was made to build a township on Manhattan Island, which had been discovered by the company's English navigator, Henry Hudson, in 1609.

In 1647, the building became a men's hostel and, in 1826, was mostly rebuilt for a Lutheran orphanage. Restored in 1984, this is now the James Adam Institute.

The Haarlemmerstraat façade dates, in its entirety, from the 1826 period, and comprises a stuccoed main building, flanked by brick pavilions. Deep ground floor windows, Ionic pilasters, and the pediment, decorated with a swan on a pedestal, are elegant features.

*Follow the section of Herenmarkt that skirts the east side of the building, and enter the courtyard, right, where all the façades maintain their 17th-century aspect.*

In the centre, the statue of Pieter Stuyvesant, Dutch Governor of New Amsterdam, 1647-64, was presented by the Turmac Tobacco Company, to mark their 60th anniversary. England acquired New Amsterdam in 1664 and re-christened the town New York, in honour of the Duke of York, later James II. A plaque, on the east wall of the courtyard, commemorates the decision, made here in 1625, to develop New Amsterdam.

*Continue southward. First left Brouwersgracht.*

A tablet at **no. 52**, dated 1749, is inscribed Nooyt Volmaakt (Never Perfect) and depicts three chairs. One wonders if this was the excessively humble announcement of a furniture maker.

Stone dolphins flank the neck gable of **no. 48**.

*Return westward. Second left Keizersgracht. Follow the west thoroughfare.*

One of Vincent van Gogh's uncles, J. P. Stricker, lived at **no. 8,** 1881-86. More important, Vincent's cousin, Kee, whom he adored, moved here to live with her parents after her husband had died. A sad case of unrequited love, the young lady refused even to meet Vincent when he came to woo her.

**Numbers 40-44** are good examples of restored, step-gabled warehouses.

From 1940-45, at **no. 58**, the Judenrat (Jewish Council) administered the measures introduced by the German occupying forces for controlling, and later deporting, Amsterdam's Jews. The members of the Council were Jews themselves and their work gained them some protection. Accused of collaboration, after the war, the defence that without their intervention Jews would have suffered even greater hardship was accepted. It was also conceded that they, like most other Jews, believed the German explanation that the deportees were being taken to labour camps.

*Return to Brouwersgracht and continue directly ahead, following Binnen Brouwerstraat. First left Haarlemmerstraat.*

The Gothic/Romanesque Revival **Posthorn Church** (Posthoornkerk), at nos. 124-6 was designed by P. J. H. Cuypers in two stages, 1860-63 and 1887-89. It no longer functions as a church, being converted to offices in 1989, and is generally closed to visitors.

Rhenish inspiration is immediately apparent, particularly in the twin spires.

*Continue westward, where, following the next intersection, the street becomes Haarlemmerdijk.*

## 2. Haarlemmerdijk

Haarlemmerdijk is gradually regaining its former status as a principal shopping street, which it lost when the tram routes were altered following the end of the Second World War. At present, Haarlemmerdijk, with its wide variety of shops, has much of the atmosphere of a small town's high street.

Closing the vista at the far end, Willemspoort evokes Berlin's Brandenburg Gate.

(Buiten Oranjestraat, first right, leads beneath the railway track to Bickerseiland and Realeneiland, the linked Western Islands, the development of which formed part of the city's 17th-century extension. Sections remain picturesque, but local authority housing, without great appeal, intrudes. Although lacking outstanding interest, there is a nautical atmosphere, and those with time to spare may enjoy wandering along the canals in sunny weather.)

At **no. 56**, **J. G. Beune** will make cakes to order that incorporate a photograph, reproduced in brown or red edible dye; computerised equipment is involved in the process.

**The Movies,** at no. 161, is an art-film cinema, built in 1928 and restored in 1974. Most films shown are foreign, with sub-titles in Dutch.

When the town wall was repositioned in the 17th century, one of the new gates was known as **Haarlemmerpoort**, because the road to Haarlem stretched from it.

The Civic Guard Company of Captain Coq was on duty at Haarlemmerpoort in September 1638, when Marie de Medicis visited Amsterdam, and it has been suggested that this occasion may have provided the setting for Rembrandt's famous *The Night Watch*.

That gate was replaced in 1840 by the present **Willemspoort**, designed by C. Allewijn and C. W. M. Klijn, in Classical style. Within, local taxes were assessed and collected. The building was converted to provide residential accommodation in 1986. Something obviously went wrong with the design of the columns, as they taper far too abruptly. De Koningh, who carved the capitals of the Madeleine in Paris, was also responsible for these Corinthian examples.

*Proceed southward, third left Brouwersgracht. Cross the first bridge, to the south side and follow Palmgracht directly ahead. Amsterdam's quarter, known as the Jordaan, has now been entered.*

## 3. The Jordaan

Between Prinsengracht and Singelgracht, the moat created outside the new town wall in the 17th century, a hexagonal area was set aside to accommodate workers and poor immigrants. Existing paths became streets, and some of the ditches were deepened to serve as narrow canals; all were set at an oblique angle to those further east.

Originally, the Jordaan was known as Nieuw Werck (New Project), but the many street names referring to flora soon led to the present appellation. It is believed that French Huguenots referred to it as 'the garden' (le jardin in French), later corrupted to de jordaan. Restricted sites meant that the houses were high and narrow, many being subdivided.

At an early stage, and in spite of the difficulties, it was the Jordaan that witnessed the first social housing projects built in the city. These took the form of almshouses (hofjes), sponsored by charitable institutions, most of which still physically survive.

Apart from a few canals, the Jordaan degenerated rapidly, pollution caused by new light industries creating a slum, which remained until the Second World War had ended. However, due to its central position and environmental protection, this is now a fashionable area in which to live, and restaurants and bars proliferate.

Unfortunately, most of the Jordaan's picturesque canals were filled in the late 19th-century, to combat cholera and typhoid epidemics.

House numbering of the main, north-east/south-west streets begins at the Brouwersgracht and Prinsengracht ends. Although short, many cross streets have lengthy names as they end with Dwarstraat (Cross Street) and begin with their position (from east to west), eg. Erste (First), Tweede (Second), Derde (Third). The name of the street that they cross comes between.

The Jordaan's area is defined, clockwise from the north, by Brouwersgracht, Prinsengracht, Leidsegracht and Lijnbaansgracht.

**Palmgracht**, now filled, was formerly a narrow canal. Numbers 20-26 were built as **Bossche Hofje**.

Over the doorway (generally closed) of nos. 28-38 are carved the initials 'PA' and a turnip (raep), indicating that here Pieter Adiraensz Raep founded the **Raep Hofje**, for elderly ladies and orphan children. Above this is inscribed the date of the building '1648', together with the establishment's arms. The original cross windows survive.

*Continue westward to the end of Palmgracht. Left Lijnbaansgracht. First left Palmstraat.*

A brightly-coloured identity stone, made in 1982, continues the Amsterdam tradition at nos. **110-150**, although this is a modern building.

*Return to Lijnbaansgracht, left. Third left Lindengracht.*

# 4. Lindengracht

Now also filled, this was formerly the Jordaan's most important canal, apart from Rozengracht to the south, and maintained its residential popularity throughout most of the area's unfashionable period.

'Cat in the Vineyard' is the name given to **no. 160**, due to the subject of its identity stone.

Above the central doorway of **nos. 55-57**, with its twin bell gables, is a humorous tablet, decorated with: ''t Hcargnednil' (Lindengracht spelt backwards), the year upside down, and fishes swimming in trees, all depicting a topsy-turvy world. It is the modern work of sculptor Hans 't Mannetje.

Below the top floor windows of **no. 53**, 1687 is inscribed on carved linen. A plaque depicts a reel, two monkeys and a dog.

Centrally situated in the north end of the street, the statue of **Kees de Jongen** depicts a character from a book by Theo Thijssen, who taught in the Jordaan. Every Saturday morning a general market is held at this point and, during the third week of September, many activities that contribute to the Jordaan festival take place here.

*Continue ahead to the Brouwersgracht/Prinsengracht intersection.*

Constructed in the 17th century as the first stage in the Canal Girdle project, **Brouwersgracht** is one of Amsterdam's most attractive waterways, particularly where it links with others. From here may be viewed, on the north side, spout-gabled former warehouses, which have been converted to apartments; their original hatches are now glazed.

*First right, follow the west thoroughfare of Prinsengracht.*

# 5. Prinsengracht

Many regard Prinsengracht as the finest of the Canal Girdle waterways because more of its original houses remain unaltered. Apparently, the 'princes' referred to have no connections with members of the House of Orange, as some believe; the name was chosen to indicate that the houses were less grand than those built on Keizersgracht (the Emperors Canal). Houseboats occupy the northern stretch as far south as Rozengracht.

On the Brouwersgracht corner, nos. 2-4, dated 1641, is the step-gabled **Papeneiland Café**, one of Amsterdam's oldest brown bars. Within, an ancient stove and small Delft tiles are evocative features.

*Remain on the west side.*

A painted post-horn above the door decorates **no. 7** (on the east side).

**Number 9** bears a plaque inscribed Nooit Weer (Never Again), referring to the difficulties that its owner had in removing a tenant who lived in the adjacent building.

A fisherman in a boat is depicted on the plaque of **no. 35**.

Noordermarkt (North Market), created around North Church, interrupts the range of Prinsengracht houses on its west side. *Follow the north side of the square.*

# 6. Noordermarkt

Markets are still held: Monday a flea market, Saturday morning a bird market and food (mainly organic) market, where farmhouse yoghurts and cheeses are popular.

Number 4, **Woutertje Pieterse**, a coffee shop, is named to commemorate a character in an autobiographical Multatuli novel: a statue in front of no. 8 depicts Woutertje Pieterse and Femke, in tribute to Multatuli (1820-87).

On the north corner of Noorderkerkstraat, first right, **Ziekenfondsbrillen**, at no. 18, sells spectacle frames and sunglasses at very reasonable prices. They are not second-hand, most form part of unsold batches, often bankrupt stock.

Next-door-but-one, at **no. 14**, 'Geloof Hoop en Liefde' (Faith, Hope and Charity) is inscribed on the plaque above the shop front.

*Return to Noorderkerkmarkt and continue anti-clockwise.*

**Number 21**, below its second floor window, displays a ship.

A cow, a chicken and a sheep appear respectively on the gables of **nos. 17, 18 and 19**.

**Hegeraad**, at no. 34, is a delightful brown bar, one of the Jordaan's most popular locals. It is described as a Tapperij Slijterij (Off-Licence), but no longer operates as such.

A stone on the façade of **nos. 39-41**, depicts a scene from a fable by Fontaine, the French writer of fairy tales.

## 7. North Church (Noorderkerk) Hendrick de Keyser, 1620-22

44-48 Noordermarkt

Open Saturdays 10.00-12.00. Sunday services 10.00 and 19.00.

To attend at least part of one of the Sunday services at North Church is an engrossing experience. Several hundred regularly participate, and the preacher still wears mid-19th century dress. To many it will evoke a period film, set in the United States.

### History
This was the last church that de Keyser designed, its construction beginning at the same time as West Church, but completed in two years. Here, the plan of the building evolves around the all important pulpit. Whereas West Church, further south, was intended for the wealthy, North Church was regarded as a place of worship for the poor of the Jordaan. Bonders, a Calvinist sect, now hold their services here, and some worshippers travel long distances, ensuring unusually large congregations for church services in Amsterdam. Conventional dress is insisted on, women being required to cover their heads. Much-needed restoration is planned, 1992-98, and it is not yet clear if the church will open throughout this period.

## Exterior

It is obvious that the status of this church is humbler than that of West Church. There is no great tower, decorative stonework is minimal, and a squat appearance is emphasised by the houses that fill each corner. Identical, balustrated gables to the four façades are domestic in nature, their trapezoid shape and hipped roofs adding to the general squatness. Window tracery retains Gothic inspiration.

A plaque, attached to the east end of the south façade, commemorates the general strike against the German deportation of Jews. This protest took place on 24 February 1941, beginning at Noordermarkt with a Communist-led rally.

A monument depicting three bound figures stands near the entrance to the church, at its south-west corner. Inscribed 'Eenheid de Sterkste Keten' (The Strongest Chains are of Unity), the 1934 riots in the Jordaan against proposals to reduce dole money by 20 per cent during the Depression are commemorated.

## Interior

The Greek Cross plan of the church, with all elements subservient to the centrally-located pulpit, was an innovative development. Londoners might reflect that, even 10 years later, their St. Katherine Cree was being designed to a traditional Gothic layout, and that it was not until Wren was well into rebuilding the post-Great Fire City churches (c. 1680) that a Greek Cross plan was permitted in England.

Concentric rows of pews, all original, surround the pulpit, having been brought forward from the walls where they initially stood, accommodating up to 1,000 worshippers. Also facing the pulpit is the organ, with the church warden's pew below. Plain stone pillars and bare brick walls contribute to the rather subdued atmosphere.

*From the west corner of Noordermarkt, Lindenstraat runs southward.*

At **nos. 4, 6** and **19** stone tablets depict King David playing his harp.

Lindenstraat leads to **Karthuizerstraat**, the name of which commemorates the Karthuizer convent, which stood here until the Alteration.

The five restored gables of **nos. 11, 13, 15, 17 and 19** are inscribed, respectively (in Dutch of course), 1537, Winter, Summer, Spring and Autumn.

At nos. 61-191, the courtyard of **Huys-Zitten Weduwenhofe**, designed by the City Architect Daniel Stampaert in 1650, may generally be entered. Built for poor widows, these were an early Amsterdam example of almshouses. As is usual, they are in the form of one-room units grouped around a courtyard. All was faithfully restored in 1991.

The roof pediment displays the names of the donors.

Above the door, a smaller pediment is dated 1650 and bears the establishment's title. Entered from the archway is the attractive garden courtyard, where two ancient pumps have been retained. Pediments facing the courtyard display, respectively, the old and new arms of the city.

*From Karthuizerstraat, follow, first left, Tichelstraat. First left Westerstraat.*

**Westerstraat's** former name, Anjeliersgracht, reflects that it was originally a canal. A second-hand clothes market is held under canvas on Monday mornings.

Much of the south end of the street comprises 1985 conversions of tenement blocks, designed by P. J. Hamer, 1862-64. Like their predecessors in England, the architectural style is revivalist and eclectic.

*Return northward. First right Tweede Anjeliersdwarsstraat leads to Tweede Tuindwarsstraat.*

At no. 8, **Flying Objects** exhibits opened-up kites, all for sale, in its compulsive shop window.

*Second left Egelantiersstraat.*

**Number 52** displays a plaque depicting a hand writing with a quill pen, thus commemorating a schoolmaster with calligraphic skills who lived here in the 17th century.

**Taveerne Claes Claesz**, at nos. 24-26, serves Dutch food, but dinner only and not Mondays, Tuesdays or Wednesdays!

A passage, right of the building, leads to **Claes Claesz Hofje**, nos. 18-50, where 23 former 17th-century almshouses were converted, from 1968-73, to provide accommodation for students of the Music Conservatory.

The houses feature a variety of gables, and are grouped around three courtyards, which are linked by passageways that lead eventually to Eerste Egelantiersdwarsstraat.

*Follow Egelantiersstraat northward to Prinsengracht, right.*

Interestingly, on the opposite side, **no. 151**, behind its eclectic 1850 façade, which originally fronted a school, was rebuilt in 1980 to provide housing.

**Zon's Hofje**, at nos. 157-71, is another 17th-century almshouse, rather leafier than most.

**De Twee Zwaantjes** (Two Cygnets), no. 114, is the top venue for music-hall favourites, sung in various languages. Opened in 1928, there is also a cabaret and a bar, but the most important ingredient of the evening is the 'sing along'. Understandably, the 'Song of the Jordaan', to an accordion accompaniment, is extremely popular with the locals. Open Fridays and Saturdays from 19.00, Sundays from 18.00.

*Return northward. First left Egelantiersgracht; follow its north thoroughfare.*

Fortunately, **Egelantiersgracht** has escaped conversion to a street, thus avoiding the fate of most of the Jordaan's canals.

**Café 't Smalle**, at no. 12, is a rare example of an Amsterdam brown bar that sells 'pub' food in the English style (the apple cake is exceptional). Founded by Pieter Hoppe in 1780, gin and liqueurs were originally distilled on the premises, including Hoppe genever, which is still available. Panels and beams create a venerable atmosphere. Open daily from 10.00, the interior is candle-lit at night.

First left, **Eerste Leliedwarsstraat** boasts several art galleries, and affords a splendid view of West Church, with its famous tower.

On the corner with Nieuwe Leliestraat *(first right)*, **Café de Reiger**, at no. 34 Nieuwe Leliestraat, is popular with the Jordaan's youngsters. Open at 17.00, good home-made soups and sandwiches are served.

*Continue ahead. First right Bloemgracht.*

## 8. Bloemgracht

Due to its gabled 17th-century houses, Bloemgracht is known as the Herengracht (Gentlemen's Canal) of the Jordaan.

**André Coppenhagen 1001 Kraben**, at no. 38, is another of the city's extraordinary specialist shops (closed Monday). The 1001 kraben (beads) are all displayed by colour range in glass jars – a veritable bead rainbow.

By tradition, the three identical step-gabled houses at **nos. 87, 89** and **91** are the work of Hendrick de Keyser, and for this reason known as 'The Three Hendricks'. Their original names are as indicated respectively on the tablets: the townsman, the countryman and the seaman. They are good examples of 17th-century burgher houses.

**Number 116** displays a plaque inscribed 'Godt alleen d'eere' (Honour God alone).

*Return northward. Second right Eerste Bloemdwarsstraat.*

**De Stalhouderij**, at no. 4, is Amsterdam's smallest theatre, seating a maximum of 40. Formerly a livery stable (stalhouderij), there is an upstairs bar. Plays are performed in English.

On the corner of Bloemstraat (first left) **Café Chris**, 42 Bloemstraat, was founded in 1624 and is Amsterdam's oldest bar. Its wooden interior has been well preserved.

*Continue southward. First right Rozengracht.*

Formerly the Jordaan's most important canal, **Rozengracht** was filled in the 19th century to provide a link road with the newly laid out Raadhuisstraat.

**Lonny's,** at no. 46, is one of Amsterdam's most popular Indonesian restaurants. (Evenings only; see also restaurant listing.)

Adjacent, **toko**, an Indonesian delicatessen, is run by Lonny's Restaurant.

**Bols Tavern** occupies a 17th-century house, at nos. 106-108, which lies back from its open courtyard. (Evenings only and shut Sundays; see also restaurant listing.)

After his insolvency, Rembrandt moved to Rozengracht, which, by the 1660s had already degenerated into a poor area. A detour to the site is not recommended, as the house has gone and only a plaque on its replacement (no. 184) commemorates his occupancy.

*Return northward to Prinsengracht.*

On the far corner, no. 283, **De Kalkhoven**, another brown bar, opens daily at 11.00.

*Follow Prinsengracht northward.*

**De Keyser**, at no. 180, has sold tea and coffee on the premises since 1839.

Number 170, **Gallerie d'Arte**, is where the genuine, and very expensive, ceramic delftware may be purchased in Amsterdam.

*Return southward to the Rozengracht intersection and cross, left, to the east side of Prinsengracht, which broadens at this point to become Westermarkt.*

## 9. West Church (Westerkerk) Hendrick de Keyser 1620-31

281 Prinsengracht

Church open daily throughout the day. Tower open June – mid-September, Tuesdays, Wednesdays, Fridays and Saturdays for guided tours on the hour 14.00-17.00. Admission charge.

Still an important church, to many an Amsterdammer the tower of West Church symbolises the city; views from its summit are Amsterdam's finest. Rembrandt and his son Titus both lie within.

### History

West Church, the second church to be built in Amsterdam specifically for Protestant worship, was completed 28 years after the first: South Church. De Keyser was responsible for designing both, but he died in 1621, shortly after construction of this building had begun. More restrained and fluent than South Church, West Church shows the French influence on de Keyser's late style, which was a precursor of Dutch Classicism.

It was the extension of the city westward from Singel, with houses built on the new canals for wealthy merchants, that led to the construction of West Church. The most important burials within are those of Rembrandt, in an unknown grave, and his son Titus. Queen Beatrix married Prince Claus here in 1966.

Complete restoration of the body of the building began in 1985 and the church reopened five years later; completion, however, is not expected until 1992. The tower, which is now the responsibility of the state, was not included in the scheme.

## Exterior

A Gothic inheritance is apparent in the building's vertical emphasis and its window tracery. However, an anti-clockwise tour of the exterior will reveal the symmetry of West Church, which, together with the small pediments surmounting the gables, proclaims that this is not a Gothic building.

Facing Westermarkt, at the south-east corner of the church, stands a commemorative bronze statue of **Anne Frank** (1929-45), by Mari Andriessen. Anne, who took refuge nearby, referred to the bells of West Church in her diary.

Behind the church may be seen a very unusual monument, in the form of three marble triangles set, respectively, in the pavement, on the pavement and beside the canal. Known as the **Homomonument**, it was designed by Kavin Daan in 1987 to commemorate all homosexual men and women who have suffered persecution. Evidently, this site was selected for the monument because Holland's most famous meeting place for gay men, a public urinal, had stood here until it was removed in 1966, amidst protest, immediately prior to the wedding of Queen Beatrix in West Church.

Although entirely Classical, the tower is sited, in the Gothic manner, in a central position at the west end. It was not completed until 1638, 17 years after De Keyser's death.

At just under 300 feet, this is the highest tower in Amsterdam, and views from the top are the finest that the city has to offer.

Above the brick section, the entire steeple is built of wood, clad initially in sandstone, and then lead for the upper part. Sections, incorporating columns, are reduced in size at each upward stage. The imperial crown surmounts the structure.

Amsterdam's heaviest bell, at seven tons, is housed in the tower, but it has never yet been rung. The carillon, restored in 1959, now consists of 42 bells. Those ascending the tower must climb 160 steps

– but there are six levels for resting and views are worth the effort.

*Enter the church from the west, Prinsengracht, façade.*

## Interior

Large, clear windows and white walls combine to produce an extremely light interior. As is common in Amsterdam, the roof is a timber barrel vault. Columns and the edging are of sandstone, a hallmark of de Keyser's late style.

Original fittings of oak include the canopied pulpit, box pews and the splendid east door. The chandeliers are copies of the 17th century originals, looted by the Germans and now lost.

At the west end, the organ shutters, painted by Gerard de Lairesse, were restored in 1991. Depicted are David dancing before the Ark, and the Queen of Sheba bearing gifts to Solomon. The organ itself has been frequently extended and restored since it was made in 1686. For the many recitals held in the church it is usually the choir organ, a smaller instrument, which is played.

Attached to the second bay's column, right, a plaque of 1906 commemorates Rembrandt's burial in the church on 8 October 1669. Due to his poverty, the great artist was interred in a rented tomb shared with two others and, unfortunately, its location was not recorded. However, the recent installation of underfloor heating has led to the discovery of several skeletons, one of which may prove to be Rembrandt's. Tests were begun at Leiden University in 1991 on the bones of nine possible skeletons, in a search for traces of the lead that Rembrandt's paints would have deposited.

Rembrandt's son Titus, who died on 7 September 1668 (aged 27), a year before his father, also lies in the church. His tomb, however, is known: it is located in front of the pulpit, generally covered by a carpet.

The tearful young ladies, who frequently occupy the pews, are not generally mourning a loved one, but giving vent to their emotions after visiting The Anne Frank House nearby.

*Exit from the church, right, to Westermarkt.*

René Descartes, the French philosopher, lived at **no. 6** during his sojourn in Amsterdam from 1628-49.

*Follow Prinsengracht northward.*

## 10. The Anne Frank House (Anne Frankhuis)

263 Prinsengracht

Open Monday – Saturday 09.00-17.00. Sundays 10.00-17.00. From May – August the museum remains open daily until 19.00. The admission charge includes an informative folder, incorporating a room plan.

More than half a million visitors each year make a pilgrimage to this house, the most poignant Amsterdam reminder of the Holocaust. Few have not heard of *The Diary of Anne Frank*, as the best-selling book has also inspired a play and a film. Rooms are relatively small, and the narrow stairway steep. At peak times, therefore, queues can be long, and the atmosphere within claustrophobic.

### History

Anneliese Frank was born at Frankfurt am Main in Germany on 12 June 1929; her Jewish parents were Otto and Edith. Anne's sister Margot, was three years older. With great prescience, the family left Germany for Amsterdam on Hitler's appointment as Reich Chancellor in 1933, and lived in Merwedeplein. Otto Frank set up a wholesale herb and spice business in this house in Prinsengracht, now the museum, in 1940, just before the German occupation of Holland began during May that year.

It soon became apparent that, to escape deportation to Germany, Jews would have to go into hiding and, early in 1942, Otto concealed the entrance to the two upper floors and attic of the annexe with a hinged bookcase. At the rear of the house, the windows had been blacked out already for the benefit of the stored herbs, and the annexe windows, apart from that of the attic, were now hung with thick net curtains; furnishings were brought from the Merwedeplein house.

This annexe became the secret hideaway of the Frank family from 6 July 1942, some of Otto's former employees who were still working below supplying their everyday needs, at great personal risk to themselves. The van Daan family shortly moved into the annexe with the Franks. Anne recorded her daily life in the diary that she was given for her 13th birthday, 12 June 1942. In November that year, a Jewish dentist friend, Mr. Dussel, joined the fugitives.

An anonymous telephone call to the Gestapo led to the discovery of the hideaway on 4 August 1944. Ironically, the occupants were amongst the last batch of Jews to be deported to German concentration camps from Westerbork, the German labour camp in the north of Holland. Mrs. Frank died of starvation at Auschwitz, Mr. van Daan was gassed, and Pieter van Daan disappeared when the SS vacated Auschwitz. Mr. Dussel died at Neuengamme, and Mrs. van Daan died at Bergen-Belsen. Anne and Margot Frank also died at Bergen-Belson, both of typhoid and within a few days of each other, in March 1945, just two months before they would have been liberated. Miraculously, Otto Frank survived Auschwitz and lived until 1980.

The proposal to demolish the annexe, in 1957, led to the establishment of the Anne Frank Foundation, and the museum was opened three years later.

A flat cornice hides the gable of this merchant's house, built in 1635.

## Interior
Stairs lead directly to the second floor, where a permanent exhibition deals with the rise of fascism and the Second World War.

A link room to the annexe (1740) retains blackout paper on its windows.

The bookcase, which concealed the entrance to the hideaway, is kept ajar; a map hid the top of the door.

The first room served as the bedroom of Anne's parents and her sister Margot. Original to the room is the map of Normandy, with the Allies' advance indicated. Beside it, marks on the wall measure stages in the growth of the teenagers, also original.

Anne shared the next room with Mr. Dussel. The pictures that she cut out of journals and pasted down as wall decoration are original. For English visitors, in particular, it is touching to note that photographs of Princess Elizabeth (now Elizabeth II), Princess Margaret, and the chimpanzees' tea party at London Zoo, are included amongst those of film stars.

Due to noise, the adjacent toilet/washroom could only be flushed when the offices below were closed; not all those employed there were in on the secret.

Stairs lead to Mr. and Mrs. van Daan's bedroom, which, due to its size, also served as the communal kitchen and living room.

Window blocks, behind which the nightly blackout slats had to be placed, survive.

From Pieter van Daan's small room, stairs lead to the attic, where meagre supplies of food were kept.

The attic window, due to its concealed situation, was the only one in the annexe that could be opened without risk of discovery.

A modern corridor, added for the museum, leads to the top floor of the main house, all of which is devoted to an **Anne Frank and her Diary exhibition**. A video performance, in English, includes readings from the diary.

The original, hand-written diary is the most important exhibit. Before the Gestapo returned to ransack the annexe, the office staff who had aided the fugitives took away items that they thought might be of value. Miep, a typist, kept Anne's possessions and presented them, including the diary, to Otto Frank after the war. The diary was first published in 1947, under the title that Anne had chosen, *Het Achterhuis* (The Attic). It has since appeared, as *The Diary of Anne Frank*, in more than 50 languages, in excess of 13 million copies having been sold.

Only two of the brave Dutch who had helped Anne and her companions throughout the 25 months of what was in effect their imprisonment were punished; they were sent to a Dutch concentration camp, but survived the ordeal.

Steps lead down to the first floor of the house, where temporary exhibitions are held. A bookshop/information office is passed before the descent to the exit is made.

*Return southward along Prinsengracht.*

It will be noted that houseboats are not permitted on the canal south of the Rozengracht junction.

Number 377, **Café van Puffelen** is a popular brown bar, which opens at 14.00 (16.00 in winter). Food is served from 18.00.

*First right, Berenstraat leads to Elandsgracht.*

**Elandsgracht** was formerly an important canal in the Jordaan.

At **no. 109**, the block is divided into passageways occupied by stalls of a flea market, excellent for haberdashery. Open Monday to Thursday 11.00-17.00 and Saturdays 09.00-17.00.

Any street from the east side leads to Looiersgracht, where, entered from no. 38, a market known as **Rommelmarkt**, with rotating themes, is held daily from 11.00-17.00 except on Fridays. Speciality days are Mondays: coins and stamps, Tuesdays: books and records and Thursdays: clothing.

*From the north end of the street follow Prinsengracht southward.*

Bell-gabled, **no. 300** was built in 1767 but much restored in 1959. Above the entrance to the timber lower frontage, a red fox is depicted with a bird in its mouth. Another fox appears below the hoist beam.

**Molenpad**, no. 653, a brown bar, is open daily from 12.00 and offers attractive views over the canal from its windows.

Built around two courtyards, on the site of a former orphanage, the **Palace of Justice** (Paleis van Justitie) at no. 436, was designed by the City Architect J. de Graaf, 1825-29. Corinthian pilasters and balustrades are features of the building, which is laid out as three pavilions. Windows maintain the Empire style.

Although well preserved, the interior is rather stark.

*Continue to the Leidsestraat junction and cross to the south-west corner.*

**Dikker and Thijs**, no. 82 Leidsestraat, is an hotel with its entrance and Brasserie Bar facing Leidsestraat. Previously, the ground floor accommodated Amsterdam's most exclusive delicatessen, but this has now been relegated to a small area in the city, on the Prinsengracht side. Nevertheless, if caviar, foie gras or smoked salmon are what you are looking for, this is still the best place to find them.

*Trams 1, 2 and 5 pass Leidsestraat.*

ROUTE 6

# Maritime Amsterdam and The Plantage

Amsterdam's former dockland retains a great deal of its 17th-century charm, the undoubted highlight being the Maritime Museum. The Artis Zoo and Botanical Gardens are both situated in the Plantage, an area developed in the 18th century with 'country' villas for Amsterdam's wealthy citizens.

## Timing
- Fine weather is really essential, due to the open nature of the area. However, the Maritime Museum, Tropenmuseum and much of the Botanical Gardens are under cover.
- The Maritime Museum is closed on Sunday mornings and Mondays.
- East Church is closed on Thursdays, Saturdays and, apart from services, on Sundays.
- 't Kromhout Shipyard/Museum is closed at weekends.
- The Tropenmuseum is closed on Saturday and Sunday mornings.
- At weekends, the Botanical Gardens are not open until 11.00.

## Locations for Route 6
1. Angle Tower
2. Maritime House
3 Entrepotdok
4. Maritime Museum
5. East Church
6. 't Kromhout Shipyard/Museum
7. Tropics Museum
8. The Plantage
9. Artis Zoo and Planetarium
10. Former Dutch Theatre
11. Botanical Gardens

## Start: Stationsplein:

*Proceed eastward to Prins Hendrikkade, and continue north of St. Nicolaaskerk.*

# 1. Angle (or Weeping) Tower (Schreierstoren)
1482

94-95 Prins Hendrikkade

This tower was built in 1482 as one of the bastions in Amsterdam's defensive wall. Before Prins Hendrikkade was laid out, it faced the open sea, at a point where two canals, Oudezijdskolk and Geldersekade, met at a sharp angle (schreie), hence its name.

A stone tablet of 1569 depicts a ship at sea and a weeping woman. This probably gave rise to the untrue tradition that sailors' loved-ones bade them farewell from the tower as they departed on their long and hazardous voyages. Because of this, the building's alternative name is the Weeping Tower.

Left of the door are two bronze plaques. The one presented by the Greenwich Village History Society, in 1927, commemorates the Englishman Henry Hudson's departure from a point near the tower in his ship *De Haelve Maen* (The Half Moon) on 4 April 1609, in search of a quicker passage to the East Indies. Instead, he inadvertently discovered Manhattan Island. The other plaque was given in 1945 by the New York Port Authority.

Above the doorway of **no. 95**, the stone tablet was inserted in 1945 to commemorate the 300th anniversary of the first Dutch voyage to the East Indies. The top floor and the rear extension were later additions to the tower, which was originally surmounted by a battlement above the round-arched frieze. The gilded weathervane is in the form of a sailing ship.

**Geldersekade**, the wider of the two canals that the tower overlooks, retains many 17th-century houses.

**Oosterdokskade** forms the bridge that crosses Oosterdok to the north.

Facing the bridge, from its south-east corner, a large bust, now weathered to pale green, depicts **Prince Hendrik** of the Netherlands (1820-79), the youngest son of Willem II. He enthusiastically supported seafaring merchants and was nicknamed 'the seaman'.

Permanently sited on the north side of Oosterdok can be observed *Sea Palace*, a 700-seater floating restaurant, obviously inspired by the pagoda-roofed *Jumbo* in Hong Kong. Interiors, and a lengthy menu, are Chinese, but Indonesian specialities (in Chinese style) may also be ordered. Prices are high but the interior is luxurious. Open daily 12.00-23.00.

Immediately east of the bridge, Maritime House occupies the triangular corner block. It is best viewed from the north side of Prins Hendrikkade.

## 2. Maritime House (Scheepvaarthuis)
J. M. van der Meij 1911-16

108-11 Prins Hendrikkade

Maritime House incorporates late examples of the Neue Kunst (Dutch Art Nouveau) style but is also regarded as the first work by the Amsterdam School. It was from this point, in 1645, that the Dutch fleet departed on their first voyage to the East Indies. Now the headquarters of the municipal transport authority, the block was originally designed to accommodate six shipping companies.

It is said that the sharp point of the building represents the prow of a ship, but the shape of the site probably determined it in any case.

Sculptures represent nautical themes in a medieval manner: explorers, sea horses, dolphins, etc. Architects P. L. Kramer and M. de Klerk assisted in the work.

A stone plaque, above the ground floor window of **no. 131 Prins Hendrikkade**, depicts Michiel Adrienszoon de Ruyter, the 17th-century admiral who lived in the house.

The next canal, **Oude Schans**, was called Schans Bulwark in 1516, when it served as a moat to Amsterdam's defensive wall on the east side. Oude (Old) was added when the wall was moved further east.

*Proceed southward, following Kalkmarkt, which forms the first stretch of the west thoroughfare of Oude Schans.*

At the second junction (with Oude Waal) stands the **Montelbaans Tower** (Montelbaanstoren), built as a defensive tower in 1512 to protect merchant ships sailing on Oude Shans. It now accommodates the Amsterdam Water Authority.

The lower part is original, but Hendrick de Keyser added its octagonal upper section and lead-clad wooden steeple in 1606.

It was around the Montelbaans Tower that Amsterdam's first planned expansion took place in 1585.

*Return northward and cross to the east corner of Oude Shans and Prins Hendrikkade.*

At **no. 1 's Gravenhekje** the four trapezium-gabled warehouses were built in 1642, work attributed to Pieter de Keyser. Oval and circular windows light their attics.

The warehouses were commissioned by the Geoctroyeerde Westindische Compagnie, founded in 1621 to trade with Central and South America. Initially, piracy was enthusiastically indulged in, a Spanish consignment of silver being captured off the Cuban coast in 1628 by Pieter Hein. However, when such acts became impossible, following the peace treaty with Spain in 1648, the West African slave trade took their place as the company's main earner. Between 1626 and 1650, 70,000 were forcibly deported to serve as slaves in Holland's Caribbean colonies.

*Continue following Prins Hendrikkade eastward to Peperstraat (first right).*

Pepper was the most valuable spice imported from the East Indies in the 17th century and **Peperstraat** was named from the pepper wharf, which stood further south, on the Rappenburg intersection.

**Number 159 Prins Hendrikkade** bears traces of Art Deco work. It was built as offices for the former Holland West Africa Line.

The roof level centrepiece of **no. 171** features a ship, a globe and Jacob's staff – an instrument for determining the position of latitude. Built in 1753, the house was commissioned by a prosperous grain merchant.

The block of warehouses, at **no. 176**, on the Foeliestraat corner, was designed for the Dutch East Indies Company in 1602. Original shutters survive and the roofs project to cover the hoist beams.

*Second right, Schippersgracht leads to Rappenburgerplein.*

Founded in 1638, **De Druiff**, at no. 83, was formerly the oldest Likeurstokerij (Off-licence) in Amsterdam. Although off-sales were discontinued in 1982, the ancient still remains in the cellar.

The name De Druiff means the grape, but this is more a beer and spirits house than a wine bar. Ancient barrels blend with the venerable appearance.

De Druiff is open daily 11.00-01.00 (02.00 Friday and Saturday). The patron made me promise faithfully to record that the intimate nature of his bar precludes the admission of large groups.

Just south of De Druiff, on the east side of the canal, lies Entrepotdok.

## 3. Entrepotdok

To promote Amsterdam's warehousing trade, goods in transit to other parts were exempted from excise duty, and this, the greatest warehouse complex in Europe at the time, was built to accommodate them in 1827; its architects were J. de Greef, C. W. M. Klein and G. Moele. The state purchased the warehouses in 1857, refurbishing and extending them. Recently, they have been adapted to residential/ office accommodation, each unit being given, in alphabetical order, the name of a town in Holland or Belgium.

From Laagtekadijk, a central courtyard, Kadijksplein, may be entered to the rear of the units. The administrative blocks were added in 1857; their Doric colonnade survives but has been filled in.

*Follow Nieuwe Herengracht, which begins south of De Druiff.*

**Number 143,** built in 1750, has a white-painted façade, flanked by rusticated pilasters. Its central section and eave corbels are decorated in Baroque style.

**Number 103** was built in the 17th century, but its façade remodelled in 1751. Here, the decoration is more Rococo in style and the ironwork of a high standard.

*Return northward to the open expanse of Oosterdok, right.*

**Oosterdok (East Dock)** is now earmarked as a maritime recreation area, with activities centred on the Shipping Museum. Boats of historic interest are now permanently moored at the east end of this inland lake.

*First left Kattenburgerstraat leads to the Maritime Museum.*

## 4. Maritime Museum (Scheepvaart Museum)
1 Kattenburgerplein.

Open Tuesday  – Saturday 10.00–17.00. Sundays and holidays 13.00– 17.00. Admission charge.

Model ships, with the biggest model of them all a full-sized replica of *Amsterdam*, are the greatest attraction to most visitors. Much of the museum is naturally devoted to Holland's greatest naval period, the 17th century, when its great fleet was regularly in combat with the English. It is strange to reflect that the century ended with a Dutchman on the throne of England.

Daniel Stalpaert designed the building as a great naval storehouse for the Admiralty, called the Zeemagazijn (Sea Arsenal). It was completed in 1656 and, from here, newly-built ships, and vessels in dock, were supplied with their requirements, which included armaments, sails, ropes, food and fresh water. The Dutch navy transferred its bases to North Sea ports comparatively recently, and this building then lost its purpose. Remodelling for the present museum, founded elsewhere in 1916, took place from 1974-81. Ten years later, a full-sized replica of *Amsterdam*, an 18th-century merchant vessel, was moored in Oosterdok as part of the museum, and is now its greatest attraction.

Although severely Classical, due to its commanding position and size, the precisely square, former storehouse is an imposing building, with each façade incorporating a large pediment, carved with nautical themes by Artus Quellien. The building is entered from Kattenburgerplein, via the inner courtyard, where 17th and 18th century cannon are displayed.

All the exhibits have now been captioned in English, and complete reorganisation was begun in 1992, a task that will take eight years.

As is occurring in so many museums throughout the world, a change from chronological to thematic order will be effected. All aspects of Dutch maritime history are dealt with, illustrated by models, paintings, instruments, maps, display panels etc.

From the ground floor, many will wish to proceed directly ahead to board *Amsterdam*. Throughout the 17th and 18th centuries, the Dutch East India Company (Verenigde Oostindische Compagnie), was the world's largest trading and shipping corporation. One of its ships, *Amsterdam*, was lost off the south coast of England, at Hastings, on its maiden voyage in 1749; what remains of the wreck may still be visited at low tide. Fortunately, most of the crew and cargo were saved.

The original ship took less than two years to build, but its replica involved many unskilled workers, as an employment scheme, and work that began in 1985 was not completed until 1991: the mayor of Hastings was invited to the opening ceremony.

For increased security, all Dutch merchant vessels sailed in convoy and were heavily armed. A ship such as *Amsterdam* would have had a complement of 230 on the outward voyage, but only 70 of them made the return journey, as East Indiamen had to complete seven years' service overseas. Many would also die on the boats through sickness or misadventure during the eight month journey.

Although the ship's master and mates had their own cabins, the crew slept between the guns on the main deck, in suspended hammocks, where possible, or else lying on mattresses. At all times, approximately one-third were employed on deck.

On the outward journey, the cargo consisted of gold and silver (mostly in the form of coins), textiles, wine and items for general use by the company in their Asian offices that could not be obtained locally. Return cargoes included saltpetre, spices, dyestuffs and eastern objets d'art.

*Return to the ground floor of the museum.*

Little alteration is expected to this floor, where temporary exhibitions are held. In the south-east corner, the royal barge is displayed. Powered by oarsmen, the sovereign used the vessel on ceremonial occasions. The barge, designed by C. J. Glavimans, and built at Rotterdam in 1818, will never float again, its last journey having been to transport Queen Juliana and Prince Bernhard on their Silver Wedding day in 1962. A figurehead of Neptune is flanked by Triton, and, at the stern end, Holland's coat of arms and allegorical figures of Fame are depicted.

By the summer of 1992, a new and enlarged display on the first floor featured the Dutch East Indies Company; adjacent windows overlook the ship *Amsterdam*.

The museum continues on the second floor, where it is virtually certain that the reconstructed cabins and dining rooms of pre-Second World War ocean liners will remain.

Paintings displayed include works by the two Willem van de Veldes, father and son, and a very patriotic depiction of the Battle of Gibraltar (1622) by Cornelis van Wieringen, in which the Dutch fleet gained a memorable victory over the Spanish.

Immediately north of the museum, the entrance to the long brick building, facing Kattenburgerstraat, leads to the former **Naval Wharf**.

From May 1877 to July 1878, the 24 year-old Vincent van Gogh lived here, in the house of his uncle Johannes van Gogh, known as Jan, who was a rear admiral, the highest ranking naval officer in Amsterdam and director of the wharf. His house, then numbered 3 Grote Kattenburgerstraat, formed part of the naval establishment. At present, the complex is rather dilapidated and the public are not permitted to enter.

*Return southward. First left Kattenburgergracht leads to Wittenburgergracht.*

## 5. East Church (Oosterkerk) Daniel Stalpaert, 1669

25 Wittenburgergracht

Open Mondays, Tuesdays, Wednesdays and Fridays 10.00-14.00 and for Sunday services.

Like de Keyser's North Church, Daniel Stalpaert designed this building to a Greek Cross plan, eminently suitable for centralising the position of the pulpit. The main feature of the façade is its roofline balustrade.

*Enter the church from the rear.*

An attractive blend of undecorated, pale-gold stone and white paintwork gives a luminous quality to the interior. The original pulpit, carved with a serpent theme, has the usual great sounding board found in Dutch Reformed churches.

A deep cornice, which runs around the walls of the church, appears to be of stone, but is, in fact, of wood.

Although the building serves primarily as a welfare centre, after a 20-year period, services are held here once again, as the parish church recently burnt down. Six offices, with glass partitions, have been created in the aisles, and there is generally a small exhibition.

*Leave the church and continue eastward, following Wittenburgergracht, which leads to Oostenburgergracht.*

Number **77, Oostenburgergracht**, a warehouse of 1660, retains the VOC monogram of the Dutch East Indies Company in its pediment.

Immediately right, the trapezium gable exhibits good plasterwork, also executed in 1660.

Closing the vista ahead, at the far east end of the Nieuwe Vaart canal, is the city's last windmill to survive on the eastern periphery. Erected in 1814, the **De Goyer windmill** stands in Zeeburgerstraat; its ground floor has been remodelled as a shop. If there is sufficient wind, the sails revolve on the first Saturday in the month. In former times, there were many windmills around the perimeter of the city, as can be seen from ancient maps. Their main tasks were to pump water and grind wheat. Windmills were never built in towns, as the buildings decreased the speed of the wind.

Adjoining the windmill, the smallest brewery in Amsterdam provides a highly acclaimed lager.

*Return to the west end of Zeeburgerstraat. Left Sarphatistraat. First right Hoogte Kadijk.*

## 6. 't Kromhout Shipyard/Museum (Museumwerf 't Kromhout)

147 Hoogte Kadijk

Open Monday – Friday 10.00-16.00. Admission charge.

A strong smell of tar indicates the presence of the shipyard, half way along the north side of Hoogte Kadijk. Personally, studying the history of marine engines, and observing the repair of stricken vessels, comes low in my order of priorities during a visit to Amsterdam, but those with greater mechanical and nautical interests will no doubt find 't Kromhout intensely fascinating.

On this wharf, one of the oldest still working in the city, 't Kromhout made ships of iron and steel, initially powered by steam engines. From 1873, steam power was also used in the manufacturing process. Expansion led to a move to a larger shipyard in North Amsterdam, but repair work continued here. Both structures that form the yard are covered by a cast-iron roof, erected c. 1890.

A museum in the former workshop describes the company's most important mechanical developments during the last two centuries.

Exhibited is the Kromhout 12 horse power paraffin engine. Of simple and efficient design, this was the most popular power source employed by vessels operating on the inland waterways of the Low Countries; a semi-diesel engine replaced it and was equally successful. Stairs lead to further displays and a café.

*Return eastward, following Hoogte Kadijk to its end. First right Sarphatistraat. Third left Alexanderplein.*

Facing the square and the Tropical Institute, **Muiderpoort** was built as a gateway in the city wall, by Cornelis Rauws, in 1771. The gateway is Classical in style and surmounted by a cupola, its lantern displaying a clock. Doric columns support the pediment, which has been carved with the city's arms, by K. Ziesenis.

Ahead stands the great bulk of the Tropical Institute, incorporating, to its north, the Tropical Museum.

## 7. Tropics Museum (Tropenmuseum) J. J. and M.
A. van Nieukerken

2 Linnaeusstraat

Open Monday – Friday 10.00-17.00. Saturdays and Sundays 12.00-17.00. Admission charge. An exhibition plan in English is provided.

It must be explained immediately that this museum is not connected with tropical plants or the arts and crafts of tropical countries. The prime function is to demonstrate the simple way of life of a significant proportion of the world's people, all of whom subsist well below the poverty line drawn by affluent nations. When they commissioned this great complex, the present Royal Tropical Institute was called the Colonial Institute, but times, of course, have changed.

The great pile is constructed of brick, and designed in a vaguely Dutch Renaissance Revival style, but with towers surmounted by pointed Gothic roofs. Keystones and capitals are profusely carved with themes that refer to Holland's interests in tropical countries throughout their colonial period.

**(Opposite)** *A full-sized reproduction of 'Amsterdam', a 17th-century merchant ship, is a recent acquisition of the Maritime Museum.*

*Continue northward. First right Linnaeusstraat.* Immediately right, the entrance façade of the museum is flanked by towers, decorated with reliefs that depict the world's most important religions.

Major crops from former Dutch colonies: rice, rubber, sugar and tobacco are also illustrated. Each tower has a weathervane. That to the right is in the form of the Garuda, a bird-god that has given its name to Indonesia's national airline. To the left, the vase depicts a Makara elephant head, symbolising wisdom to Hindus.

Decorative carving continues within the museum, all the work of Louis Vreugde.

The hall of the ground floor is surrounded by arcades, while the first and second floors consist of arcades only; principle themes are: Ground floor Man and Environment, Man and Technology; First floor South Asia, South-East Asia, Music, Drama and Theatre; Second floor Africa and Latin America.

Several village streets have been constructed, including local stores, the meagre contents of which are a good indicator of the low standard of living of its customers.

*Return to Alexanderplein and proceed westward. Second left Plantage Muidergracht. Cross the first bridge left to Nieuwe Achtergracht, right. Cross the front bridge, right, to the north thoroughfare of Nieuwe Achtergracht, right. First left Nieuwe Prinsengracht.*

*Alternatively, if not visiting the Geology Museum, proceed ahead from Alexanderplein, crossing the bridge to Plantage Middenlaan. First right Plantage Kerklaan and Artis Zoo.*

The **Geology Museum** (Geologisch Museum), at 130 Nieuwe Prinsengracht, open Monday to Friday 09.00-17.00, will appeal to those interested in rock formations and gemstones; entrance is free.

*From the museum, follow Nieuwe Prinsengracht westward. First right Roetersstraat leads to Plantage Kerklaan.*

**(Opposite)** *'Girly' shows are explicitly promoted in Amsterdam's surprisingly bucolic red light area.*

## 8. The Plantage

The Plantage quarter is bounded by Entrepotdok, Plantage Muidergracht and Nieuwe Herengracht.

In the 17th century, the Plantage was a pleasure garden and considered too important to permit Nieuwe Keizersgracht, Nieuwe Kerkstraat and Nieuwe Prinsengracht to be extended through it. Remnants of the garden survive as the Artis Zoo and the Botanical Gardens, but the rest was lost in the 18th century, when a high-class housing development was begun. Wealthy Amsterdammers built country villas on large plots of land, approached from leafy lanes, high walls or fences being compulsory. One original house survives (at no. 72 Middenweg) and its gardens are open to the public in summer. The Plantage, with its large, stuccoed houses, remains popular with well-heeled Amsterdammers in retirement.

## 9. Artis Zoo and Planetarium

38-40 Plantage Kerklaan

Open daily 09.00-17.00 (closes at 18.00 in summer). Admission charge.

Founded in 1838, Amsterdam's is the oldest public zoo in Europe. An English guidebook is in preparation but not expected to be available until 1994.

Wherever possible, animals are protected from human beings by a ditch, rather than iron bars, and this park-like zoo, with its stunning floral displays, gives the impression of being far away from the centre of a great metropolis.

Most animals normally expected in an important zoo are on view but the aquarium, built by the Salm brothers, in Neo Classical style, is exceptional. Also not to be missed is the reptile house.

Within the complex, but involving an additional admission charge, the new Planetarium includes a permanent exhibition. Shows are held regularly throughout the day.

*From the zoo, exit left and follow Plantage Kerklaan southward. First right Plantage Middenlaan.*

## 10. Former Dutch Theatre (Hollandse Schouwburg)

24 Plantage Middenlaan

Open throughout the day. Admission free.

In 1941, the Dutch Theatre was given to Amsterdam Jews, then numerous in the Plantage, in which to perform their own plays, but, in June the following year, Hitler's 'final solution' was put into effect and the building became a transit camp for deportees. More than 50,000 Jews were assembled in the former theatre, before being transported, after long waits in appalling conditions, to Westerbork labour camp, from whence trains took them to German concentration camps.

After the Second World War, the building was presented to the city with the condition that a memorial chapel should be created within; in the event, the entire site became a memorial.

Only the façade and, at the rear, sections of the walls of the stage, have survived, the remainder was in a poor condition and demolished.

Within the small chapel, a flame burns in a bronze wall bracket. The stone slabs, symbolising a father, a mother and a child, stand in earth brought from Israel. Inscribed in the wall, in Hebrew and Dutch, are words from Psalm 119 'My soul melteth for heaviness, strengthen thou me according to thy word.'

A cloistered garden has replaced the auditorium. At its end survive parts of the walls of the stage. In the centre of where this had been, stands a basalt column on a Star of David base. Behind it are the words 'To the memory of those taken from here'.

Opposite the building, at **no. 27** the IVKO teacher training college now occupies the building that had served as a crèche for young Jewish children from 1942-45. Some escaped deportation with the aid of Dutch sympathisers, and a plaque 'to those who saved the children' records their help.

*Exit left and follow Plantage Middenlaan to its west end.*

## 11. Botanical Gardens (Hortus Botanicus)

2 Plantage Middenlaan

Open Monday – Friday 09.00-17.00. Saturdays and Sundays 11.00-17.00. From 1 October until 31 March the gardens shut daily at 16.00. Admission charge.

The gardens include tropical and sub-tropical specimens, most of which are under glass. In 1682, the area was laid out as pleasure grounds for residents of the Plantage, eventually including a herb garden for medical use. Exotic specimens were brought back from the East Indies by merchants, and these formed the basis of the display.

On the wall of the former Orangery, now a coffee shop, the names of the varieties in bloom that day are listed.

In Palm House F, a 400-year old cycad (palm fern) is believed to be the world's oldest potted plant in existence. A lotus tank and carniverous plants are features of the Tropical House.

*Exit left. First left Nieuwe Herengracht. First right Weesperstraat leads to Mr Visserplein. First left Waterlooplein. Waterlooplein Metro Station may be entered from the east side of the Opera House/ Town Hall complex.*

ROUTE 7

# The Great Art Galleries and Vondelpark

The Rijksmuseum, incorporating the world's most important collection of 17th century Dutch painters, and the Vincent Van Gogh Museum, Amsterdam's greatest tourist attraction, are included on this route. However, unless the visitor is very selective, or excessively pressed for time, to enter both on the same day is not advisable. Fortunately, these galleries, together with the Stedelijk (for Impressionist and later modern masters) are conveniently situated, and return visits to this 'museum quarter' are easily made.

## Timing

- Apart from Vondelpark, the locations on this route are particularly suitable if the weather is poor.
- The Rijksmuseum is closed on Mondays, as is the Vincent Van Gogh Museum, apart from the Easter to September period. Both museums are also closed on Sunday mornings.
- After remodelling, the Film Museum will probably close again from Saturday to Monday.

## Locations for Route 7

1. Rijksmuseum
2. Coster Diamonds
3. Vincent Van Gogh Museum
4. Stedelijk Museum
5. Concertgebouw
6. Film Museum
7. Vondelpark
8. Dutch Riding School

## Start: Stadhouderskade (Rijksmuseum)

*Trams 6, 7, 10 or, to Leidseplein, trams 1, 2, 5 and then a short walk eastward.*

## 1. Rijksmuseum

42 Stadhouderskade

Open Tuesday – Saturday 10.00-17.00, Sundays and holidays 13.00–17.00. Admission charge.

Many art lovers come to Amsterdam chiefly to visit the Rijksmuseum, such is its renown since it opened here in 1885. The great painting collection is the museum's chief attraction, as it includes the world's finest display of Dutch works from the 17th century 'Golden Age'. Rembrandt, of course, takes pride of place, his immense *The Night Watch* serving as the Rijksmuseum's *Mona Lisa*, so to speak. Foreign painters are sparsely represented, as the museum does not rival international collections such as those at London's National Gallery or the Louvre, in Paris.

Louis-Napoléon was responsible for consolidating much of the present collection in the Royal Palace from 1808. Works were gradually added and, in 1815, the Rijksmuseum was established at Trippenhuis.

P. J. H. Cuypers, the architect of Central Station, was commissioned to design the present building, and work began in 1877, lasting eight years. Cuypers, a Catholic, was much influenced by Viollet-le-Duc, the French architect responsible for restoring many of his country's Gothic monuments.

Steeply-pitched roofs and pointed towers are 16th-century Gothic features, but Renaissance elements are also to be found. As at Central Station, sculptures and tiles depict applicable themes, symbolising, in this case, the arts, Dutch history and the glorification of Amsterdam. The general layout of the building, constructed with four corner pavilions around two courtyards, is remarkably similar to that of the Royal Palace, although, of course, its detailing is quite different. Both courtyards have been roofed to provide additional exhibition space.

A completely remodelled entrance from Stadhouderskade was completed in 1991, in time for the special Rembrandt exhibition. It replaced, not before time, a revolving door, that had always restricted entrance to and exit from the building. However, if queues are long, the alternative entrance, at 19 Hobbemastraat (basement level), may still be more convenient.

A museum plan is available, at a nominal price, which shows that exhibits are displayed on the basement, ground and first floor levels.

At the reception desk, on presentation of a passport, a complimentary ticket to visit the Six Collection (in Amstel) may be obtained.

When the Rembrandt exhibition ended, in March 1992, a complete reorganisation of the Rijksmuseum was begun. At the time of writing, details of repositioning are not available, nor is the timetable for the changes. It is not, therefore, possible to indicate the locations of the works, which will eventually be grouped thematically.

In addition to around 5,000 paintings, from the 15th to the late 19th century, the museum covers Sculpture and Applied Art, Dutch History (up to and including the Second World War). Asiatic Art, and Study Collections. Temporary Exhibitions are also held.

## The Night Watch

Every first-time visitor to the Rijksmuseum will want to see Rembrandt's *The Night Watch*, which once more faces down the gallery of honour on the first floor, a position that it occupied when the museum opened, in 1885. This painting will probably not be moved during the museum's reorganisation; a nearby display relates its history.

'The Company of Captain Frans Banning Cocq and Lieutenant Willem van Ruijtenburch', as *The Night Watch* is officially entitled, marks the culmination of Dutch painters' efforts to breathe life into group portraits of the Civic Guard Companies. These paintings were commissioned to hang in the Great Hall (Doelen) of the Company, and members depicted paid the painter according to the prominence that they received. Captain Cocq's Company was the Kloveniers, a kloven being a 16th-century firearm, predecessor of the musket. It has been said that when the painting was completed, in 1642, it was not well received by the Company, but there is no justification for this allegation.

Eventually, Civic Guards were disbanded, and the Kloveniers Great Hall became an auction room. In 1715, the painting was transferred to the Town Hall, where it was cut down on all four sides to fit a space between two doors. From old copies, we learn that the greatest damage was to the left-hand side where two figures were lost.

When the Rijksmuseum was inaugurated, at Trippenhuis, in 1815, *The Night Watch*, as the painting had been called for just seven years, due to discolouration, immediately became a popular exhibit. Anticipating the German proclivity for acquiring works of art for the fatherland during the Second World War, *The Night Watch* was hidden in several locations between 1939 and 1945. Soon after the danger had passed, cleaning revealed that the painting could not possibly depict a nocturnal scene; however, the established name has stuck and virtually nobody ever uses the correct, lengthy appellation. In spite of being cut down, *The Night Watch* remains one of Rembrandt's largest works. Much of its fame rests on the dramatic use of chiaroscuro, combined with the extraordinary sense of vivacity that the artist has achieved.

### Rembrandt van Rijn 1606–69

The Rijksmuseum possesses 19 paintings that appear to be bona fide works by Rembrandt; London's National Gallery boasts 20. As in several other museums, examples that were once believed to be genuine no longer are. Throughout his career, Rembrandt was primarily inspired by Biblical themes and the human face, particularly elderly subjects. His dramatic, Baroque use of chiaroscuro was unique, as was his ability to probe the depths of his sitters' personalities.

Particularly renowned, in addition to *The Night Watch*, are; *The Anatomy Lesson of Jan Deyman, The Syndics of the Drapers Guild, Portrait of Saskia van Uylenburgh* (his wife) and *The Jewish Bride*. It has been suggested that the two paintings, *Tobit and Anna*, and *Hannah*, may both feature portraits of Rembrandt's mother, but this is not certain.

### Frans Hals 1581/1585(?)–1666

The first great Dutch painter of the 17th century, Hals does not appear to have painted until he was nearly 30. During the 50 years that he worked, his themes were restricted to portraiture or genre paintings, emphasising figures. Outstanding works include: *Lucas de Clercq and his Wife, Feyntje van Steenkiste, The Meagre Company* (its right hand side completed by Pieter Codde), *The Merry Drinker, Nicolaes Hasselaer,* and *Sarah Wolphaerts van Diemen.*

### Johann (Jan) Vermeer 1632–75

Generally regarded as Holland's greatest 17th-century master, after Rembrandt, only 31 works by Vermeer (of Delft) survive; there are no drawings, letters or even notes. He was the master of domestic interiors, a velvety softness of both line and chiaroscuro being his hallmark. Vermeer was converted to Roman Catholicism c.1653.

Among the works displayed are: *Young Woman Reading a Letter, The Love Letter, The Kitchen Maid* and *A Street in Delft*.

### Pieter de Hooch 1629–after 1688

A contemporary of Vermeer, de Hooch was another genre painter from Delft. Only work from his middle period, 1655-62, is regarded as inspired; on his move to Amsterdam the spark of genius left him. His best works are reminiscent of Vermeer, but he bathed his scenes in a golden light that contrasts with Vermeer's coolness - colours are also deeper and more brilliant. Exhibits from his great period include *The Pantry* and *The Linen Cupboard*.

### Johannes (Jan) Steen 1625/1626(?)–1679

Jan Steen, who was born and died at Leiden, was itinerant throughout his career, never, however, residing in Amsterdam. He is famous for depicting roisterous scenes and chaotic interiors; like Vermeer, Steen was an innkeeper. The most prolific of the great Dutch masters, literally hundreds of his paintings survive, not all of them, however, of the highest quality. Splendid examples at the Rijksmuseum include: *The Feast of St. Nicholas, After the Drinking Bout, Christ at Emmaus, The Adoration of the Shepherds, Young Lady Pulling off her Stocking* and *The Laughing Baker's Shop*.

### Jacob van Ruisdael 1628/1629(?)–1682

Holland's greatest landscape painter, van Ruisdael introduced a greater strength into Dutch paintings of this type, particularly noticeable when compared with the work of his uncle, Salomon van Ruysdael. In his last period, 1670-82, Ruisdael's work followed the general decline in Dutch painting, marked by weaker composition. Not to be missed are: *Windmill at Wijk*, *View of Haarlem* and *Winter Landscape*.

It is perhaps invidious to select works from the other great masters represented, particularly as much depends on personal taste, however, the following will impress most – for varying reasons:

Albert Cuyp, *Landscape with two Horsemen*
Pieter Saenredam, I*nterior of St. Bavo Church*
Willem van der Velde, the Younger, *The IJ at Amsterdam*
Hendrick Cornelisz Vroom, *Battle of Gibraltar*
Jan van der Cappelle, *The State Barge Saluted by the Home Fleet*
Joannes Verspronck, *Girl in a Light Blue Dress*

Adriaen van Ostade, *Fish Seller*
Jan van der Heyden, *Martelaarsgracht*
Batholomeus van der Helst, *Portrait of Andries Bicker* and *Portrait of Princess Maria Henrietta Stuart*
Ferdinand Bol, *Portrait of Elizabeth Bas*
Hendrick Avercamp, *Enjoying the Ice*

Outstanding from the Gothic period are:
The Master of Alkmaar, *Seven Works of Charity*
The Master of Brunswick, *The Birth*
Jan Vermeyen, *Wedding at Canaan*
Geertgen tot St. Jans, *The Adoration of the Magi* and *The Tree of Jesse.*

A small foreign collection includes works by Fra Angelico, Veronese (an attribution), Goya, Jordaens and Rubens.

In the Dutch History section, a huge *Battle of Waterloo*, by Willem Pieneman, depicts Wellington in the centre, whilst the wounded Prince of Orange is born away on a stretcher. There are also Meissen porcelain figures, huge dolls houses from the 17th century, and Asiatic Art, all superb but more specialised attractions, which many will wish to view on later visits.

*Exit from the museum left, following Stadhouderskade. First left Jan Luijkenstraat. First left Hobbemastraat. First right Paulus Potterstraat. Coster Diamonds occupies the corner building.*

## 2. Coster Diamonds

2-4 Paulus Potterstraat

Open for guided tours daily 09.00-17.00. Admission free.

This is one of the largest of the many diamond merchants in Amsterdam that are open to the general public. A little is learned about the stages involved in producing a cut diamond, but the main purpose is to sell stones to the visitors, not to instruct, a fact that quickly becomes obvious.

The diamond trade in Amsterdam evolved in 1586, when established Jewish merchants fled the Spanish occupation of Antwerp, fearing the Inquisition.

A guide will explain that an uncut diamond is first bisected and then given a 'brilliant' cut, to provide 58 facets - the tiny surfaces, set at angles, that give the stone its light-reflecting qualities. The less colour that a diamond has, the greater its value. Visitors are not permitted to view the cutting process; however, polishing, the final stage, is demonstrated.

The Koh-i-Noor diamond, since 1937 the centrepiece of Queen Elizabeth the Queen Mother's Crown, was recut and polished for Queen Victoria in 1852 by two members of Costers' staff, to enhance its brilliance. Work, lasting 38 days, was commissioned by Garrard's and executed at their London premises. The Duke of Wellington witnessed part of the proceedings, which reduced the diamond's weight from 186 carats to approximately 109 carats (one carat = 0.2 grams).

*Exit left and follow Paulus Potterstraat southward.*

## 3. Vincent van Gogh Museum

7 Paulus Potterstraat

Open Tuesday – Saturday (Also Mondays Easter – September) 10.00–17.00. Sundays and holidays 13.00–17.00. Admission charge.

Such is the current popularity of Vincent van Gogh, that this museum has become Amsterdam's top tourist attraction. More than 200 paintings are on permanent display.

Vincent Willem van Gogh was born at Zundert, South Holland, in 1853. Although regarded as one of the great modern masters, it is a surprise to most to learn that he saw nothing of the present century, dying at Auvers-sur-Oise, northern France, in 1890. Equally surprising is the fact that van Gogh made his first drawing as late as 1880, aged 27, and produced his first oil painting two years later. Therefore, all of van Gogh's works – a legacy of 800 oil paintings and 700 drawings – were accomplished during the last 10 years of his life.

Vincent, the eldest of six children born to a pastor, also proposed to follow a career in the Dutch Reformed Church, but could not pass his exams. Although he worked for art dealers in London and Paris in his early twenties, apparently van Gogh was not immediately inspired to paint himself. Like most Dutchmen, he was an accomplished linguist and taught languages in London, in addition to lay-preaching. Whilst there, Vincent fell in love with an English girl, but suffered the first of his many rejections, events that may have led to his subsequent mental disorder.

Missionary work in Borinage, the coal-mining region of Belgium, brought van Gogh into contact with abject poverty, and he was inspired to give all his possessions away, an act that sowed the seeds for his own perpetual lack of money. In the same year, 1880, he began to draw, at last discovering his true vocation.

Although beginning to experiment with oils in 1882, Vincent's work, until 1884, consisted mainly of drawings and watercolours. In 1885, he spent three months studying art at the Antwerp Academy. It was during his stay, with brother Theo, in the Montmartre quarter of Paris, from March 1886 to February 1888, however, that van Gogh's palette brightened due, no doubt, to the influence of the Impressionists, most of whom he met. Towards the end of his stay, with the painting of *Père Tanguy*, Vincent had finally developed his mature style, founding Post Impressionism and pointing the way for the Expressionists. However, sales of his works did not transpire, and it was only the fraternal generosity of Theo that enabled Vincent to continue as an artist.

In February 1888, van Gogh left Paris for Arles, in the South of France, and was immediately enchanted by the clarity and brightness of the Provençal light. It was now that his truly great work began. In October that year, Paul Gauguin shared accommodation with Vincent at Arles and they stayed together until the end of December. It appears that their relationship soon became strained, possibly due to van Gogh's developing mental problems. On Christmas Eve, Vincent, apparently in remorse for threatening Gauguin with a cut-throat razor the day before, sliced off part of his left ear; not surprisingly, Gauguin decided it was time to go.

Within four months, the artist, at his own volition, was admitted to the lunatic asylum at St. Rémy-de-Provence. Here, he continued to paint at a furious pace, his line becoming even more vigorous and uninhibited.

Discharging himself in May 1890, Vincent returned to the Paris region, but, as Theo had married, resided with Dr. Gachet, a homeopathic specialist, at his home in Auvers-sur-Oise. By 29 July, Vincent was dead, shot by his own hand, beside his last painting, in the fields of Auvers. Its subject, a menacing flock of black crows, seems ominously prophetic. Six months later, Theo was also dead – of a chronic disorder of the kidneys.

During his lifetime, only one painting by Vincent van Gogh was sold, and only one critic referred to his work. By the turn of the century, however, his position as a modern master was already assured. Experts disagree on the extent to which Vincent's mental depression affected his work; the artist contracted syphilis, but it seems likely that loneliness, leading to excessive introspection, also played an important part.

Most of the exhibits displayed originated as the collection of Theo van Gogh, and the museum opened in 1973 in the present five-storey building, which was commissioned from G. T. Rietveld and Partners.

Two hundred paintings, 500 drawings and 700 letters form what is by far the world's largest collection of van Gogh's work.

Temporary exhibitions are held on the ground and third floors (lift available), whilst graphic works by Vincent and other artists are displayed, thematically, on the second floor. However, most will wish to proceed directly to the first floor, where van Gogh's paintings are supplemented by the works of contemporary artists that he had collected himself.

Although many of the paintings, which are displayed chronologically, are well-known through popular reproduction, the latter, of course, lack the third dimension, a particularly important feature of Vincent's oils, due to his heavy impasto. Important works not to miss include: *In the Field,* 1883; *Peasant Woman in a Red Bonnet,* 1885; *The Potato Eaters,* 1885; *Skull with a Cigarette,* 1886; *View of Arles with Irises* 1888; *Self-Portrait in Front of an Easel,* 1888; and *Pietà,* 1889.

During the April 1991 robbery from the museum, three paintings were damaged before the haul was recovered the following day; these are being restored but will probably not be exhibited until 1993.

*Exit from the museum left and continue southward.*

## 4. Stedelijk Museum

13 Paulus Potterstraat

Open daily 11.00-17.00. Admission charge.

The Stedelijk municipal museum is primarily an art gallery. Its exhibits continue from the late 19th century, the point at which those in the Rijksmuseum end. There are three floors, but most of the space is given over to temporary exhibitions, which are altered every four to five weeks. Unless the subject of the temporary exhibition attracts, most will wish to proceed, by lift, directly to the second floor, where, in rooms 223-27, works by modern masters are displayed. A leaflet is provided that explains the layout of the museum and the location of the permanent collection, by artist.

The permanent collection of the Stedelijk Museum is based on that of Sophia Augusta Lopez-Suasso, with later additions. It is housed in a building designed by A. Weissmann (1885-95).

An enormous late Matisse cut-out (1952) covers the entire wall of room 225A, left of the stairwell. It is entitled *La Perruche et la Sirène* (Parakeet and Mermaid).

Room 223 includes a *Mont Ste Victoire* and a *Still Life*, by Cézanne, four van Gogh's, one of which is the famous portrait, *La Berceuse*, and a study by Monet for *A Bar at the Folies Bergère*, surprisingly different from the final version in London's Courtauld Institute Galleries.

Piet Mondrian, Holland's most famous painter of the present century, makes his first appearance in Room 224, but in works that pre-date his renowned 'neo-plastic' period, which began c. 1920.

Five magical crayons, by Odilon Redon, illuminate Room 225.

Abstracts by Mondrian, in Room 226, are the only examples of his 'neo-plastic' work that can be seen in Amsterdam. Here also are paintings by Malevitch.

Finally, in Room 227, Picasso and Rouault are represented.

Approached only from van Baerlestraat, which runs immediately south of the Stedelijk, sculptures are displayed on a small lawn. They include a Henry Moore reclining figure of 1957.

Opposite, on the van Breestraat corner, **Small Talk** is one of the few Amsterdam restaurants where brown bean soup served with smoked ham, a Dutch speciality, can be obtained throughout the year.

*Proceed eastward towards the Concertgebouw.*

**Restaurant/Bodega de Keyzer** occupies the J. W. Brouwerstraat corner, at no. 96 van Baerlestraat. It opened in 1905 and retains much of the original, fin-de-siècle decor, with dark woodwork relieved by ferns predominating.

## 5. Concertgebouw A. L. van Gendt 1888

2-6 Concertgebouwplein

Booking office open daily 10.00-19.00

Due to the exceptional acoustics of its concert hall, and the consistently high quality of its conductors, the Royal Concertgebouw orchestra has gained a world-wide reputation in the field of classical music. During the summer months, however, it is more likely that a visiting orchestra will be performing.

The Concertgebouw Orchestra was founded in 1888 by Willem Kes, who insisted that audiences should be seated in rows rather than, as formerly, at tables attended by waiters. Willem Mengelberg, just 24 years old, was appointed chief conductor in 1895, a position that he held until 1954. Mengelberg created a distinctive sound for the orchestra, thereby establishing its fame. Edward van Beinum took over, but his reign was much shorter, as he died at rehearsal in 1959. Bernard Haitink and Eugen Jochem then became joint chief conductors, but finally, in 1963, Haitink was appointed the orchestra's sole chief conductor, and remained so for 25 years. On his transfer to London, as conductor of the Royal Opera House orchestra, the first non-Dutchman replaced him, the Italian, Riccardo Chailly.

Central European theatres, Vienna's in particular, have inspired the design of this Neo-Classical building, completed in 1888 by A. L. van Gendt. Structural problems became apparent in 1983, and the original piles had to be replaced. Work began two years later on transferring the 10,000-ton edifice to new piles, necessitating the closure of the hall until 11 April 1988, when it was re-opened with a gala concert.

To mark its centenary, Queen Beatrix awarded the Concertgebouw Orchestra the prefix Royal. Architect Pi de Bruijn added basement-level facilities and a wing, facing Concertgebouwplein, which incorporated a new entrance foyer and an upper, projecting gallery, supported by piers. Fronted in glass, the latter feature was much criticised as being unsympathetic to the style of the original building.

Prior to this extension, the entrance to the Concertgebouw had been from Van Baerlestraat; what is now Concertgebouwplein was then known as J. W. Brouwersplein, its name being changed in 1988 to mark the centenary of the building. Bookings for concerts may be made up to one month in advance.

*Return westward. Second left Willemsparkweg.*

**Number 15** is a violin shop of great charm.

*Return to Van Baerlestraat, left. Fifth left Vondelstraat. Take the first entrance, left, to Vondelpark.*

## 6. Film Museum (Nederlands Filmmuseum)

3 Vondelpark

Opening times are yet to be established, but these will probably be Tuesday – Friday 10.00-17.00. There is an admission charge.

The museum, situated just within the park, is housed in a splendid building, Vondelpark Paviljoen, by P. J. and W. Hamer (1881). Wholesale alterations began in 1991 and it is unclear, at the time of writing, exactly what the museum will comprise when this has been completed. Formerly, the museum occupied only the ground floor, exhibits including early methods of creating the illusion of movement, and a stereoscopic 'Kaiserpanorama' (Emperors Panorama).

Video presentations described the history of the cinema and the work of restoring old nitrate film stock. Three or four films were shown daily in a small cinema, many of them from the 1920s; a free monthly programme gave details.

*Exit to the park.*

## 7. Vondelpark

Open 24 hours daily. Admission free.

Although not Amsterdam's largest open space, Vondelpark is the most popular in the entire country, receiving almost eight million visitors each year.

Formerly open fields, Z. D. Zocher began to lay out the park in 1865, L. P. Zocher and J. J. Kerbert giving assistance. Peaty soil proved a major difficulty, due to its tendency to sink, and much of the present top soil had to be brought from elsewhere to raise the level, work taking 12 years to complete. The Zocher family specialised in the removal of Holland's ancient town walls and converting their ramparts to parks.

Vondelpark stretches northward, beneath Huygensstraat, almost to Singelgracht, where the main gates, designed by A. Linneman in 1883, are to be found.

A statue near the Film Museum commemorates Holland's greatest poet **Joost van den Vondel** (1587-1679), after whom the park is named. It is the work of L. Royer, 1867, and stands on a pedestal designed by P. J. H. Cuypers.

During fine weather, from June to August, concerts are given afternoons and evenings in the **Open Air Theatre** (Openlucht Theater), admission free.

Refreshments may be obtained from the pre-war **Theehuis** (Tea House).

On Queens Day (April 30) and Liberation Day (5 May), traders are permitted to set up stalls in the park.

*Exit to Vondelstraat.*

## 8. Dutch Riding School (Hollandsche Manege)
A. L. van Gendt, 1881

140 Vondelstraat

Open most of the day. Admission free.

Built by the Concertgebouw's architect, a charming, 19th-century atmosphere prevails and visitors are most welcome. A long passageway leads to the rectangular sandpit, where riders parade their horses. All is Baroque Revival in style, with two ends balustrated.

Ascend the stairs, left, to the first floor café, from where there are good views of the proceedings.

*Descend and exit left.*

Closing the vista to the north, in the centre of an oval circus, stands the former **Vondelkerk**, by P. J. H. Cuypers, 1872-80. Entirely Neo-Gothic, it is regarded as the masterpiece of this architect, who was also responsible for designing the houses in the circus.

Unfortunately, the interior of the church was vandalised, 1979-85, whilst locked up, and conversion to offices took place in 1986.

*Continue northward. Second right Huygensstraat. Third left Pieter Cornelisz Hooftstraat.*

This is Amsterdam's most chic shopping street, (usually abbreviated to **P. C. Hooftstraat**), refreshingly, many of the fashion goods offered are Dutch in origin, the shops of greatest appeal mostly being located at the north end. Style and high quality are their hallmark.

Little is of exceptional interest architecturally, although **no. 118**, remodelled by the American Post-Modernist, Robert Stern, using Art Deco themes, has an amusing 'tulip' entrance.

A higgledy-piggledy shop 'display', at no. 62, comprises cotton reels and buttons, in startling contrast with the sophisticated presentation of luxury items to be admired in the neighbouring windows. Apparently, the venerable owner declined the blandishments of property developers, preferring to stay put and continue her old-established business.

**Sama Sebo**, no. 27, is one of the city's most popular Indonesian restaurants in the higher price range (also see restaurant listing).

*At Singelgracht, ahead, Stadhouderskade, right, leads to the Rijksmuseum and trams 6, 7 and 10. Alternatively, and for most visitors preferably, follow Stadhouderskade westward to Leidseplein, second right, for trams 1, 2 and 5.*

ROUTE 8

# Leidseplein and South Amsterdam

I must confess to regarding most of this route as a 'mopping-up' operation, intended for those who have spent a lengthy time in, or already made many visits to, the city. Few are likely to treat it as an itinerary. Nevertheless, enthusiasts of modern architecture will certainly want to see the examples of work by the Amsterdam School, concentrated around Amstelkanal, and most visitors enjoy the lively, if overpriced, ambience of Leidseplein.

## Timing

- The former Heineken Brewery may be visited Monday - Friday 09.00-10.30, and, from time to time, at 13.00. Saturday visits are being considered.
- The Albert Cuypstraat market functions Monday - Saturday.
- The Resistance Museum is closed Mondays, Saturdays and Sunday mornings.
- The Tram Museum operates from Easter to late October, Sundays 10.30-17.30 – and also, in June and July, Tuesdays, Wednesdays, Thursdays and Saturday afternoons.

## Locations for Route 8

1. Leidseplein
2. Municipal Theatre
3. Former Heineken Brewery
4. Albert Cuypstraat Market
5. Sarphati Park
6. Amsterdam School Architecture
7. Resistance Museum
8. Electric Tramline Museum
9. Amsterdam Woods

## Start: Leidseplein

Trams 1, 2, 5, 6, 7, 10.

## 1. Leidseplein

Although larger and more open in nature, Leidseplein is, in some ways, the Leicester Square of Amsterdam. Once a high class shopping and entertainment area, it is now the fast-food outlets, buskers and terraced cafés that dominate. Prices charged for quick sustenance are the highest in the city, partly due, it is claimed, to the high rentals that the vendors have to pay.

Because of the vast quantities of chips and mayonnaise sold and consumed, the square has been referred to by its detractors as 'La Place de la Mayonnaise'. Nevertheless, the large crowds of tourists and normally well-behaved youngsters that throng here throughout most of the year impart a lively quality, and Leidseplein is still regarded with affection by the majority of Amsterdammers. In winter, Leidseplein becomes an ice rink and skates may be hired.

Progressing anti-clockwise from its north end, the oldest feature in the square, at no. 24, on the Korte Leidsedwarsstraat corner, is the **'t Swarte Schaep** restaurant, occupying a 17th-century building. It is one of the few top-grade restaurants near the city centre to open for lunch (also see restaurant listing).

On the south-east corner of Kleine-Gartmanplantsoen stands a Classical Revival building, by A. Jacot, 1911. This was commissioned by Hirsch, a very large department store, but has been converted to offices and a ground floor bank.

At no. 28, in the south-west corner, the **American Hotel**, designed by Willem Kromhout, was built 1898-1902. Kromhout played a major part in the development of the Amsterdam School, preferring, like Berlage, to eschew the then fashionable revival of former styles. The juxtaposition here of loggias, castellated oriel windows and vaguely Dutch Renaissance dormers demonstrates Kromhout's Expressionist tendencies.

Internally, the famous café is no longer quite so impressive, nevertheless, its stained glass windows, depicting birds and medieval figures, the vaulted ceiling and the Art-Deco lighting have survived the modifications intact.

## 2. Municipal Theatre (Stadsschouwburg)

J. L. Springer, 1894

26 Leidseplein

Daily guided tours in summer.

The architect, Springer, who was assisted in this work by A. L. van Gendt, returned to Amsterdam from London, where he had participated in the design of Frascati's restaurant in Oxford Street, demonstrating his decorative talents. Here, a Renaissance Revival building was stipulated, which would display a great deal of ornate embellishment, depicting theatrical themes. Unfortunately, cuts in the budget precluded most of the decoration, which might have brought the building to life. On completion, the design of the theatre was heavily condemned, virtually ending the distraught Springer's career.

It is unfortunate that the building projects so far, disturbing the rectangular format of the square.

Internally, the auditorium has been likened to an iced wedding cake. Basically Classical, pillars, gilded figures and velvet upholstery result in an agreeable if 'sugary' appearance.

*Follow Lange Leidsedwarsstraat eastward from the north end of Leidseplein.*

**Lange Leidsedwarsstraat** is now mainly devoted to restaurants in the lower price range. Best known, as it remains open until the early hours of the morning, is **Bojo**, at no. 51. Purporting to offer Indonesian dishes – most of which should be fiery - only the bland Dutch taste is catered for. Asking politely in advance if my beef rendang could be spiced-up to approach the genuine article, I was advised to go away and eat chips instead. I did, and had a better meal. Definitely not recommended unless ravenous at two o'clock in the morning.

At the end of the street, Spiegelgracht runs northward to link with Nieuwe Spiegelstraat. Between them and Kerkstraat, which crosses the latter street, they offer what is claimed to be the world's highest concentration of antique shops. If searching for a vintage map or print of Amsterdam, **Old Prints**, at no. 27, generally has a splendid selection.

*Proceed to the south thoroughfare of Prinsengracht, which marks the junction of Spiegelgracht and Nieuwe Spiegelstraat. Turn right and follow the canal eastward.*

**Deutzenhofje**, nos. 857-897, was built as almshouses for poor female members of the Dutch Reformed Church, by Pieter Adolfse de Zeeuw, in 1695. The entrance pilasters and the cornice, decorated with putti, predict the coming 18th-century taste.

*Return westward to Weteringstraat, first left. First right Eerste Weteringdwarsstraat.*

Numbers 11-43, with identical bell gables, were built as **Grill's Hofje**, for elderly ladies, 1721-31. The entrances to pairs of houses are shared.

*Return to Weteringstraat and turn right. Second left Derde Weteringdwarsstraat.*

**Weavers houses**, at nos. 27-33, built by Philips Vingboons in 1670, are survivors from the 400 that once stood in Amsterdam. The entrance frontage is still of timber.

*Continue ahead to Vijzelgracht, first left.*

Just before the Prinsengracht intersection (third left), no. 2, the **Consular Général de France**, a plain Classical block, is the work of Adriaan Dortsman, 1669.

*Return southward, following Vijzelgracht, to the south side of Singelgracht. First left Stadhouderskade.*

## 3. Former Heineken Brewery

78 Stadhouderskade

Open Monday – Friday 09.00-10.30, sometimes also 13.00. Saturday opening is under consideration. Admission charge (nominal).

A revised two-hour presentation for visitors to this former brewery was inaugurated in 1991, to coincide with the opening of the new entrance (visits formerly began at the Eerste van der Helststraat gate).

Since the transfer to other locations in 1988, it has no longer been possible to observe, in Amsterdam, the brewing of Heineken beer, or activities directly connected with it. The new tour, subject to alteration, consists of an audiovisual presentation, visits to the stables and the old brew house, a film show and a reception. Tickets may only be purchased on the day, and a maximum of 100 people can be catered for at any one time. Prospective visitors should consider whether the complimentary lager and cheese sandwiches are important enough to warrant spending so much time taking part in what is now little more than a public relations exercise. At the time of writing, Heineken was available in the United Kingdom, as lager brewed in Holland, but also, in virtually indistinguishable bottles, as British imitation lager, brewed in England, a marketing nightmare for the company.

*Exit right. First right Eerste van der Helststraat.*

**Kokenbier**, no. 51, although not particularly venerable, is a popular brown bar for the Albert Cuypstraat market stallholders, and lacks the 'museum' feel that some of this genre possess. The ceiling is a good brown example, but the tiled bar and floor are modern.

At the south end of the street, a small square, **Gerard Douplein**, retains some low-rise buildings that predate the 19th-century development of the area, which is known as **De Pijp** (The Pipe). The reason for this name is a mystery: it has been suggested that the gently curving route followed by many of the streets, resembling the shape of a ceramic Gouda pipe, is its source, but this is conjecture.

Prior to the commencement of speculative building in 1868, the area was mostly open fields interspersed with canals, beside which stood windmills operating wood saws. Owners of the mills were able to delay the filling of the canals until 1889.

*Follow Albert Cuypstraat eastward from the south side of the square.*

## 4. Albert Cuypstraat Market

It is claimed that the market, which has operated in this street since the 1920s, is the largest of its type in Europe. Open every day except Sunday, many stalls are doing business by 08.00, and goods are sold until 17.00; some side streets are also involved on Saturdays, when the market is expanded. A wide variety of goods are offered, but it is the fruit and vegetables that attract most Amsterdammers, late Saturday evening being the bargain time, particularly for perishable fruits.

Albert Cuypstraat is significantly wider than other streets in De Pijp; this is because it was originally a major canal, named Zaagmolensloot, a reference to the sawing mills that lined its banks.

*First right Eerste Sweelinckstraat leads to Sarphati Park.*

## 5. Sarphati Park

Opened in 1885, the name of the park commemorates Dr Samuel Sarphati, a town-planner, who was responsible for much of the appearance of south-east Amsterdam.

Included in Sarphati's plans was this park, but he envisaged a much larger area. However, Amsterdammers are lucky to have an open space here at all, as it was originally planned that Central Station would be built on its site instead of in the harbour.

Sarphati Park has been compared with Parc Monceau, in Paris, but there is a long lake and trees rather than follies, and it is more reminiscent of London's St. James's Park. There is, as might be expected, a monument to Samuel Sarphati, erected in 1886.

A children's zone occupies the south-east corner.

Many North Africans and Turks have lived in the area since the 1960s and, at times, the park may appear to be an Islamic enclave.

*Ceintuurbaan runs north-eastward from the south side of Sarphati Park.*

**Numbers 251-55**, a Neo-Gothic pile, built by A. C. Boerma in 1885, is referred to as the House of the Gnomes, referring to the two figures playing ball at upper level.

*Continue ahead to Amsteldijk, right.*

On the opposite side of the river (unnecessary to cross) at no. 23, Weesperzijde, **IJsbreker** (pronounced and meaning ice-breaker) is a café with an adjacent concert hall that is renowned for live performances of modern music. The terrace is always popular in fine weather.

*From the Amsteldijk bridge, fifth right Tolstraat.*

The **NINT Science and Technology Museum**, (Technologie Museum NINT) 129 Tolstraat, is Amsterdam's 'David' to the London Science Museum's 'Goliath', and possesses few items of major importance. It is only really of interest to technically- minded, Dutch-speaking, schoolboys. Open Monday to Friday, 10.00-16.00 and Saturdays and Sundays, 13.00-17.00. Admission charge.

*Return to Amsteldijk, right. Third right Jozef Israëlskade.*

## 6. Amsterdam School Architecture

Jozef Israëlskade, the north thoroughfare of Amstelkanal, is the focus of an area, much of which is regarded as a landmark in 20th- century architecture and town-planning.

Penseelstraat, the second turning right after the first bridge has been passed, leads to **Henriëtte Ronnerplein**. This comprises idiosyncratic work by Michael de Klerk, 1921-23. Very influential, de Klerk was a major exponent of the Amsterdam School, which, for the first time, attempted to give character to low-cost municipal housing. Not all, however, approve of his relatively small windows.

*Return to the canal, right.* Immediately before the second bridge, **Pieter Lodewijk Takstraat**, right, was developed 1921-22 by Piet Kramer, one of the earliest of the Amsterdam School architects. Tall chimneys emphasize a fortress-like quality, but parallel glazing bars stress its essentially horizontal nature.

Further south, Paletstraat leads from the canal to another square, **Thérèse Schwartzeplein**, also by de Klerk, and complementing his Henriëtte Ronnerplein.

*Return northward and cross the first bridge to Amstelkade, left. First right Waalstraat. First left Churchillaan leads to Victorieplein.*

Most of the housing in this area was built in the 1930s as part of Amsterdam's 'South Plan', devised, in 1917, by H. P. Berlage. Seventy-five per cent of the accommodation was earmarked for workers.

In **Victorieplein** stands a commemorative statue of the architect **Hendrik Petrus Berlage** (1856-1934).

From the west side of Victorieplein, the short Deltastraat leads to **Merwedeplein**. Anne Frank lived here with her family from 1933 until 1942, when they left to take refuge from the occupying Germans in the Prinsengracht annexe. Their house survives, at **no. 37**, but there is no commemorative plaque.

*From Merwedeplein, Waalstraat, first left, crosses Rooseveltlaan. First left Lekstraat.*

## 7. Resistance Museum (Verzetsmuseum)

63 Lekstraat

Open Tuesday–Friday 10.00-17.00. Saturdays and Sundays 13.00-17.00. Admission charge.

Having visited The Anne Frank House and other locations directly connected with the iniquitous behaviour of the Nazis in Holland during the Second World War, some visitors may baulk at yet more horror. However, this is certainly a very different type of museum, modern sound and visual techniques imparting a slightly 'Madame Tussaud' ambience.

Housed in a former synagogue, many aspects of the five-year German occupation (of Holland not just Amsterdam) from May 1940, are covered, including the undeniable collaboration that took place between a sizeable minority of Dutchmen and the oppressors (remember that Anne Frank was betrayed by a Dutch Nazi sympathiser as late as 1944).

Straight reporting of the facts, without comment, increases the repugnance that most visitors will feel. All types of resistance, from passive to extremely active, are dealt with, including forgery of papers, sabotage, assistance to Jews and strikes. The grim reprisals for such acts are also recorded.

Many fail to appreciate that not only Jews went into hiding: by the end of the war, there were more than a quarter of a million Dutch fugitives. Most foreigners are equally surprised to learn that although the Allies had swept into the German heartland by 1944, opening of the sluices had left Amsterdam isolated, and it was therefore bypassed, remaining occupied until the day before the armistice.

*Exit left and return to Waalstraat, tram 4, or return to Victorieplein, trams 12 and 25.*

Vintage transport enthusiasts may wish to explore South Amsterdam further from the Electric Tram Museum, continuing to Amsterdam Woods, or even beyond, to Amstelveen and, possibly by 1992, Bovenkerk. The museum is sited at the former Haarlemmermeer station, and is reached by tram 6 from the Tropical Museum via the Rijksmusum and Leidseplein, or tram 16 from Central Station via Muntplein and the western section of Albert Cuypstraat.

## 8. Electric Tram Museum (Electrische Museumtramlijn)

Former Haarlemmermeer Station, 264 Amstelveenseweg

Open Sundays from Easter until end October 10.30-17.30 (tram departures every 20 minutes). Also Tuesdays, Wednesdays, Thursdays and Saturdays during July and August (tram departures 13.00, 14.15 and 15.30). Admission free. Cost of tram ticket depends on distance travelled.

The 'museum', created by amateur enthusiasts, is really the trams themselves. Examples of electric trams from Holland, Germany, Austria and Czechoslovakia were built between c.1910 and 1950 and have been restored to their original appearance; all are in working order but there are no double-deckers. Some of the trams were presented to the museum merely for the price of their scrap iron value. Those who have visited Lisbon in recent years will have travelled on similar models already and may wonder what all the fuss is about. However, readers are requested to bear in mind that, as has already been admitted, the author is not technically minded.

Haarlemmermeer station operated from 1913-1950, steam trains running from the terminus to Amstelveen, Aalsmeer and Uithoorn. Conversion to a museum, leased free of charge, was completed in 1975, with a threequarter mile track, since extended to four miles, which connects Amsterdam Woods (van Nijenrodeweghalt), Amstelveen and Bovenkerk. The return trip for the entire journey takes two and a half hours. Many, however, prefer to take a shorter, 15-minute journey and explore Amsterdam Woods if the weather is fine.

*From van Nijenrodeweg halt follow the path, right, over a bridge to enter Amsterdam Woods. Be sure to check times for the return journey. Bicycles may be hired near the entrance for periods from two hours to one day.*

## 9. Amsterdam Woods (Amsterdamse Bos)

For long-term visitors desperate for a break from the urban scene, a visit to Amsterdam Woods by vintage tram is the simple answer. The man-made woods were created 1934-37 to provide labour for the many unemployed in the city during the Depression. Much of the land was reclaimed in the form of sand polders. An important feature is the Bosbaan rowing course, opened by Queen Wilhelmina in 1937. It is six lanes wide and stretches 2,000 metres.

Most pedestrians will prefer to keep to the north of the course, as motor cars cruising along its south bank tend to diminish the rurality. An afternoon tour, keeping within the woods but parallel with the water, and returning along the water's edge, is popular. At the south-west end of the course, one and a quarter miles distant, a path leads northward to **Boerderij Meerzicht** restaurant, where pancakes are served in a former farmhouse; there are also outdoor barbecues in good weather.

Nearby, the **Bosmuseum** (Woods Museum) describes the woods and its formation. Popular with children is the museum's Diorama, as they can crawl through a tunnel excavated through tree roots, to the accompaniment of wild animal noises.

A short distance further north is the expanse of the **Nieuwe Meer** (New Lake). As has already been suggested, an attractive return to the tram halt follows the rowing course.

Scale 1: 615 000

| 0 | 10 | 20 | 30 | 40 | km |

# Excursions from Amsterdam

## Introduction

Unfortunately, most visitors to Amsterdam are able to make few excursions from the city, due to the limited time that they have available, thus they never see the smaller Dutch cities that are really more typical of, as well as being significantly older than, the capital. Holland is a small country and, to detail every day trip of interest that can be made from Amsterdam requires an 'all Holland' book. However, I have made a selection of the most outstanding locations that can be reached within approximately half an hour by public transport. These are as follows: Bulbfields/Keukenhof, Aalsmeer, Marken/Volendam/Edam/Monickendam, Haarlem, Utrecht, Leiden and Alkmaar.

On arrival at Haarlem, Leiden or Utrecht, an immediate call on their respective VVV Tourist offices is recommended for maps and up to date information. All are near the stations.

## Bulbfields/Keukenhof

Many visit Holland primarily to see the bulbfields, between late-March and late-May. Daffodils, which make a splendid show throughout April, are then followed by the much more spectacular tulips.

Although, left to nature, the tulips would be at their best towards the end of May, it is then that their blooms are lopped off, in order to conserve the strength of the bulbs, the raison d'être for the flowers' existence. It is the bulbs that are sold, bringing in a significant boost to Holland's income; the blooms are just an ancillary bonus for the tourist industry.

Coach trips from Amsterdam take visitors through the bulbfields, which are concentrated between Haarlem and Leiden, around the town of Lisse. On the way, a 'commercial break' is made to a bulb-seller, where orders are taken. Here, the extravagant blooms may be closely inspected, even when most of the bulbfields have been denuded. Visits terminate at the **Keukenhof**, 65 acres of landscaped grounds and glasshouses. As may be expected, the tulips are allowed to flower in the gardens until deterioration begins. The Keukenhof is open daily from 08.00 to 19.30, but only from the end of March to the end of May. Not only is a coach tour a convenient way of seeing the bulbfields, but the raised seats in the vehicles give a much better view than can be gained from a motor car.

Flower enthusiasts may also wish to visit the town of **Aalsmeer**, where the world's largest flower auction takes place every weekday at no. 313, Legmeerdijk, from 07.30 to 11.00. In addition, Holland stages a Floriade, at a different venue, every 10 years. This is an enormous flower show, that lasts from mid-April to mid-October. In 1992, it takes place just north of the Hague, and coach operators will transport visitors to it from Amsterdam in around three quarters of an hour; trains from Amsterdam take around 30 minutes. If possible, of course, a sunny day should be selected for any of these trips, although Holland's north-European climate may well preclude this.

## Marken/Volendam/Edam/Monickendam

A visit to these small towns is, apart from the bulbfields, the most popular excursion from Amsterdam. Coach tours operate to them, but they are quite easily visited by public transport, beginning with a short train journey to Volendam.

**Volendam** remained a small fishing village, until the Zuiderzee was enclosed by its great dike in 1932 and its industry thereby ended. Soon, tourism took over, and the main reason for a visit is that local costume, in particular clogs, baggy trousers and winged, lace caps are still worn. Conversely, Volendammers are renowned for their up-to-date tastes, and the interiors of their picturesque houses have been completely modernized. Volendam remained Roman Catholic after the Alteration, Protestant zealots deciding that the small population which still primarily consists of 10 families, was not worth the bother of reforming.

**Marken**, until the causeway was built recently, remained an island and, in consequence, a traditional way of life was retained. Now, however, its character is consciously maintained, and a sense of artificiality prevails. The former island may still be reached by boat from Volendam, an attractive trip in fine weather. Needless to say, both towns offer souvenirs in abundance, few of which are the cheapest in Holland. If Marken is visited first, bus 110 proceeds to Volendam, continuing to the town of Edam, famous for its cheese.

**Edam** is equally pretty, and, to many, more attractive than its touristy neighbours. In the 16th century, it was still more prosperous than Amsterdam, and the quality of the ancient buildings reflects this. The most important, **St. Nicolaaskerk**, however, was almost entirely rebuilt after a fire in 1602. The 18th century **Raadhuis**, in the central Damplein, possesses delightful plasterwork internally. Edam's cheese, wrapped in red cellophane, is renowned for its lack of flavour and has given Dutch cheese in general an undeserved bad name. Visitors are informed that the Dutch themselves rarely eat it; virtually all is sent abroad.

On returning to Amsterdam, travellers are recommended, if possible, to make a stop at **Monickendam**, an unspoilt town on the IJselmeer, where excellent fish dishes are available at harbourside restaurants. Much 17th-century architecture survives in Monickendam, which is virtually a mini-Amsterdam.

## Haarlem

Tours of the bulbfields give visitors a tantalising glimpse of this ancient city, just 12 minutes by train from Amsterdam. There is, however, a great deal to see, and a whole day, at least, can be spent most enjoyably in its museums, churches and ancient thoroughfares.

Highlights are the Frans Hals Museum, the picturesque Grote Markt square and the Great Church of St. Bavo. The VVV office lies right of the station exit, facing Stationsplein.

Situated on the river Spaarne, Haarlem is the provincial capital of Noord-Holland. Following a seven-month siege, in 1572 the city was sacked by the Spanish army, led by Frederick of Toledo. Willem-the-Silent recaptured it five years later, but most of the population had been massacred, including all the Protestant clergy.

Streets lead southward from the station to the historic centre of Haarlem, which is almost entirely surrounded by waterways. **Donkere Begijnhof** marks the medieval goldsmith's quarter and leads, via some 'girly' alleyways, to the former Begijnhof. Until 1568, the **Waalsekerk** was the Begijnhof's chapel and it is the oldest religious building in Haarlem. Open for Sunday services, frescoes date from c. 1400, and a Gothic structure of timber roofs the sacristy.

Further south lies the outstanding **Grote Markt**, a cobbled square that retains a medieval character, due to its extensive collection of Gothic and Renaissance buildings that are unparalleled elsewhere in Holland. A statue of **Laurentius Costers** c. 1370 – c. 1440 commemorates a local printer – the world's first say Haarlemmers, although most historians still attribute printing's invention to Gutenberg of Mainz.

**St. Bavokerk**, or the Grote Kerk (Great Church), dominates the square, but is entered from 23 Oude Groenmarkt. Visitors to Amsterdam's Rijksmuseum may recall Berckhyde's many paintings of the building. St. Bavo was built around an existing church, consecrated in 1100, but damaged by fire. The chancel was completed in 1390, the transepts in 1455, the nave in 1481 and the tower in 1518. Internally, the late-Gothic style is in evidence, although all is now rather bare, with the usual white-painted walls. The timber roof of the nave is exceptionally high. At the west end, the organ of 1738 was played by Müller, this is one of the largest examples in the world and comprises 5,000 pipes.

Allegorical carvings of Poetry and Music, below the organ, are the work of Jean-Baptiste Xavery and the finest in the church. Pieter Saenredam, the painter, is buried in the south ambulatory, and Frans Hals lies beneath the floor of the chancel, (slab no. 56) marked by a lantern.

West of the church are the **Vishal** (fish market), rebuilt in 1768, and the **Vleeshal** (meat market), an outstandingly decorative Renaissance work, by Lieven de Key. Internally, however, only its columns are original.

Further west lies the 14th-century, Renaissance-style **Stadhuis** (Town Hall); its main façade was rebuilt in 1630. Lieven de Key designed the Zijlstraat wing of 1622.

Near the Post Office, at 32 Gasthuisstraat, the former **Civic Guard hall** (Kloveniersdoelen), of 1612, survives, now adapted to a library.

Continuing southward, almost to the Kampersingel waterway, **New Church** (Nieuwe Kerk) represents a Classical rebuilding, by Jacob van Campen, 1649. Its steeple is the earlier work of Lieven de Key, 1613; within lies the great landscape painter Jacob van Ruisdael.

The **Frans Hals Museum**, 62 Groot Heiligland, Haarlem's greatest tourist attraction, displays paintings of the Haarlem School, including eight large group paintings by Hals. The museum is open daily 10.00 to 17.00, but with the usual Sunday opening of 13.00. Frans Hals (1580-1666) was born in Antwerp, moving to Haarlem with his parents before reaching his teens. He is believed to have spent his last years in this former almshouse, built by Lieven de Key in 1618.

Hals was a member of the Militia Company of St. George, and he included himself in the painting of its officers (top left-hand corner). Apart from old master paintings, there is a reconstructed pharmacy, in which 18th-century delftware is displayed, a collection of 18th-century dolls houses, and, in the former refectory, fittings from demolished Haarlem houses. Works by modern artists, including Appel, are housed in a new wing. The entrance archway of 1679 incorporates statues of Hals and Lieven de Key, made when the museum opened in 1913.

Return towards the city centre, following **Grote Houtstraat**, the most important shopping street in Haarlem. Just north of the Gedempte Oude Gracht junction lies the **Proveniershuis**, of 1577, built as the headquarters of the Civic Guard Company dedicated to St. George. **Almshouses** are approached from its rear courtyard.

By proceeding eastward, the Binnen river is reached. Overlooking it, to the north, are the ancient **Weigh House** (Waag) and the **Teylers Museum**, at 16 Spaarne. This eclectic museum is open Tuesday to Saturday 10.00 to 17.00, and Sundays 13.00 to 17.00. Pieter Teyler van der Hulst, a philanthropic merchant, arranged for the museum to be founded, following his death in 1778, and it is the oldest in the country. Exhibits include fossils, ancient scientific instruments, crystals and Dutch coins and medals. However, it is the former collection of drawings that belonged to Queen Christina of Sweden that attracts most. Works by Michelangelo, Raphael and Rembrandt are the highlights.

On the opposite side of the river, in Spaarnwonderstraat, survives a turreted **14th-century gate** from Haarlem's city wall.

# Utrecht

Four trains per hour whisk visitors from Amsterdam to this ancient city in less than 30 minutes. The centre is well preserved and ringed by picturesque 'sunken' canals. Holland's National Collection of Ecclesiastical Art and the Gothic cathedral, Domkerk, are highlights.

From the station, a lengthy walk through Europe's largest completely covered shopping centre, **Hoog Catharijne**, constructed in 1983, must be made before emerging. The main VVV office lies left of the exit, in Vredenburg. Continuing eastward, the attractive central part of Utrecht is reached, providing a dramatic contrast to its rather humdrum approaches.

**Oudegracht** (old canal) was excavated in the 12th century. Originally, the canals of Utrecht were not sunken, but, as the ground built up gradually on either side, another thoroughfare was laid out, 10 feet above, and parallel, with the lower. The upper street fronts houses, whereas the lower fronts former warehouses, many of which are now cafés and bars.

By following the canal southward, the **Stadhuis** is reached. This Classical building of c. 1824 replaced a medieval structure, which stood on the site and in which the Union of Utrecht, establishing Holland's present boundaries, was proclaimed, and the Treaty of Utrecht with Louis XIV signed.

Continuing ahead, following the canal but crossing to its west side. Buurkerksteeg leads to the former **Buurkerk**.

Accommodated in what was Utrecht's oldest parish church, dating from the 13th century, is the **Speelklok tot Pieremont Museum**, open Tuesday to Saturday 10.00 to 16.00, and Sundays 13.00 to 16.00, with guided tours on the hour. Founded in the 10th century, the church was partly rebuilt in both the 14th century and 15th century. In 1586, its chancel was demolished for the construction of Choorstraat (Choir Street). Sister Berken, famous for her religious tracts, retired, heartbroken, to spend the last 57 years of her life in a small cell in the church, on discovering that she was the illegitimate daughter of a cathedral canon; she died in 1514. Displayed within is a collection of musical boxes, fairground organs, pianolas and an early juke box.

Ahead, the **Cathedral's tower**, at 367 feet, is the highest in Holland. It may be ascended throughout the year, with a guide, on the hour, Saturdays and Sundays 12.00 to 17.00, April to October also Monday to Friday 10.00 to 17.00. The tower was built in French Gothic style, on the site of two earlier churches, from 1321; the octagonal lantern was added in 1383. As early as 700, St. Willibrord was appointed Bishop of Utrecht, and the city wielded great power in the Middle Ages. The archbishopric status of Utrecht, which it gained, briefly, in

1559, was only revived in 1851. The body of **Utrecht Cathedral** was constructed from 1254 to 1520, but only its church and two bays of the nave's south aisle survived the hurricane of 1674. It is open Monday to Saturday 10.00 to 17.00 (closing at 16.00 October to April) and Sundays 14.00 to 16.00. Internally, white walls are typical of Holland's Calvinist churches, but some 13th-century paintings have recently been discovered in the chapels of the chancel. The pews, pulpit and windows of the transepts date from the 1936 restoration. The white marble tomb monument of Admiral van Gendt, who died in battle in 1672, is the work of Verhulst.

Extending southward, the cloister was built from 1340 to 1495 and links with the **former chapter house**, at the south end. This building was constructed in 1495 and it was here that the historic Union of Utrecht was signed in 1579. Utrecht University, Holland's largest, now uses the ancient hall as their auditorium; it may only be entered by appointment (tel: 030 394252).

Slightly to the east lies **St. Pieterskerk**, open June to September, Tuesday to Saturday 11.00 to 16.30. A combination of Romanesque and Gothic styles proclaims the venerability of this church, consecrated in 1048. Its original west front and flanking towers were lost in the 1674 hurricane and the façade rebuilt. Internally, Romanesque features, Holland's oldest, are of great interest. They include capitals to six of the columns, bas-reliefs c.1170 on either side of the church, discovered in 1965, and, in the crypt, the sarcophagus of the founder of the church, Bishop Bernold (died 1054). The baptismal font comes from Maastricht.

Further south, in Pausdam, survives **Paushuize**, built in 1517. This was assigned, as the papal lodging, to Holland's only pope, Adriaan VI, but he remained pontiff for just one year, dying in 1533, and never resided in the house. Since 1959, the building has provided accommodation for the provincial authority.

By following Nieuwegracht southward, the **Catherijneconvent Museum** is reached at no. 63. Open Tuesday to Friday 10.00 to 17.00, and Saturdays and Sundays 11.00 to 17.00. The buildings that formerly housed the convent now accommodate Holland's national collection of ecclesiastical art. In the Kloostergebouw (cloister) the earliest exhibits are to be found, and these are the most impressive. It is poignantly apparent just how much Holland lost artistically through Calvanist iconoclasm. A highlight is the superb *Virgin and Child*, by van Cleve. Incorporated in the complex is the late-Gothic former church of the convent, founded by Carmelites in 1468. Floral decoration within is outstanding; this is now the cathedral church of Holland's Roman Catholics (press the button beside the door to enter).

At the far end of Nieuwegracht is the **Centraal Museum** (not very central), open Tuesday to Saturday 10.00 to 17.00, and Sundays 13.00 to 17.00. It is accommodated in the former St. Agnes Convent, founded in 1420. Exhibits are eclectic, but concentrate on items related to the history of the city. Included is the municipal collection of paintings, dominated by the works of Jan van Scorel (1495-1562) 'the Leonardo of the North'. A large doll's house c. 1680, and the Viking 'Utrecht Ship', discovered in 1930, are other important exhibits.

In spite of Utrecht's 20,000 university students, the city is not particularly lively in the evening, most of them making the short journey to Amsterdam for night life.

## Leiden

Leiden is a similar distance from Amsterdam as Utrecht, there are three trains per hour and the journey takes just over 30 minutes. Holland's oldest and most renowned university still plays an important part in the town's activities, and Leiden also houses the national museum of antiquities, not to be missed. Much of the town remains picturesque, 35 ancient almshouses surviving.

From the mid-14th century until the 18th century Leiden was a flourishing centre of the cloth industry. In 1573, a one-year siege by Philip II's army began, Leiden only being relieved when Willem the Silent breached the dykes and sent in the Dutch fleet; the date, 3 October 1574, is commemorated each year with a fair and fireworks. The VVV Tourist office faces the station exit, slightly to the right. Follow Stationsweg southward, crossing the first canal. Immediately left stands a former windmill.

**Valk's Windmill Museum** (Molenmuseum de Valk), at Binnenvestgracht, is open Tuesday to Saturday 10.00 to 17.00, and Sundays 13.00 to 17.00. Twenty windmills for grinding corn once surrounded Leiden, and this example c. 1743 was restored c. 1900, following the death of de Valk, the last miller, to serve as a museum of the windmills' history in the Netherlands. The sails usually turn, wind permitting. Continue southward to the west canal, Oude Singel.

**De Lakenhal Museum** – open Tuesday to Saturday 10.00 to 17.00, Sundays 13.00 to 17.00. Built in Palladian style by Arent van 's Gravensande in 1640, the museum's premises served as the Cloth Hall until 1800; plaques on the façade depict aspects of the wool trade. The hall then became a hospital and was converted to a museum in 1870. Leiden's history and artistic heritage are depicted. Of particular interest are the reconstructed period rooms, including a Dutch kitchen, a surgeon's room and the Brewers' Room, with great murals of 1723, taken from the old Brewers' Guild Hall. A monumental fireplace from Leiden's old town hall, and panels of Dutch tiles also impress. Many paintings are displayed throughout.

By following Turfmarkt southward and crossing De Rijn (the river Rhine), Rapenburg is reached.

The **Rijksmuseum van Oudeheden**, 28 Rapenburg, is open Tuesday to Saturday 10.00 to 17.00, and Sundays 13.00 to 17.00. Arranged on three floors, the museum houses Holland's foremost collection of antiquities, with outstanding examples, chronologically displayed, of Egyptian, Greek and Roman work. Most descriptions are now in English as well as Dutch. From the entrance hall may be seen the Nubian Temple of Taffeh, presented to Holland by the Egyptian government, in thanks for its financial help in saving monuments from being engulfed by the Nile, after the construction of the second Aswan Dam. Dating from the first century, the building was remodelled in the fourth century for the worship of Isis. Four hundred years later, it became a Christian church. Between 1910 and 1960, the temple had been primarily under water, due to the construction of the first Aswan Dam. Items from a 2nd century Roman temple, discovered by fishermen at Zeeland in 1970, are also of interest; the temple had been dedicated to a local goddess of seamen, Nehellenia. In 1987, the Royal Coin Collection was presented to the museum.

A little further south appears the bulk of **Pieterskerk**, Leiden's biggest church, but now deconsecrated. Rutger van Kampen completed this Gothic building c. 1500 although work had begun in 1330. Its bell tower collapsed in 1512 and was never rebuilt. Exhibitions, concerts and a Saturday antique market are now held in Pieterskerk and there is an admission charge. Fittings of interest include a late-Gothic pulpit, the chancel screen, with a Renaissance frieze of 1525, and the organ of 1641. Buried within is John Robinson, an English preacher, who led the Pilgrim Fathers.

Immediately south of the church, at 21 Kloksteeg, is the **Jan Pesijnhofje almshouse**, built in 1683 on the site of the house where John Robinson lived from 1611 until his death in 1625; he never made the trip to America with his flock, who set sail in 1620.

Following Kloksteeg westward, the Steenschuur canal is crossed to Rapenburg. Ahead, at no. 73, lies the original premises of **Leiden University**. Willem-the-Silent presented the university to Leiden in recognition of the valour of its citizens throughout the Spanish siege, in which half the population perished. It was founded here in 1581, in the former chapel of a convent, now the Academie Gebouw, open Wednesday to Friday 13.00 to 17.00. A small museum occupies the ground floor. To the rear, visitors may wander through the botanical gardens, laid out in 1594 for growing medicinal herbs.

*Return eastward, continuing to Breestraat.*

A fire destroyed most of the **Town Hall** (Stadhuis) in 1929, but it was possible to save the exuberant, late-16th century Renaissance façade of Lieven de Key, and restoration was completed eight years later. Most of de Key's surviving buildings are to be seen in Haarlem.

*Cross the Nieuwe Rijn, behind the Town Hall, and proceed southward to Nieuwestraat.*

**Hooglandsekerk** is open May to September, Mondays 13.00 to 15.30, and Tuesday to Saturday 11.00 to 15.30, Sunday service at 10.00. This late-Gothic church retains its original 14th-century nave, but the remainder dates from subsequent rebuilding. As may be expected, temporary exhibitions take up much of the space. A Baroque memorial to Pieter Adriaansz van der Werff stands at the south-east pillar of the crossing. Van der Werff was burgomaster of Leiden during the Spanish-siege, and it is said that he offered his body as food to the starving citizens; they refused, but, inspired by his self-sacrificial offer, continued their resistance with renewed vigour.

North of the church, on an artificial mound (Saxon or Roman) stands the **Burcht**, overlooking the confluence of the old and new Rijn's. This fortress was built for the Counts of Holland, but there is little left of great interest apart from the views. The **Nieuwstraat gateway** of 1658 displays coats of arms of burgomasters from 1651 to 1674.

By following the old Rijn westward, on route to the station, and crossing the Rapenburg junction, Rembrandtbreeg is reached.

**Weddesteeg** provides the south approach to the bridge and it was in one of its houses, now lost, that Rembrandt van Rijn was born in 1606. The great painter's father was a miller, and his grandparents owned two nearby windmills for grinding corn.

After crossing the bridge and continuing past the windmill to the first crossing, immediately left, stands **Morspoort**, the western gate in the former city wall.

*Continue ahead to the station.*

## Alkmaar

This town, north-west of Amsterdam, is visited primarily for its cheese market, established in the early 14th century. It operates every Friday morning from mid-April to September and is very popular with coach tours – arrive before 1000 to get the best views. There are also two trains per hour to Alkmaar from Amsterdam and the journey will take 30 minutes. Most cheeses bartered appear to be great discs of Goudas. The market takes place on the **main square**, where there is also a **Cheese Museum** and a **weigh house** (Waag) with an extravagant gable, added in 1573 to celebrate the defeat, locally, of the Spaniards.

# Architectural Glossary

Definitions are given as applicable to Amsterdam where appropriate.

**Aisle**   Parallel areas subdivided by arcades.

**Altar**   Table of stone at which Mass is celebrated in a church or chapel. The most important altar, generally situated at the east end, is known as the high altar. None survive in Dutch Reformed churches.

**Altar frontal**   Covering of the front of the altar facing the worshippers.

**Altar rail**   Low structure protecting the area in which the high altar stands.

**Ambulatory**   Passageway in a church formed by continuing the aisles around the chancel.

**Amsterdam School**   A uniquely Dutch architectural style, created c. 1912 by P. L. Kramer and others, in which form was regarded as more important than function. Decorative brickwork and towers are characteristics. Many examples of municipal housing in this style survive in South Amsterdam.

**Apse**   Semi-circular or polygonal extension to a church.

**Architrave**   Internal or external moulding surrounding an opening.

**Art Deco**   In vogue from the mid-1920s, and dominant throughout the 1930s, this style was characterised by simple, streamlined areas, decorated with stylised, geometric ornamentation.

**Art Nouveau**   An art style, popular c.1890-1910, adopting sinuous, organic lines.

**Ashlar**   Large blocks of smoothed stone laid in level courses.

**Attic**   Low, top storey of a building.

**Baroque**   Exuberant 17th-century development of the Classical style, little favoured in Holland architecturally.

**Bay**   Compartments of a building, divided by repeated elements.

**Boss**   Ornamental descending projection covering the intersection of ribs in a roof.

**Buttress**   Structure attached to a wall to counter an outward thrust. Rarely used in Amsterdam, due to the light weight of the buildings.

**Capital**   Top section of a column or pilaster, usually carved in the distinctive style of a Classical Order.

**Chancel**   The section of the church built to accommodate the clergy, but no longer used as such in Dutch Reformed churches.

**Cladding**   Material added to a structure to provide an external surface.

**Classical**   Styles following those of ancient Greece or Rome.

**Clevestory**   Upper section of a wall, normally in a church, which is pierced with windows to provide additional light.

**Crossing**   The intersection, in a church, of the nave, transept and chancel.

**Convent**   A complex housing a monastic community, male or female.

**Corbel**   Wall bracket, generally of stone, supporting a beam, for example.

**Corinthian**   Greek Classical Order. Columns are slender and their capitals intricately decorated with carved leaves and small spiral scrolls (volutes).

**Cornice**   A projecting decorative feature running horizontally at a high level.

**Cupola**   Small domed roof, often surmounting a turret.

**Doric**   Classical Order, the oldest and sturdiest. The capitals of Doric columns are virtually undecorated.

**Dormer window**   Window protruding from a sloping roof.

**Dutch gable**   Decorative gables built in Holland from the mid-16th century.

**Eave**   Horizontal edge of a roof overhanging the wall.

**Fanlight**   Oblong or semi-circular window above a door.

**Finial**   Decorative terminal to a structure, eg. spire or gable.

**Fluted**   Vertical grooving of a column or pilaster.

**Gable**   Upper section of wall at each end of a building (the Dutch refer to the entire wall as the gable).

**Gallery**   Upper level storey, always open on one side, and usually arcaded. Alternatively, a long room for displaying works of art.

**Gargoyle**   Decorative protruding spouts that drain rainwater from roofs. Often carved as beasts or demons in Gothic buildings.

**Gothic**   Architectural style from the 12th to the 16th centuries, employing the pointed arch.

**Gothic Revival**   Attempt to reproduce the Gothic style in the 19th century.

**Grisaille**   Grey monochrome decoration developed by Jacob de Wit in the 17th century.

**Ionic**   Classical Order. Columns are slenderer than those in the Doric Ordering and capitals decorated at corners with spiral scrolls (volutes).

**Jetty**   An upper floor or floors, extending above a lower. Rare in Amsterdam.

**Keystone**   Central stone at the apex of an arch, or where the ribs of a vault intersect. Frequently elongated to form a boss (see above).

**Lady Chapel**   A chapel dedicated to the Virgin Mary.

**Light**   Section of a window filled with glass.

**Lintel**   Horizontal section of stone or timber spanning an opening to distribute the weight that it bears.

**Misericord**   'Mercy' seat provided by a shallow surface for resting purposes that protrudes horizontally when the seat itself is tipped up. Supporting brackets are often richly carved with various subjects, not always religious. Generally in the form of Gothic choir stalls, good examples survive in Old Church.

**Moulding**   Decorative addition to a projecting feature, such as a cornice, door frame, etc.

**Mullions**   Vertical bars dividing a window.

**Murals**   Wall paintings, examples of which survive in Old Church and New Church.

**Nave**   Body of the church, built to house the congregation, but no longer divided from the chancel in Dutch Reformed churches.

**Neck gable**   Narrow, vertical extension to the gable, usually surmounted by a pediment. Favoured by the Vingboons brothers, c. 1625, who also developed the raised neck gable, which often encompassed three storeys and was linked to the façade by volutes.

**Nieuwe Kunst**   Dutch Art Nouveau (*sic*), rarely whole-hearted in Amsterdam.

**Oratory**   Small private chapel.

**Oriel window**   Window projecting as a bay but at an upper level.

**Order**   Classical architecture, where the design and proportions of the columns and entablatures are standardized.

**Palladian**   Classical architecture, following the style of the Italian Andrea Palladio in the 16th century.

**Pediment**   Low-pitched triangular gable, generally built over a portico, door or window but, in Amsterdam, also frequently used to surmount a neck gable.

**Pier**   Solid structure supporting a great load.

**Pilaster**   Shallow, flat column attached to a wall.

**Pinnacle**   Vertical decorative feature surmounting a Gothic structure.

**Portal**   Important doorway.

**Portico**   Classical porch of columns supporting a roof, usually pedimented.

**Pulpit**   Timber structure from which the preacher speaks. The most important fixtures in Dutch Reformed churches, where they invariably have sounding boards.

**Quoin stones**   Dressed stones fitted externally at the angles of walls to give added strength.

**Rationalism** (or Functionalism, or Modernism)   Twentieth-century architecture, incorporating modern materials, where the design is dependent on the function of the building.

**Renaissance**   Rebirth of Classical architecture, as evolved in Italy in the 15th century.

**Reredos**   Decorative structure, usually standing behind the altar in a church or chapel. Generally made of wood, but occasionally of stone. None survive in Dutch Reformed churches.

**Rib**   Protruding band supporting a vault. Occasionally purely decorative.

**Rococo**   Last phase of the Baroque style in the mid-18th century, with widespread use of detailed ornamentation, little found in Holland.

**Rood Screen**   A screen between the nave and chancel in Roman Catholic churches. The rood is a carved Crucifixion scene standing on the beam of the screen.

**Romanesque**   Style of architecture featuring semi-circular arches.

**Rustication**   Use of stonework on the exterior of a building to give an impression of strength. The jointing is always deep.

**Sacristy**   Room in a church for storage of sacred vessels and vestments. Generally used for robing. Also known as a vestry.

**Sarcophagus**   Carved coffin.

**Spout gable**   Simple triangular gable, with no decoration.

**Step gable**   Developed in the mid-16th century, to give an appearance of greater width to the steeply pitched roofs by extending the 'steps' on either side. Many examples are decorated with scrolls. Popular until the late 17th century.

**Transomes**   Horizontal bars dividing a window.

**Trapezium** (or Trapezoid) gable   The trapezium shape was introduced by Hendrick de Keyser early in the 17th century. Examples are constructed from soft red brick, decorated with yellow Bentheimer stone.

**Trompe l'oeil**   Painting that 'tricks the eye' into believing it is three-dimensional work.

**Trophy**   Decorative sculptured arms or armour.

**Tuscan**   Classical Order. Roman adaptation of the Greek Doric.

**Tympanum**   Semi-circular or triangular space between the lintel of an opening and the arch above it.

**Vault**   An arched structure forming a roof.

**Vestibule**   Entrance hall or anteroom.

**Volute**   A spiral scroll carved in stone, which forms a distinctive element of the Ionic Order. In Amsterdam, volutes frequently decorate gables.

# INDEX